San Francisco Opera

San Francisco Opera

THE FIRST

SEVENTY-FIVE YEARS

JOAN CHATFIELD-TAYLOR

CHRONICLE BOOKS

SAN FRANCISCO

Page 180 constitutes a continuation of the copyright page.

Distributed in Canada by Raincoast Books
8680 Cambie Street
Vancouver, B.C. V6P 6M9

10 9 8 7 6 5 4 3 2 1

Design and composition by Juliette Robbins, Danielseed Design.

This book is set in Adobe Garamond, customized for Danielseed
by the Macktez Corporation. Adobe's Bell Gothic Light has been
used for the captions. Sean Cullen customized it to accommodate
the many diacriticals present in this subject matter. Matthew
Carter's Snell Roundhand is the display font.

Printed in Tokyo

Chronicle Books
85 Second Street
San Francisco, CA 94105

Web Site: www.chronbooks.com

Library of Congress Cataloging-in-Publication Data:
Chatfield-Taylor, Joan.
    San Francisco Opera : the first seventy-five years
    / Joan Chatfield-Taylor.
        p.   cm.
    Includes index.
    ISBN 0-8118-1368-1
    1. San Francisco Opera—History.   2. San Francisco
Opera—Pictorial works.   3. Opera—California—San Francisco.
I. Title.
    ML1711.8.S2S352 1997
    792.5'09794'61—dc21   97-5085
                                                         CIP
                                                         MN

dedication

For RICHARD J. COHEN and NIMA A. GRISSOM, who believed that this book was possible. And for my children, CHRISTINA and MATTHEW, as always.

Several years ago, Lotfi Mansouri and I had a conversation about a book on the subject of the San Francisco Opera. I thank him not only for remembering the conversation, but also for providing the support and enthusiasm that made writing this book a joy.

My endless thanks also go to Kori Lockhart, publications editor for the opera, whose patience, humor, courtesy, and encyclopedic knowledge were crucial to the completion of this project. It is impossible to name all the other people at the San Francisco Opera who took time from their hectic schedules to talk to me about their work, but I assure them that I remember their contributions with profound gratitude.

Margaret Norton, Kirsten Tanaka, and Matthew Buff were among the staff members at the San Francisco Performing Arts Library and Museum who patiently and cheerfully helped me to gather material. My thanks also go to the staff in the microfilm department of the San Francisco Public Library, and to Robert Tuggle, archivist of the Metropolitan Opera. Sarah Billinghurst, James Schwabacher, and Nancy Adler Montgomery gave generously of their time and knowledge.

More gratitude is owed to my agent, Fred Hill, and to editors Jay Schaefer and Kate Chynoweth, who shepherded this project through the complexities of the publishing process. Copy editor Judith Dunham's careful reading, good ideas, and positive attitude were an inspiration. Designer Juliette Robbins's love and understanding of opera is apparent on every page. Finally, for unfailing support at difficult moments, I thank my friends, who know who they are.

contents

ORDER OF APPEARANCE

foreword OVERTURE

A great love affair is going on in San Francisco—a romance that began nearly 150 years ago. It is the city's overwhelming passion for opera, and two extraordinary events in 1997 prove beyond a shadow of a doubt that "our love is here to stay": the San Francisco Opera's landmark seventy-fifth season and the completion of the extensive renovation of the company's home, the magnificent War Memorial Opera House.

It would be impossible in a single volume to capture all of the history and stories that have made the San Francisco Opera one of the world's great opera companies. It is a combination of the great artists, the masterpieces performed, the audience that loves them, and the scores of people who have worked diligently behind the scenes, all creating an exciting tradition of legends and legacies.

For seventy-five years, the San Francisco Opera has entertained, challenged, educated, unified, and served the Bay Area. In so doing, it has risen to be counted among the great opera companies of the world. This book offers an affectionate look at opera in San Francisco and the rich history of the San Francisco Opera. It is filled with fascinating anecdotes and photographs that recall the past golden ages of opera and give us a good look at our current golden age. This book also offers an opportunity to get to know some of the people and events that have brought us this far, as we look forward to the next seventy-five years.

LOTFI MANSOURI
General Director

First Annual Music Festival
and

Grand Opera

at

Stanford Stadium

Stanford University
California

GAETANO MEROLA, Director

BENEFICIARIES:

Stanford University Endowment Fund   Stanford Clinic in San Francisco
Fund for Enlargement of Organ in Memorial Church
Home for Convalescent Children on Stanford Campus

ALL SEATS RESERVED

NOW ON SALE at Sherman, Clay & Co., San Francisco, Oakland, San Jose;
Crandall's, Palo Alto, and Book Store on Campus

prologue

OPERA IN SAN FRANCISCO

1851-1922

"We came by boat, arriving in the late afternoon. We made a tent of our bedsheets and camped on Telegraph Hill. Then we erected a knock-down house and added a lean-to kitchen which also serves as a dining room for our meals."

The year was 1850, and the writer was a French-born opera singer named Alfred Roncovieri, who arrived in San Francisco on the heels of the first gold prospectors. His destination was a bustling, raucous town whose population had exploded after the discovery in 1848 of gold at Sutter's Fort. In 1846 about 150 people lived in a scattering of primitive houses on the sandy hills around the bay, and wolves and grizzly bears roamed the land. By 1850 the harbor was crowded with ships and the town had grown to some thirty thousand people, many going to and from the gold fields on the American River.

A riot broke out among ticket-seekers when diva **Adelina Patti** came to San Francisco in 1884, and hordes of her enthusiasts followed her carriage as it proceeded through the streets.

The program for Gaetano Merola's first opera season at the Stanford football stadium pictured a semi-circular stage with a backdrop of trees. Not shown are the dozens of tents that were set up outside the stadium to serve as dressing rooms for the artists (opposite).

Impresario Thomas Maguire was tireless in his enthusiasm for opera and his willingness to keep rebuilding his theaters after they were destroyed by the frequent fires that raged through San Francisco in the 1850s. This is **Maguire's Opera House**, located on Washington Street between Kearny and Montgomery Streets. Built in 1856, it was the setting for both vaudeville and grand opera, a typical combination at the time.

When the gold miners came to town, they wanted entertainment in any form that was available. The city's insatiable craving for diversion was satisfied initially by dozens of saloons, which provided smoke-filled settings for gambling, prostitution, drunkenness and knife fights. Outside on the muddy, ill-lighted streets, acrobats, stilt walkers, and magicians attracted audiences. In this rough and violent time, crowds gathered for bloody events like cockfights and the terrifying spectacle of a chained bear pitted against a bull.

By 1850 the city boasted a dozen theaters, a development greeted with enthusiasm by the local press. One reporter wrote hopefully that the theaters would be responsible for "weaning many from the insanity of the gambling houses." On the flimsy new stages, which were often attached to saloons, the emphasis was on variety rather than quality. One evening at the rowdy Bella Union Theater, the program included popular songs, dance, a performance of "The Glorious Farce of the Siamese Twins," and two demonstrations by a tightrope walker.

There were occasional signs of interest in higher culture. Operatic arias were sometimes offered as brief intermission fare at the theaters, and a music store, purveying guitars, banjos, flutes, and sheet music, opened its doors in 1849.

The city's intense love affair with opera began on February 12, 1851, with a performance of Bellini's *La Sonnambula* before a crowded house at the Adelphi Theatre. The city's first presentation of an entire opera was given by a small group of Italian opera singers who had arrived by boat a few days earlier. The Pellegrini Opera Company, consisting of three singers and a pianist, plus a trunkful of costumes, was typical of small European troupes that sailed up and down the Pacific Coast, stopping at whichever port seemed likely to provide an audience. News of the gold rush undoubtedly inspired the Pellegrini company to sail north to San Francisco.

The company, bolstered by some local talent, followed its successful presentation of *La Sonnambula* with performances of *Norma* and *Ernani*. The performance of *Ernani* came only seven years after the premiere of the Verdi opera in Venice, although it would be a mistake to make too fine a comparison between what went on at the Adelphi Theatre and what had transpired seven years earlier at La Fenice. The San Francisco production of *Ernani* was a box-office success in spite of the fact that the baritone role was sung by a mezzo-soprano.

The Pellegrini troupe stayed until May 1851, performing a series of concerts in Sacramento in addition to opera in San Francisco. That May, an enormous fire broke out in the center of the city. Some eighteen hundred buildings, including all the city's theaters, were destroyed in a few hours. The Pellegrinis, left without a stage for their efforts, departed by ship as the ashes cooled. In those few months, however, the little troupe had sowed the seeds of San Francisco's lasting enthusiasm for grand opera.

The city's early operatic performances were colorful events. Although the construction of the wooden theater buildings was quick and inexpensive, considerable effort was made to ensure that the interiors gave an impression of color and richness. The effect was undoubtedly heightened by the dim and uneven lighting. Electricity did not arrive in San Francisco until 1854, so the first audiences saw opera in the flickering light of candles or whale oil lamps. The latter apparently were more dependable than wax tapers but had a distinctive smell not usually associated with high-toned culture.

The scene at the Pellegrinis' first performance of *La Sonnambula* was very likely noisy and informal. Gold miners came as they were, with their pants stuffed into their high leather boots and their wide-brimmed hats firmly on their heads. Peanuts were sold in the aisles of San Francisco theaters, and it was considered perfectly acceptable to crunch on them throughout the performance. Spitting was a common activity, and the patrons occasionally expressed their enthusiasm by throwing gold on the stage.

It was a raucous scene, particularly to anyone familiar with the staid conventions of East Coast opera houses like the Academy of Music in New York, which existed as showplaces for the conservative wealthy to show off their clothes, their jewelry, and their coaches. The eastern and western audiences did have some points in common. The primary one was money, whether it was in the form of discreet bank accounts in the East or bags of gold nuggets in California. In San Francisco, opera tickets were occasionally auctioned off for more than a thousand dollars apiece, a small fortune at that time.

With so much money in circulation, it is not surprising that the enterprising Pellegrinis were followed by many other entertainers eager to make their own fortunes in the burgeoning city. Beginning in 1852, a succession of sopranos dazzled local audiences. An American, Eliza Biscaccianti, was the first to inspire the kind of adulation that later became a civic habit. She arrived in 1852 and gave a series of triumphant concerts. Later the same year, she was overtaken by an Irish-born soprano, Catherine Hayes, poetically known as the Swan of Erin, who came to town under the aegis of showman Phineas T. Barnum. Two years later, the object of San Francisco's musical affections was an Englishwoman, Anna Bishop, who starred in the city's first performances of Donizetti's *Don Pasquale*.

Although attempts to establish a local company were sporadic and unsuccessful, entrepreneurs continued to build theaters to welcome traveling companies. Preeminent among them was Thomas Maguire, who arrived from the East in 1849, built his first theater above a saloon in 1850, and became the city's most important impresario. Maguire loved opera, even when he lost money on it, and presented hundreds of performances to large audiences during the first decade after the discovery of gold. According to the Works Progress Administration survey of music and theater in San Francisco, compiled in the 1930s, San Franciscans had the choice of 1,043 operatic performances between 1850 and 1860. Even taking into consideration that opera and other live theatrical events had no competition from television, movies, or recordings, this is an impressive statistic.

Why did San Franciscans love opera so much? One of the WPA's anonymous writers attempted to explain: "Men's lives had an operatic quality in the fifties. Overnight, new arrivals won fortune or suffered ruin. Classes were fluid; social differences fluctuated; individual bravura was applauded; sudden reversals of fortune were experienced by almost everyone. The mood was grandiose. An air of triumph and unexpectedness pervaded the atmosphere. Grand opera was avidly seized upon as a most satisfying form of entertainment."

Perhaps this romantic explanation was true in the earliest years of operatic entertainment in San Francisco, but it was not long before opera became a symbol not of individual bravura but of a desire for conventionality and community. In a rapidly changing society, opera played a significant role. As the city grew, the new residents began to want symbols of civilization, particularly highly visible responses to the violence and unconventionality of the very recent past. No one wanted the facade of culture more than the nervous newly rich, desperate to erase their obvious signs of low birth.

As astonishing as the rapid growth of San Francisco was the speed with which the new city took on airs of respectability. By 1859 it was possible to live a relatively conventional life in the city, perhaps in a house with a garden at some distance from the noise and crowds of downtown. Churches, among them St. Mary's Church on California Street and the French community's Notre Dame des Victoires on Bush Street, flourished in spite of the city's reputation for debauchery. A sort of society scene rapidly developed, allowing those who were so inclined to attend reassuring rituals like debuts and charity balls. The ships in the harbor brought fashionable items from Europe, and the newspapers soon filled up with advertisements for French champagne and white kid gloves.

In San Francisco and throughout the West, opera houses, ostentatious and redolent (their owners hoped) of European sophistication, sprang up wherever there was a concentration of money. They opened in frontier towns like Abilene and Butte and Virginia City. In the Mexican town of

The Tivoli Opera House grew from modest beginnings in 1875 as a German beer garden on Sutter Street to the large theater seen here, which was the setting for decades of grand opera seasons that attracted many of the world's great singers. In the beginning of the twentieth century, the Tivoli was the busiest musical theater in the United States, offering both grand and light opera as well as popular music.

Guanajuato, at one point the world's primary source of silver, the columned facade and intricately painted pseudo-Moorish interior of the Juarez Theater still astonish the eye. In truth, many of these edifices were labeled opera houses because the name was more respectable than the racier connotations of "theater." The fare offered onstage was far more often light opera, operetta, burlesque, or vaudeville than Verdi and Bellini.

To some extent, this was also true in San Francisco. During the economically depressed decade of the 1870s, San Franciscans fell in love with light opera, and performances of the works of Jacques Offenbach, Reginald de Koven, and Victor Herbert outnumbered presentations of grand opera.

Nevertheless, opera never died out in San Francisco as it had in New Orleans, once the American capital of opera.

The difference between San Francisco and most of the other communities with their grandiose opera houses was the knowledgeable audience for music, beyond the gold miners in search of spectacle, beyond the befurred and ostrich-feathered patrons whose main interest was the social scene. Although the gold rush drew thousands of ruffians, it also attracted more cultivated people from well-educated East Coast families and from Europe.

Both on the stage and in the audience, the city's thriving foreign enclaves had a particular influence on San Francisco's cultural development. Alfred Roncovieri, the Bordeaux-born bass who set up his tent on Telegraph Hill, not only rushed to San Francisco at the height of gold fever but stayed here to sing with various traveling and local companies until 1873. He was part of a busy French community, which founded the first local opera organization, the French Opera Company, in 1853. The city's many music-loving Germans were noted for forming active choral groups as soon as they arrived. These ensembles were the source of choristers for visiting opera companies.

The Italians supported opera from the start. The Pellegrinis were Italian and presented only Italian works. A few years later, another Italian couple, Eugenio and Giovanna Bianchi, began presenting opera fairly regularly at the opera house of impresario Tom Maguire. Italian artists came frequently with traveling companies, and Italian opera dominated the repertoire, particularly the stirring melodies of *Il Trovatore*, the most performed opera in nineteenth-century San Francisco. Opera came to have such an Italian accent that many of the Italian names one saw on the program were pseudonyms thought up by Americans who feared that their Yankee names were not suitable for their chosen art form.

As the city's Italian population grew, so did their importance as members of the audience. In the early decades, they were criticized by other members of the audience for their exuberant enthusiasm, particularly for their then unfamiliar habit of throwing bouquets at the curtain calls of their favorite divas. Later, as attending the opera became an increasingly elitist affair, society writers sniffed about the "Italian fruit vendors" who filled the balcony seats. Condescension aside, the presence of the knowledgeable Italian audience meant that opera was not a flash in the gold pan but an essential facet of the city's cultural brilliance.

The foreign-born music lovers contributed to the comparatively democratic flavor of opera-going in San Francisco. Although the unbuttoned rowdiness of the 1850s peanut crunchers was short-lived, audiences in San Francisco never achieved the pretentious snobbism of nineteenth-century audiences in New York, where the press dwelt endlessly on the feud between the old families of the Academy of Music and the nouveaux riches who founded the Metropolitan Opera. In New York, too, opera houses were intentionally designed not only for the maximum comfort of the subscribers but for the maximum discomfort and discouragement of middle-class patrons.

In contrast was San Francisco's most successful musical theater, eventually known as the Tivoli Opera House. In 1875 a German immigrant, Joseph Kreling, established a beer garden in an abandoned building at the corner of Sutter and Stockton streets and named it Tivoli Gardens. The first entertainment was provided by a group called the Spanish Students, a theatrical troupe from Mexico stranded in San Francisco due to lack of money. They performed Gilbert and Sullivan's *H.M.S. Pinafore* for 104 consecutive nights. As Tom Maguire had done decades before, Kreling filled his seats by keeping ticket prices low.

In 1879, following a fire that destroyed the Sutter Street premises, Kreling opened the Tivoli Opera House, where the principal attraction was operettas rather than steins of beer. He soon added grand opera to the repertoire of light music, starting with *Faust* and going on to more extravagant works, including *William Tell*, *Don Giovanni*, and *L'Africaine*. In 1895 the Tivoli had its first separate

San Francisco's most beloved diva around the turn of the century was unquestionably **Luisa Tetrazzini**, who was a little-known Italian soprano on tour in Mexico when William H. "Doc" Leahy, manager of the Tivoli Opera House, heard her. He brought her to San Francisco to perform at his theater, where she won instant adoration.

grand opera season, lasting eight weeks the first year and soon extending to as many as twenty weeks. Its success contributed to another fabulous statistic: 2,225 opera performances took place in San Francisco in the first decade of the twentieth century.

The Tivoli was responsible for the debut of the most adored opera singer in San Francisco history. William H. "Doc" Leahy, who became manager of the Tivoli in 1893, heard a little-known Italian soprano, Luisa Tetrazzini, in Mexico and invited her to come to San Francisco. In 1905 she made her appearance as Gilda in *Rigoletto* and earned a screaming, stamping ovation after "Caro nome." Tetrazzini subsequently sang to great acclaim around the world, but she kept a soft spot in her heart for San Francisco.

Her most memorable performance came on Christmas Eve of 1910, when the city was still recovering from the earthquake and fire of 1906. In the early afternoon people began to gather at the corner of Market, Third, and Kearny streets, and by early evening a crowd estimated variously at between one hundred thousand and two hundred fifty thousand people filled the surrounding streets. They had come to hear Tetrazzini, visible from afar in a white sequined dress and an enormous ostrich feather boa, sing a concert that included the Waltz Song from Gounod's *Roméo et Juliette* and "The Last Rose of Summer."

"Where else could I sing on Christmas Eve?" she wrote later. "This I shall always remember as my night of nights. No setting, no audience, no scene has ever so deeply moved me."

Tetrazzini knew how to play the role of the diva. A newspaper account of her death in Milan reported that "for several days, Madame Tetrazzini has been unable to take nourishment other than occasional sips of champagne."

She was not the only diva to attract an adoring following in San Francisco. Opera singers, into the early twentieth century, were the ultimate media stars, inspiring the same kind of irrational adoration that sports figures and rock stars inspire today. In spite of the long train trip or ship voyage from the East Coast, many of the world's greatest singers came to San Francisco. When the revered Adelina Patti came to town in 1884, crowds followed her carriage down the street. The crush of people attempting to buy tickets to her recital was so great at Sherman Clay and Company, the city's most prominent music store, that windows were broken and pianos damaged. Not surprisingly, Sherman Clay asked her impresario to find someone else to sell tickets on her behalf in the future.

San Franciscans also treasure the story of Enrico Caruso, who came to San Francisco for the last time in April 1906 as part of a Metropolitan Opera troupe that also included Marcel Journet, Louise Homer, and Marcella Sembrich. On the evening of April 17, Caruso dazzled the local audience with his performance as Don José in *Carmen*. Early the next morning, the great earthquake shook him out

TETRAZZINI SINGING IN THE OPEN AIR. CHRISTMAS EVE
SAN·FRANCISCO, CAL.

of his sleep at the Palace Hotel. He spent the day in terror, sitting on his suitcases in the street and finally hiring a cart to take him and his luggage out of town. He swore that he would never return to the city where he had always enjoyed browsing through Chinatown shops, and he kept that promise.

Opera thus became part of the fabric of the city, as an art form, a social manifestation, and a source of beloved legends. The only thing that was missing was a permanent, resident grand opera company.

One of San Francisco's legendary operatic moments came on Christmas Eve of 1910, when **Luisa Tetrazzini** stood on a platform near Lotta's Fountain, at the corner of Market, Third and Kearny Streets, and sang a program of arias and popular songs to a crowd that filled the surrounding streets.

Merola

chapter one GAETANO MEROLA

In 1922 San Francisco was bubbling with optimism. Sixteen years after the 1906 earthquake, four years after the end of the Great War, the city had rebuilt itself and was growing vigorously. On April 1, the *San Francisco Chronicle* financial section blazed with encouraging headlines: "SAVINGS DEPOSITS GAIN—OIL SHARES ADVANCE—STOCKS RISE SHARPLY." Another headline cheerily announced "PROSPEROUS CALIFORNIA—Not Elsewhere on Earth Is There So Little Distress as Right Here."

The city was alive with new projects. The auto industry, only twenty-four years old, was transforming the city's streets. Traffic jams appeared regularly along Post Street, and motorists demanded that more streets be paved to allow smoother progress for their vehicles. Buildings were going up all over town, and real estate sales for the month of March set a record of $13,735,695, the highest figure since the earthquake and fire.

Into this hotbed of builders and dreamers stepped one of the supreme optimists of all time. In 1922 a dashing Neapolitan conductor named Gaetano Merola launched the San Francisco Opera, convinced that the city could support its own opera company rather than depend on the visiting troupes that had provided musical entertainment since 1851.

Gaetano Merola, after visiting San Francisco many times as conductor for traveling opera troupes, came to believe that the city deserved and could afford its own opera company. With the help of a handful of music-loving philanthropists, he put together the first season at Stanford University in 1922. The following year, he presented a fall season of nine operas at the Civic Auditorium.

The church of Sant' Andrea della Valle was created in beautifully painted canvas drops for the production of *Tosca* that opened the War Memorial Opera House in 1932 (opposite). The production was recreated by designer Thierry Bosquet for the opening of the 1997 season in the newly refurbished opera house.

PROGRAM

Saturday Evening, June 3rd, 1922, at 8:15 sharp

"I'PAGLIACCI"

(In Italian)

Two Acts by R. LEONCAVALLO

CANIO..Giovanni Martinelli
TONIO..Vicente Ballester
(Taddeo in the play)
SILVIO...Marsden Argall
BEPPE..A. Neri
(Harlequin in the play)
NEDDA...Bianca Saroya
(Colombine in the play)

Chorus of Peasants

followed by BALLET DIVERTISSEMENT

Dances directed and arranged by NATALE CAROSSIO

(a) Indian Fantasy........................by Rimsky-Korsakov
(b) Voice of Spring..by J. Strauss
(d) Dance of the Hours, from the opera "La Gioconda"
....A. Ponchielli

Conductor — GAETANO MEROLA

Exchange Ticket   No.14873 B

Music Festival At Stanford Stadium

STANFORD UNIVERSITY, JUNE 1922

—— BENEFICIARIES ——

STANFORD UNIVERSITY ENDOWMENT FUND—FUND FOR ENLARGEMENT OF ORGAN IN MEMORIAL CHURCH—STANFORD CLINICS IN SAN FRANCISCO—HOME FOR CONVALESCENT CHILDREN ON THE STANFORD UNIVERSITY CAMPUS

This ticket may be exchanged for Reserved Seat at box offices of Sherman-Clay & Co's, San Francisco, Oakland, San Jose; Crandall's Palo Alto, or at book store on the Campus, at full value, or it will be accepted to apply on purchase of tickets of higher value.

PERFORMANCES	TWO DOLLARS
Sat. Evening, June 3rd, "I'Pagliacci"—8 p.m.	$2.00
Wed. Evening, June 7th, "Carmen"—8 p.m.	
Sat. Evening, June 10th, "Faust"—8 p.m.	
Fri. Evening, June 16th, "Carmen"—8 p.m.	No War Tax

HANCOCK BROS., SAN FRANCISCO

Born in Naples in 1881, Merola was the youngest son of a violinist at the royal court of Naples. At sixteen, the young Gaetano graduated with honors from the Conservatorio San Pietro a Majella. When he was nineteen, he was off to America, where he started his career with a year at the Metropolitan Opera, working as assistant to Luigi Mancinelli, a noted composer and conductor of Italian opera.

From this position Merola moved to various touring opera companies, including the Henry W. Savage Opera Company, the San Carlo Opera Company, and the Oscar Hammerstein Opera Company, one of the most active producers of musical theater throughout the United States and abroad. He became known as a conductor of operetta, and he was on the podium for the world premieres of two of the most successful examples, Victor Herbert's *Naughty Marietta* and Rudolf Friml's *The Firefly*. He polished his English during a three-year stint in London, as director of the Hammerstein operation in England.

He first came to San Francisco in the spring of 1906, as the accompanist to singer Eugenia Mantelli. Unfortunately, Mantelli's concerts had to be canceled, because Luisa Tetrazzini, the West Coast's favorite diva, was drawing sellout crowds to her own performances at the city's Tivoli Opera House, the most active musical theater in the United States at the time.

A subsequent trip to San Francisco in the summer of 1909 was far more successful. Merola arrived as the conductor of the International Opera Company of Montreal, which settled in for a six-week season at the Princess Theatre. His first review, for his conducting of the company's opening performance of *La Traviata*, was brief but favorable. A reviewer wrote, "The chorus was very excellent, the orchestra under G. Merola worthy of highest praise." Less lucky was his first wife, mezzo-soprano Rosa Duce Merola, whose performance as Carmen was criticized as "too obvious."

The highlight of the 1909 season was the West Coast premiere of Mascagni's *L'Amico Fritz*, an event that was apparently thought up on the spot and made possible by an exchange of cables between Mascagni in Italy and his San Francisco representative, a Signor Patrizi, editor of the local Italian newspaper. Mascagni, whose *Cavalleria Rusticana* had been presented in San Francisco five years earlier to great acclaim, promptly replied, "Very pleased to have my *L'Amico Fritz* given in San Francisco. . . . I will wait confidently the opinion of the San Francisco public, whose cordial and enthusiastic reception extended to me five years ago still lives in my heart with grateful memory."

The performance was a personal triumph for Merola, who received both ovations and positive reviews. There was talk in the Italian community of trying to get him to stay in San Francisco, but the time was not ripe and he continued to travel with touring opera troupes, visiting the city frequently during the next decade and developing a local following. In 1920 he told a local interviewer, "San Francisco pays too much for opera. Last year it paid out $425,000: $250,000 to the Chicago Opera, $100,000 to the Scotti company, $75,000 to the San Carlo. Why? That amount would give San Francisco its own opera for four years. I want to come back here and produce opera."

The following year he moved to San Francisco. His patron was Mrs. Oliver C. Stine, a prominent Bay Area philanthropist and lover of the arts, whose scrapbook records the varied ways she helped Merola and his wife. On July 26, 1922, she notes, "Lent Maestro $2000." On October 1, "Merolas move into an apartment that I furnished for them," followed by a list of the furnishings and their value, such as "coal scuttle $20, pewter ashtray, $1.50," commenting, "All the following winter took care of the Merolas. A JOB." Her generosity extended beyond that first season. An invoice dated October 9, 1925, lists a lengthy array of props for *Madama Butterfly*, including a $400 blue satin kimono and a $500 Japanese shrine, which she purchased at the city's leading purveyor of fine Asian goods.

With the help of Mrs. Stine, Merola began working as a voice teacher. At the same time he continued to develop his contacts both in the Italian community, where he frequently played cards with members of the Italian Fishermen's Association, and with the city's music-loving rich.

Thanks to the latter, he was invited to attend a football game at Stanford University in Palo Alto in

the fall of 1921. He was struck by the vivid acoustics of the stadium, commenting that he could hear each instrument of the marching band distinctly, and he decided that it would make a fine setting for musical performances. He convinced Stanford authorities to make the stadium available for a few days the following June and flung himself into the myriad tasks of presenting grand opera, starting with loans of thirteen thousand dollars from a bank and ten thousand dollars from his card-playing friends in North Beach.

From the start, he ran his opera as an international, rather than a regional, company. In spite of the newness of the enterprise and the distance from better-known operatic venues, Merola seemed to have no trouble hiring the best singers available. Giovanni Martinelli, one of the most adored tenors of the day, signed on to sing the roles of Canio in *Pagliacci* and Don José in *Carmen* and the title role in *Faust* at the football stadium. Bianca Saroya, an American soprano, agreed to sing the parts of the female heroines, while the baritone roles were taken by another well-known singer, Vicente Ballester.

An orchestra was formed from the ranks of the San Francisco Symphony, which had been founded in 1910, and Merola himself assembled an amateur chorus and began rehearsing them in the basement of a private house on Russian Hill.

By early June of 1922, all the performers were ready to go. A journalist observing last-minute preparations wrote, "Gaetano Merola still smiled although for almost two hours he had been conducting a rehearsal of *Pagliacci*. In fact, I think he has a greater variety of smiles than any other person I ever saw; from a smile of displeasure to one of highest approval." Before the inaugural performance, Merola engineered another first for San Francisco audiences—an operatic preview featuring Saroya and the chorus, broadcast on the newest technological marvel, the radio.

In Palo Alto a stage had been built at one end of the football arena, and simple scenery had been constructed. The audience, most of whom were probably familiar with the standard repertoire of the time, did not need elaborate props or massive sets to recognize the familiar settings. A Spanish facade sufficed to suggest the cigarette factory in the first act of *Carmen*, and a chimney and a fireplace were enough to describe Lillas Pastia's tavern. The smugglers' camp in the mountain was indicated by a pile of rocks. *Faust* was given the traditional candy-box setting of a tiny cottage in the midst of a garden, enhanced by real roses, live trees, and, of course, the nighttime sky filled with stars and a luminous moon rising over the rim of the Stanford stadium.

Although San Francisco itself was clammy with fog, discouraging some people from making the trip to the Peninsula, the weather in Palo Alto smiled on Merola's new venture. A *San Francisco Examiner* writer waxed ecstatic, writing, "The sky was cloudless, save for a few filmy veils floating slowly beneath a half-moon in its zenith. . . . The winds were still, and there was no intrusion of the outer world upon the fairy land of make-believe, except an interrupting whistle or two from a passing locomotive."

After the magic of the first night came the reality of ticket sales. The three-opera, week-long season, although well attended, did not break even, and the Italian businessmen who had put up their savings suggested that Merola seek out richer supporters in the future. Nevertheless, Merola was convinced that there was a future for opera in San Francisco, and he began planning immediately for a season at the Exposition (more familiarly known as the Civic) Auditorium, centrally located in the handsome new Civic Center, in the fall of 1923.

Working with Robert I. Bentley, a local businessman who was the opera's most stalwart and productive supporter throughout the next decade, Merola set about to finance the opera on a more permanent basis. Their first success was a lunch at the Pacific Union Club, where Merola gave a moving speech and persuaded fifty local businessmen to contribute five hundred dollars apiece toward the 1923 season. That, plus forty thousand dollars in advance ticket sales, laid the foundation for a permanent opera organization.

In other American cities, a coterie of rich people subsidized the opera whenever money was needed and, in turn, expected the opera to remain a province of elitism. Opera founders in San Francisco took a more democratic approach, deciding instead to ask a large number of people to become founding members at fifty dollars each. The citizens responded, with 2,441 signed up by April 1924. The newspapers crowed continuously about the less elitist system, sometimes in grave terms, other times more frivolously.

"Grand Opera in the past has usually been thought of in terms of subsidies," said the company's executive manager, Selby Oppenheimer, in a 1923 interview. "I do not believe that a few wealthy people in any community owe it to the public to subsidize grand opera by contributing to deficits. That is why the San Francisco plan has attracted so much interest everywhere among musicians and music lovers. It is the first time in the history of opera in the United States that a season of first magnitude has been self-supporting."

Lady Teazle, pen name for the *Chronicle*'s society editor, cooed in 1922, "One was delighted to observe how all classes, including the Italian fruit vender [sic] or one's favorite cafeteria cashier, to the leaders of the smart world, were all to be seen at the opera." Not all the observers were as sophisticated as they might have hoped; in the same issue of the *Chronicle*, a writer refers to Mozart's *Cossi Tan Frutte*.

Soprano **Licia Albanese** sang one of her favorite roles, Violetta, and tenor **Jan Peerce** was Alfredo in the opening night performance of *La Traviata* in 1947. Before the performance, they and the rest of the guests at Violetta's party gathered on the first-act set to celebrate **Gaetano Merola's** twenty-fifth year with the San Francisco Opera. (Above, from left to right, Merola, Peerce, and Albanese pose onstage.)

The 1933 performances of Verdi's *La Forza del Destino* had a star-studded cast: opposite from left to right, tenor **Giovanni Martinelli**, who played Don Alvaro; soprano **Claudia Muzio**, who sang the role of Leonora, shown in a typically melodramatic pose; and **Ezio Pinza**, who played the Padre Guardiano for the first of many times in San Francisco.

The setting for Merola's first opera season in San Francisco was the **Exposition Auditorium**, (above), now known as the **Bill Graham Civic Auditorium**, in the city's Civic Center. The auditorium was barnlike, the acoustics terrible, but it could seat more than six thousand people. The company revisited the Civic for the 1996–97 season, while the War Memorial Opera House was undergoing extensive seismic reinforcements and cosmetic improvements.

Knowledgeable or not, the city's elite leapt at the chance to parade themselves, their jewelry, and their furs. And why not? The City of Paris department store was advertising muskrat coats for $135. Opera patrons were also eager to show off their cars, at a time when a new record of nine hours and sixteen minutes for the Los Angeles to San Francisco run made headlines in the newspaper.

On opening night, September 26, 1923, the opera was *La Bohème*, with an all-star cast featuring Queena Mario as Mimì, Giovanni Martinelli as Rodolfo, and a young San Franciscan, Anna Young, as Musetta. A sellout crowd, some five thousand people, bought tickets for this momentous and gala moment in the city's history. Limousines, along with an occasional touring car or taxicab, swept up four abreast to the front entrance of the auditorium. The streets were packed with onlookers, who admired the well-dressed women, many of them fashionably swathed in Spanish shawls, as they descended from their cars.

Inside, the importance of the elite was acknowledged by the arc of raised boxes around the first-floor seats. These seats, high in both visibility and prestige, were part of Merola's overnight transformation of the barnlike Civic Auditorium into a temporary opera house. The work had started only the day before, but the effect was dramatic. The plain interior walls of the auditorium were masked with fabric. A heavy blue curtain flickering with concealed lights rose behind the stage, while above it, curtains of gold and blue rose to the ceiling. In the main hall, a canopy of midnight blue covered the entire ceiling.

This sort of sleight of hand was a hallmark of the Merola era, when rehearsal time was close to nonexistent. Typically, the principal singers stepped off the train three or four days before the season began, in contrast to the three weeks of rehearsal that is now typical. If they were lucky, there would be time for a couple of run-throughs before opening night. Sometimes the scenery would not be onstage until the night of the performance, a practice that occasionally led to disaster. Merola's successor, Kurt Herbert Adler, recalled much later, "We had a bad incident with *Mefistofele*, because the scenery stood in the wrong place, and the chorus got into trouble."

Significantly, contemporaneous reviews rarely even mentioned the scenery or the costumes. Audiences did not expect elaborate productions and were content with painted flats and drapes, frequently interchangeable between different operas. Singers brought their own costumes. Props, often valuable antique furniture and objets d'art, were culled from San Francisco's finest houses by a committee of socially prominent women.

What opera patrons did expect were voices, glorious voices, and Merola satisfied them in this respect from the beginning. In the first season at the Civic Auditorium, the legendary tenors

Beniamino Gigli and Giovanni Martinelli, baritone Giuseppe De Luca, bass Adamo Didur, and sopranos Bianca Saroya and Queena Mario sang in several operas apiece. For the next three decades of Merola's reign, the great singers of the world came regularly to San Francisco, often performing several roles in deference to the short season and the long travel time across the country. For European artists, the presence of a third major opera house, in addition to New York and Chicago, in the United States made it more attractive to take the long sea voyage to America in the first place.

The success of San Francisco's new opera company owed much to an immeasurable asset, Gaetano Merola's personal charm. The city was enchanted by him. Citizens rich and poor recognized him as he raced around town, handsome and well dressed, often wearing a debonair black fedora. He was exuberant, endlessly talkative in fluent English, Italian, or French, and alluringly Neapolitan at a time when the Italian community was responsible for much of the city's panache. When he stepped to the conductor's podium, he was greeted with a spontaneous ovation of pure gratitude and affection.

He brought boundless energy to the job, taking on any number of roles on a given day. In the early years, he was almost solely responsible for the administration of the company, hiring of singers, raising of funds and training the chorus. In addition, he was often in the pit, conducting all the operas in the

Gaetano Merola was considered one of the world's greatest conductors of Puccini, and at least two of the composer's works were in the repertoire in each of the San Francisco Opera's first ten seasons. The 1931 cast of *La Bohème* included, from left to right, **Audrey Farncroft** as Musetta, **Millo Picco** as Schaunard, **Ezio Pinza** as Colline, **Mario Chamlee** as Rodolfo, and **Maria Müller** in the role of Mimì.

Three stalwarts of the Merola years, from left to right, **Dorothy Kirsten**, **Ezio Pinza**, and **Claramae Turner** starred in the San Francisco Opera's first performances of Charpentier's *Louise* in 1947. Kirsten studied the title role with the composer. In spite of all his responsibilities, Merola remained at heart a musician, with a deep sympathy for his fellow artists. "This wonderful man was respected and loved by every singer who worked for him," said Kirsten. "Merola stimulated confidence in the artist. He was a perfect gentleman, a warmhearted, considerate man who was knowledgeable about the art of singing and most helpful in guiding my young career."

first two seasons, as many as half in later seasons. He even, so the story goes, put on a costume and sang with the chorus one night when its numbers were depleted. He loved airplane travel and flew to Europe often to sign up singers, particularly in the later years of his thirty-year tenure. Long before other American opera impresarios did, he concerned himself with providing opportunities to young American singers, although the formal establishment of apprenticeship programs in San Francisco would come later.

In addition to orchestrating the local season, Merola was head of the opera association of Los Angeles, where the San Francisco company presented regular seasons from 1937 to 1965. He took the company on tour throughout the West, to Portland, Seattle, and San Diego, and he presented outdoor opera in the Greek Theater at the University of California in Berkeley. He also had competition in San Francisco itself. Although the Tivoli Opera, which had been the busiest musical theater in the United States around the turn of the century, closed its doors in 1924, touring companies continued to appear, and two local companies, Cosmopolitan Opera and Pacific Opera, were active rivals through the 1950s.

The newborn San Francisco Opera was literally a family operation. Merola brought his cousin, Armando Agnini, from the Metropolitan Opera to be San Francisco's stage director. Armando's brother Alessandro took charge of costumes, and other relatives performed smaller backstage roles with the company.

In the words of Merola's niece, Carmen Fraitas, "he was a Pied Piper," entrancing all levels of society. In 1926 the opera advertised for one hundred supers for *Aida*. One newspaper recounted that three hundred aspirants "stormed the Civic Auditorium," causing sufficient disturbance that opera personnel called the police to disperse the crowd. "The affair took on quite a social atmosphere, with the presence in the waiting line of a number of those high in San Francisco's youthful social register, including Randolph Hale, Prentis Hale, Oliver C. Stine and James Colman, who recently inherited some $2 million."

For several years, Merola resigned himself to the difficulties of not having a proper opera house, presenting performances in the unwieldy Civic Auditorium and, in 1928 and 1929, at the equally unsuitable auditorium called Dreamland. He resolutely stated that it was better to have an opera company without a house than an opera house without music. The notion of having a permanent opera house

had been around for a long time. Fund-raising had begun in 1911, when the Musical Association of San Francisco pledged to raise a million dollars for a building to be constructed in the Civic Center, that grandiose symbol of the city's rebirth after the earthquake and fire of 1906.

During the next few years, progress on the project was slow. After the city announced plans to cede land to the Musical Association, the California Supreme Court ruled that the city could not legally give property to a private organization. To complicate the situation further, a private company purchased a chunk of land in the Civic Center and announced its intention to build a large warehouse there. These and other problems were finally solved when Major Charles Kendrick, a leading citizen, returned from World War I in 1919 and suggested that the opera house be constructed as a memorial to San Franciscans who had served in the war, an idea that brought in the veterans as supporters of the project.

By 1920, more than $2 million had been raised, an achievement that undoubtedly played a part in Merola's decision to move to San Francisco. Later, in 1927, a bond issue for $4 million was passed by a wide margin, and groundbreaking took place the following year. During the long gestation period, the original scheme for a single building had been changed to a plan for a more imposing pair of buildings, one for the opera house, the other for the veterans, facing each other across a courtyard. The principal designer was Arthur Brown, Jr., who had designed City Hall, with another leading local architect, G. Albert Lansburgh, responsible for the interiors and the stage.

The opera house was a handsome classical building in the Beaux Arts tradition, with wide steps and arched doorways across the main entrance on Van Ness Avenue and entrances designed for cars on the courtyard and Grove Street sides. Inside, the lobby, with its marble floors, columns, and coffered ceiling, provided a stately space for opera-goers to promenade during intermissions. Although Prohibition was not repealed until the year after the opera house's opening, ample space for bars on several levels had been included in the plans. The newspapers regaled their readers with details, from the dimensions of the huge stage to the amenities of each box, which included a call button for maid service.

Incredibly, these impressive buildings rose during the darkest years of the Great Depression, and opening night, October 15, 1932, attracted huge crowds, some watching the spectacle from the west

During World War II the audience at the War Memorial Opera House was dotted with men and women in uniform. French soprano **Lily Pons** brought the crowd to its feet in 1942 when she waved the French flag and sang "La Marseillaise" to conclude a performance of *La Fille du Régiment* (above).

In a 1952 review *San Francisco Chronicle* music critic Alfred Frankenstein wrote of Merola as "one of the world's best conductors of Verdi and Puccini. This was particularly apparent during the performance of *Bohème*. . . . It was one of the richest, warmest, most moving and memorable interpretations of this score that I have ever had the privilege of hearing. It was the kind of performance that explains why people grow sentimental, fanatical and a little unbalanced about opera in general, but particularly about *La Bohème*" (left).

steps and balustrades of the illuminated City Hall. Other spectators massed around the main entrance, kept in bounds by ropes and a squad of policemen. Tickets had been sold out for months, and there was rumor of "a rich Honolulu planter" who had offered—in vain—one thousand dollars for six tickets, printed price five dollars apiece.

Every local newspaper covered the event in copious detail. According to their accounts, the women wore slender dresses with skirts that fanned out below the knee, purchased at the finest couturiers in Paris, from Paquin and Worth to Vionnet and Chanel. The opening-night patrons became so delighted with themselves that they embarked on an unscheduled promenade, circling from the main lobby up the stairs to the box level, pausing on the balconies, then descending the wide staircases.

Not all of them managed to abandon the parade to take their seats in the boxes at curtain time, but Merola raised his baton promptly at 8:45 P.M., conducting a moving "Star-Spangled Banner" before going on to his beloved Puccini. It had been a long wait for a proper opera house, and the audience laughed knowingly when the first words of the opera—"Ah, finalmente!" (at last)—were sung by a local singer, Marsden Argall, in the role of Angelotti. Soprano Claudia Muzio, the Tosca of the evening, had also shopped at Worth in Paris for her lavish costumes.

Merola's true love was music, and he was probably happiest on those many nights when he was conducting. Although he conducted French and German opera often, his specialty was Italian opera, particularly Puccini. Listeners were touched by the warm emotionalism of his *Bohème*, comparing his version favorably with Toscanini's famous interpretation. His successor and fellow conductor Kurt Herbert Adler said that he avoided conducting *Bohème* for many years because of his memory of Merola's performances.

In the 1940s, as the opera season grew longer and the company larger, Merola's administrative tasks left him less and less time for conducting, particularly as his heart condition worsened with age. His 1953 schedule included two engagements, the first in July at the Hollywood Bowl, the second an outdoor concert at Stern Grove, the eucalyptus-shaded dell that attracted thousands to a series of summer concerts under the sponsorship of the music-loving Mrs. Sigmund Stern.

On the misty morning of August 30, just before the opening of the opera season, he went out to Stern Grove to rehearse the San Francisco Symphony orchestra for the afternoon's performance. Looking at the foggy dampness, his half-brother Ulisse Caiati turned to him and asked whether he really thought he should be conducting that day. Merola responded, "Mrs. Stern has done so much for me that I would give my life for her." All went reasonably well until he was conducting "Un bel dì" from his beloved *Madama Butterfly*. As soprano Brunetta Mazzolini sang the word "morire" (to die), Merola raised his baton, seemed to stare into space and then fell prostrate across the podium. The horrified audience watched a doctor declare him dead. An opera representative announced, "The concert is over."

Some of his favorite singers, Licia Albanese, Claramae Turner, Jan Peerce, and Nicola Moscona, augmented by the chorus and the symphony, performed Verdi's *Requiem* Mass in his memory at the opera house on April 2, 1954.

His legacy was the San Francisco Opera.

Gaetano Merola waited patiently for a real opera house, saying that it was preferable to have an opera company without a theater than a theater without an opera company. Throughout the first decade of the company's history, a small group of private citizens worked hard to raise funds, acquire a location, pass a bond issue, and invite the public to subscribe. The thousands of San Franciscans who subscribed made San Francisco the first American city to have an opera house that was not built by and for a small group of rich patrons. The War Memorial Opera House, constructed during the Depression, opened its arched doors on October 15, 1932. It was a gala occasion, and the well-dressed patrons saw a handsome production of *Tosca*, with soprano **Claudia Muzio** in the title role and baritone **Alfredo Gandolfi** as a villainous Scarpia (opposite).

chapter two HEROES

Every time that tenor Giovanni Martinelli arrived in San Francisco in the 1920s, he was greeted with the kind of adulation that today goes to rock stars, movie legends, and basketball players with multimillion contracts.

Photographers waited at the train to take his picture as he stepped onto the platform. Reporters who rushed to interview him asked him not only about his operatic career but about the Italian political situation. In the early 1920s he and fellow Italian Giuseppe De Luca had spoken highly of Mussolini, an opinion that they later changed. As the days passed, the details of his daily agenda in San Francisco were carefully reported in the newspapers. On one visit, he was invited to participate, along with the mayor and other civic officials, at a public ceremony marking the opening of a section of the Great Highway at Ocean Beach, in addition to being wined and dined by prominent San Franciscans. Amid all this activity, the adored Martinelli managed to fit in a few rehearsals at the Civic Auditorium.

Front-page attention to opera stars was not unusual in the early decades of the century. Singers were media darlings to a degree greatly surpassing the attention now lavished on the likes of Luciano Pavarotti and Cecilia Bartoli. Americans then as now loved celebrity for its own sake, and

Gaetano Merola's first superstar was tenor **Giovanni Martinelli**, who was greeted by photographers and reporters each time he returned to San Francisco (above left). Martinelli sang the roles of Canio in _Pagliacci_ and Don José in _Carmen_ and the title role in _Faust_ in the first season at Stanford University's football stadium. _Pagliacci_ was a particularly meaningful opera for him: Enrico Caruso had acknowledged the man considered his successor by giving him his clown costume after a performance at the Metropolitan Opera, saying, "Giovanni, I am giving this costume to you. I think it will fit." Martinelli had one of the longest careers in opera, particularly if one includes his final performance onstage at the age of eighty-one, when he replaced an ailing tenor in the small, half-spoken, half-sung role of the Emperor in _Turandot_ at the Seattle Opera.

Jess Thomas, here as Siegfried in _Götterdämmerung_, was both the personification of the operatic hero and one of San Francisco's favorite tenors (opposite).

Tenor **Tito Schipa** made his San Francisco opera debut in 1924 as Chevalier des Grieux in *Manon,* a role he repeated for many years. Reviewer Redfern Mason, writing in the *San Francisco Examiner,* gave a glimpse of what tenor worship was like in 1925, when Schipa repeated the role: "What Schipa would do we knew, for his reading of 'Le Rêve' is now local tradition. Last night he repeated the triumph of last year, singing the number with a refinement of tone and a perfection of diction that probably will not be equalled by any other artist in our generation. He had to sing it twice, of course, for there are occasions when the audience will not be denied." By 1929, however, the audience would be denied. Merola, feeling that encores during a performance were disruptive to the flow of the opera, had put his foot down. Another of Schipa's favorite roles was Count Almaviva (above), the romantic suitor in *Il Barbiere di Siviglia,* a role he sang in 1925, 1926, 1929, and 1935.

Baritone **Lawrence Tibbett** was something of a local boy, who lived in Bakersfield until he was six, at which time his father, the local sheriff, was killed. The family moved to Los Angeles, where he began his stage career with a Shakespearean repertory company. His acting talent contributed to his almost instantaneous success at the Metropolitan Opera in New York, where his stand-in performance as Ford in *Falstaff* made him a legend overnight. He sang a wide repertoire in San Francisco, including his first Scarpia in *Tosca* in 1928 and his first Iago in 1936 (above right), with **Giovanni Martinelli**, at left, singing his first Otello. Another memorable part was the title role in Louis Gruenberg's short-lived opera, *Emperor Jones.* Tibbett was also a success in Hollywood, where he made six movies and received an Academy Award nomination for best actor in 1930 for his artistry in *The Rogue Song.* Tibbett was a founding member of the American Guild of Musical Artists, the union that represents opera's vocal artists.

The year 1934 brought several interesting newcomers to San Francisco Opera, including Richard Crooks, Nelson Eddy, and Lotte Lehmann, but the most impressive was the great Wagnerian tenor **Lauritz Melchior**. At six feet four inches tall and 225 pounds, Melchior was an impressive figure onstage. The main attraction, however was the voice, which remained lyrical and tireless during hours of performing Wagner—perhaps aided by the special corset that he designed for himself for long roles. Melchior made history in the company's first presentation of Wagner's *Ring* cycle in 1935, sharing applause with **Kirsten Flagstad**, who was performing her first complete *Ring* ever. The photograph of the two together (opposite) became an opera classic, reproduced all over the world. The series was a sellout, causing the social elite to fret about such new dilemmas as whether evening dress was acceptable at a performance that began in the bright light of afternoon.

the personal lives of sopranos and tenors were considered diverting news by people who would never set foot in an opera house.

Of course, opera stars were as much myth as reality. There was no television to bring close-ups, gaping larynxes and all, into the living room. Radio broadcasts and recordings, both in a fairly primitive state, were the only way that most people could appreciate their favorite singers. At this remove, who could blame people for assuming that the singers, like the roles they played, were larger than life?

Fortunately for the eager press, a number of artists did their best to live up to the illusion, exercising their fine instinct for exaggeration and knack for image building. In some cases, singers were more effective actors offstage than on.

It is hard to imagine any contemporary opera star getting the kind of public attention that was lavished on Italian tenor Beniamino Gigli when he arrived in San Francisco in 1923 for the first season at the Civic Auditorium. Like other travelers, Gigli had crossed the country by train, disembarking in Oakland and then taking the ferry across the bay to San Francisco. Arriving at the Ferry Building, he was greeted by a motorcycle escort, which roared alongside his car to his hotel. He was also made an honorary chief by the San Francisco Police Department, echoing a similar tribute paid to him in New York.

American baritone **Thomas Stewart** told an interviewer, "I have never looked on opera as a singing art form. It is musical theater." In this, he was in perfect harmony with Kurt Herbert Adler's emphasis on opera as a complete art form, dramatic as well as musical. He started his San Francisco career in a big way in 1962, singing major roles in four operas, and returned many times during the next twenty-three years. In that time, he sang twenty roles, moving from Don Giovanni to Golaud in *Pelléas et Mélisande* on to Wagner, whose works he performed for ten consecutive seasons at the annual Wagner festival in Bayreuth. In San Francisco's 1972 and 1985 *Ring* cycles, he created powerful, moving portrayals of Wotan and the Wanderer (left), here in *Siegfried* in 1985. His most challenging role, he felt, was the title role in Aribert Reimann's *Lear* (opposite), in its American premiere in 1981, in which he worked with one of his favorite directors, Jean-Pierre Ponnelle. He said, "I have never sung anything so difficult; it is very atonal and is taxing to me as singer, actor, and performer as much as anything I have ever done, but I love it."

Nor was it only the major stars who were greeted by the flash of the Speed Graflex and the hurried questions of reporters. In those days before mass jet travel, the "arrival story" was the bread and butter of daily newspapers, and even slightly less glamorous singers got attention. In 1932, when Merola was moving away from an almost completely Italian and French repertoire, two eminent Wagner specialists, American mezzo-soprano Kathryn Meisle and German baritone Friedrich Schorr, both looking stolidly middle-aged, were photographed, interviewed, and prominently featured when they arrived in San Francisco.

Generally, though, it was sopranos, if they were glamorous enough, and tenors, even if they weren't always dashing, who inspired the more irrational forms of adulation. They were the ones who dodged and smiled as bouquets rained upon the stage and who received the standing ovations that lasted minutes rather than seconds. They were the ones whose public demanded encores of favorite arias in the middle of operas and mobbed the stage after a successful performance or concert.

Jan Peerce, the son of Russian immigrants who lived on New York's Lower East Side, was reportedly self-conscious about his appearance, especially his large nose and short stature. Nevertheless, he brought a lovely lyric tenor, impeccable taste and technique, and perfect diction in several languages to French and Italian bel canto roles, to Mozart, and to Rodolfo in *La Bohème*, one of the few Puccini roles he allowed himself to sing. A 1949 reviewer wrote of his Don Ottavio in *Don Giovanni*, "Peerce's singing of the role was a hair-raising demonstration, not only of beautiful tone but also of easy, floating, plastic, long-breathed vocalism that Mozart needs and all too seldom gets." Peerce, a favorite of Arturo Toscanini, sang the role of the Duke of Mantua in *Rigoletto* in his San Francisco debut in 1941. Thanks to his perfect technique, he was still pealing out high Bs when he was in his seventies and received rave notices for his final local recital in 1971. Here, second from left, he appears as Don Ottavio in a 1955 performance of Mozart's *Don Giovanni*, with, from left to right, **Elisabeth Schwarzkopf** as Donna Elvira, **Licia Albanese** as Donna Anna, and **Cesare Siepi** as Don Giovanni.

Gaetano Merola hired **Mario Del Monaco** for the 1950 season after hearing a recording of his voice and thus set up a thrilling performance of *Aida* in which both the tenor and Renata Tebaldi made their United States debuts. One reviewer carped that Del Monaco "liked to shout down the opposition...he is often tight and rasping in the middle and lower registers. But his top register can be glorious, and he often makes up in sheer strength and virility what he lacks in sensuous sound and vocal finesse." No matter—the public loved him for what *San Francisco Chronicle* music critic Alfred Frankenstein called "the fat, trumpeting clear high notes sustained until the audience yells with the excitement they engender." His movie-star looks didn't hurt either. In 1953 he was scheduled to sing five major roles, but in late August he sent a telegram canceling his appearances. Kurt Herbert Adler did not tell Merola immediately, knowing how much it would upset him. The next day Merola died at Stern Grove without finding out what Del Monaco had done. The tenor subsequently returned to San Francisco several times, concluding his career at the War Memorial in 1962, when he sang Canio in *Pagliacci* (above), with a youthful **Marilyn Horne** as Nedda.

Giorgio Tozzi took part in fifteen San Francisco Opera seasons between 1955, when he made his debut as Calkas in the American premiere of William Walton's *Troilus and Cressida*, and 1977, when he sang the role of the blind king Timur in *Turandot*. Dashingly handsome and possessing a fine lyric bass, Tozzi took on some of the roles that Ezio Pinza had sung in the preceding decades. Among those that he performed most frequently were the roles of Colline in *La Bohème* (above), Don Giovanni, and Méphistophélès in *Faust*.

Tenor **Beniamino Gigli**, one of the most revered singers of the early twentieth century, was apparently a little nervous about coming so far to Merola's brand-new opera company; he insisted that a check for a thousand dollars be deposited in his bank account before he would travel west. Merola did not have the money, but two of the company's loyal supporters, Horace Clifton and Mrs. Oliver C. Stine, came up with the funds. European singers like Gigli were lured to the United States by salaries higher than those they received at home. San Francisco, although a young opera company, was no exception. By 1930, Gigli received $3,750 a performance in San Francisco, considerably more in real dollars than similar performers are paid today. Moreover, unpaid rehearsal time for the eight operas he was to perform was short: his contract stated, "You shall place yourself at our disposal four days before the opening date in San Francisco." Additionally, it stipulated, "You agree to sing a ninth performance absolutely gratis." One of his most popular roles was the passionate poet in *Andrea Chénier* (left).

His voice was described as dark and virile, with a rich and velvety sound from boldest fortissimo to softest pianissimo, and it is remembered as one of the most thrilling sounds in opera. Baritone **Leonard Warren**, born in the Bronx, the son of Russian Jewish immigrants, had a special affinity for Italian opera. In San Francisco, where he appeared in seven seasons between 1943 and 1956, he concentrated on Verdi, singing Amonasro in *Aida*, Rigoletto, Don Carlo in *La Forza del Destino*, Simon Boccanegra, and Falstaff (above). Warren's career was cut short when he died of a stroke at the age of forty-eight onstage at the Metropolitan Opera.

Gigli was particularly well known for loving this sort of visible adoration, and one has to wonder if the following announcement in the program of one of his San Francisco concerts was intended as a true warning or was just wishful thinking. Under the headline, "Special Request," the audience was "respectfully requested to remain seated at the close of the program, and NOT TO CROWD AROUND THE PLATFORM. This practice has become obnoxious to the artists and tremendously discomforting to those in the front seats, who are entitled to enjoy complete comfort in the seats which they purchased. POSITIVELY NO ENCORES CAN BE RENDERED BY THE ARTIST IF MEMBERS OF THE AUDIENCE INSIST ON RUSHING FORWARD."

Indecorous mob scenes of this kind were not exclusive to either Gigli or San Francisco. Maria Callas experienced the same problem much later in the century.

Feuds and rivalries also contributed to the public image of certain divas and *primi tenori*. Dramatic soprano Maria Jeritza, who took the role of diva as goddess very seriously, made much of her constant feuds with her fellow artists. One night she so irritated Gigli during a squabble about curtain calls at the Metropolitan that he kicked her in the shins. With that she rushed in front of the curtain to whimper plaintively to the audience, "Mr. Gigli is not nice to me."

The curtain would not have gone up at the War Memorial in the 1930s and 1940s had there not been a group of stalwart regulars who came back again and again in an infinite variety of roles. **Charles Kullman**, shown here with soprano **Stella Roman** as Tosca in a 1941 performance, sang in the Yale University Glee Club when he was an undergraduate, then went to Europe to develop his career in Berlin, Vienna, and London. When he returned to the United States, he became a regular in San Francisco, often contributing his refined lyric tenor to Puccini's romantic heroes, but also branching out as far as the title role in Wagner's *Parsifal*. Other indispensable artists of the 1930s (below left) were Italian tenor **Dino Borgioli**, at left, and American baritone **Richard Bonelli**, at right, flanking **Claudia Muzio** as Violetta in the 1932 *La Traviata*. **Raoul Jobin** (below) had lead roles in every season from 1940 to 1949; here, he sings the role of Don José in *Carmen* in 1940, with **Marjorie Lawrence** in the title role.

Chilean singer **Ramon Vinay** brought dark-voiced power and gripping acting talent to the roles that he sang in San Francisco. Although he had started his career as a baritone, his earliest performances in San Francisco were as a tenor, as Don José in *Carmen* in 1949 and Tristan in *Tristan and Isolde* the following year. When he returned in the 1960s, he was again a baritone and a powerful stage presence in roles like Scarpia in *Tosca* (opposite) and Dr. Schön in *Lulu*.

English tenor **Richard Lewis** made his San Francisco debut in 1955 as Don José in *Carmen* and also portrayed Troilus the same season in the American premiere of William Walton's *Troilus and Cressida*. For the next fourteen years, he proved to be a highly versatile addition to the company, singing in everything from *Medea* to *Wozzeck*, with Mozart and Puccini in between. The highlight of his local career came in 1962, when he won rave reviews for his performance as Tom Rakewell in the company's first presentation of Stravinsky's *The Rake's Progress* (above).

Baritone **Robert Weede** was a favorite of the San Francisco Opera, starting with his first performance, in 1940, in the title role of *Rigoletto* and ending a quarter of a century later with his final performance as Tonio in *Pagliacci* (right). In between, he sang a host of Amonasros, Jack Rances, and Scarpias, taking time off in the 1950s to star in *The Most Happy Fella* on Broadway.

Jarmila Novotná, a Czech soprano with a lovely voice and a delicate, fine-featured beauty, received some of the most unusual tributes. Hollywood mogul Louis B. Mayer offered her a movie contract on the condition that she would quit opera. She declined to do so. A more unusual tribute came from Tomás Masaryk, the first president of independent Czechoslovakia, who put her portrait on the fledgling country's hundred-koruna notes.

Novotná was originally scheduled to make her United States debut as Violetta in *La Traviata* at the World's Fair of 1939 at Flushing Meadows, but conductor Arturo Toscanini objected to the sound of airplanes flying overhead. The performance was canceled, and Novotná made her American debut in San Francisco later the same year, singing both *Madama Butterfly* and Violetta.

Generally, though, the attention paid to opera singers was much less dignified. Although Enrico Caruso's unconventional private life, involving a married woman with whom he lived in Italy, was glossed over by an American press perhaps wary of blackening the reputation of an idol, later stars were not so lucky. For all the high-mindedness of opera as an art form, scandal involving singers was endlessly fascinating to the press and the public.

For sheer gossip value, the star of the show was Ezio Pinza, a bass who got as much attention as

One of Kurt Herbert Adler's earliest and most productive discoveries was Welsh baritone **Geraint Evans**, who came to San Francisco for the first time in 1959 in the role of Beckmesser in *Die Meistersinger*. His performance the following year of the title role in *Wozzeck* showed off his powerful acting ability and became a signature role that he performed all over the world. In addition to Wozzeck, Evans sang several other roles in San Francisco for the first time, including Paolo in *Simon Boccanegra*, the title role in *Gianni Schicchi*, Kecal in *The Bartered Bride*, and Pizarro in *Fidelio*. During his twenty years with the company, he also added special finesse and charm to roles like Papageno in *The Magic Flute* (above left), in a 1969 performance with **Margaret Price**; the title role in *Falstaff* (opposite); and a sympathetic Balstrode in *Peter Grimes*. A number of other Welsh singers, including tenor Stuart Burrows, baritone Delme Bryn-Jones, and sopranos Gwyneth Jones and Margaret Price followed in his footsteps, adding luster to the company's roster of artists during the 1960s and 1970s.

Although Italian accents were most common in the early days of the opera, to the delight of the large Italian community, San Franciscans were happy to make an exception for the long local career of **Jussi Bjoerling**. The Swedish tenor made his first appearance in the city in 1920, singing with his father and two brothers as the Bjoerling Male Quartette. He made his San Francisco Opera debut in 1940, in *La Bohème* and *Un Ballo in Maschera*. He subsequently had an active performing career in the city, giving frequent recitals, informal concerts for war veterans, radio performances, and even a duet with his wife, Anna-Lisa, at the Fol de Rol, a lighthearted gala held for many years as a benefit for the company. Bjoerling's final performance in San Francisco, in 1958, was a meeting point of two eras of operatic history: he sang his final Manrico to Leontyne Price's first Leonora in *Il Trovatore*. In 1949, Bjoerling was Chevalier des Grieux to **Licia Albanese**'s Manon Lescaut in the Puccini opera (right).

Bass-baritone **Nicola Rossi Lemeni** made his impressive American operatic debut in 1951 in San Francisco, singing the title role in *Boris Godunov*. The son of a Russian mother and an Italian father, Rossi Lemeni brought a special drama and fluency to the Mussorgsky opera. Although he sang the role in Italian in San Francisco, he sang it in the original Russian when he performed it in Russia, where he received forty-eight curtain calls. He came back to San Francisco several times, lending villainous fervor to his melodramatic portrayals of Mefistofele and Don Giovanni, and a gentler mien to the role of the Father in *Louise* (above).

Ezio Pinza was the very definition of a San Francisco Opera regular, singing in twenty out of twenty-two seasons between 1927 and 1948, lending his voice and his strong acting skills to both baritone and bass roles, including Don Giovanni (left) and the title role in *Boris Godunov* (above). He was a serious researcher who went to libraries and museums to study history, costumes, and manners for each new role. He was also a master at makeup, always doing his own from a stock of thirty-five noses, forty-seven beards, fifty-one mustaches, twenty-two pairs of ears, fifteen sets of fingernails, and forty-one pairs of eyebrows.

In 1942 Pinza, an Italian on the verge of becoming a United States citizen, was arrested as a spy and sentenced to spend the rest of the war years in an internment camp. Three months later, he was released after it was discovered that the charges, including accusations that he sent coded messages through the Metropolitan Opera's Saturday radio broadcasts, had been fabricated by a jealous rival bass in New York.

"The San Francisco Opera company, where I had performed season after season, had held up all decisions on casting until my release was official, so that they could include me in their plans," he recalled in his autobiography. Even when he arrived in San Francisco, he continued to have problems. His wife Doris wrote to her parents, "Wherever we go and any time during the day whatsoever, a detective is with us. . . . He goes to rehearsals, performances, everywhere, and is never more than five feet away from Ezio." Merola promptly complained to civil and military authorities, and the guard was eventually removed.

any romantic tenor. Although he was a serious and extremely gifted artist, respected for his extensive research into roles, it was his thrill-packed personal life that hit the front pages. Tall and rakishly handsome, the great interpreter of Don Giovanni was a Don Juan in his own right. During the fall of 1936, when he was in San Francisco to perform in five operas, he was sued for breach of promise by a young woman described as the "cloistered daughter" of a local Italian family.

Process servers hovered around the backstage area to present Pinza with summonses, and the press was not far behind. Day after day, the newspapers described the scandal with the kind of detail that implied the reporters had their ears pressed to the dressing room door. Pinza's lawyer presented an interesting defense to the woman's claim that she did not realize the dashing opera star was married. How could she not know, he asked, when Mrs. Pinza had only a year before filed a very public suit against German soprano Elisabeth Rethberg, accusing her of alienating the affections of her husband?

What was it about opera singers that inspired this kind of frenzied attention? Was all this adulation rational? Perhaps not, but neither is opera itself. The very nature of the art form, combining music with words, plays to the emotions of the audience. In a drama in which the simplest

Swedish baritone **Ingvar Wixell** made his American operatic debut in San Francisco in 1967, doing honor to the role of Belcore in the highly successful *Elisir d'Amore* directed by Lotfi Mansouri. Wixell went on to have a long career at the War Memorial, turning in gripping versions of many important baritone roles, including Germont in *La Traviata,* Scarpia in *Tosca,* Tonio in *Pagliacci,* and Simon Boccanegra. In 1985, he was a sympathetic Falstaff (above left), with **Alan Titus** as Ford.

Tenor **James McCracken** made his debut at the San Francisco Opera in 1962, starting out in two Verdi roles, the troubadour Manrico in *Il Trovatore* and the tortured Moor of *Otello,* both roles he repeated several times during his long career with the company. For the next fifteen years he brought both vocal skills and emotional intensity to many important roles. He played Hermann in the company's first production of Tchaikovsky's melodramatic *Queen of Spades* in 1963, was a powerful Samson in the 1963 *Samson et Dalila,* and sang Radames in *Aida* in 1977. His final performance with the company was as a touching Florestan in the 1987 production of *Fidelio* (above), with Irish soprano **Elizabeth Connell** as Leonore.

It didn't hurt the career of American bass-baritone **James Morris** that dozens of music critics were in town for a meeting at the same time that he sang Wotan in *Das Rheingold* for the first time (inset) and *Die Walküre*, in which he shared the stage with **Gwyneth Jones** (left). Andrew Porter, reviewer for the *Financial Times*, wrote, "Musically, the great thing was the emergence of a noble, commanding, and vocally resplendent Wotan . . . His presence was godlike. He easily lifted the Brünnhilde (Gwyneth Jones) in his arms and carried her to her place of sleep. His voice rang out with easy, unforced power and in steadily eloquent tones." Morris went on to do Wotan with enormous success at opera houses around the world. A native of Baltimore, Morris started his career by studying with retired diva Rosa Ponselle and bass Nicola Moscona, a San Francisco regular during the 1950s. Claiming that singing Wotan opened the top range of his voice, he took on some more baritone roles; in San Francisco, he sang Procida in *I Vespri Siciliani* in 1993 and the title role in Verdi's *Macbeth* in 1994.

For many San Francisco opera-goers, some of the most emotionally wrenching evenings ever spent at the War Memorial came in 1976, when Canadian tenor **Jon Vickers** sang the role of the deranged, lonely fisherman Peter Grimes in Benjamin Britten's opera. The sound of what a reviewer called "his muscular, tireless voice . . . pitted and scarred as if hacked out of a Canadian quarry" and the visible psychological agony that he brought to the stage made his the definitive interpretation of the role. His long, slow final exit, as the sailor condemned to drown himself in the sea, was one of the most moving moments in twentieth-century opera. Here he brings his intense concentration to the courtroom scene (above) and to a scene with soprano **Heather Harper**, in the role of villager Ellen Orford (left).

Although Kurt Herbert Adler combed Europe for singers, he believed strongly in developing American talent and created the company's first formal training programs for young singers. **Jess Thomas**, a handsome young man from South Dakota who was studying music at Stanford, won the Merola auditions in 1957, at the relatively advanced age of twenty-nine. He went on to become one of the world's great Wagnerian tenors. After his death in 1993, fellow Wagnerian Birgit Nilsson wrote to his widow, "He was my favorite Siegfried and Tristan." He was also the quintessential Tannhäuser, shown opposite in a 1973 performance with **Leonie Rysanek**.

Thomas was a steady friend to the San Francisco Opera, often writing letters to Adler about singers he noticed while performing elsewhere. His ultimate proof of loyalty came on December 6, 1981. Thomas was peacefully cooking brunch around noon at his house in Tiburon just north of San Francisco when Adler telephoned, asking him to sing the role of Siegmund in *Die Walküre* as a replacement for ailing James King. Thomas leapt into his car and sped across the Golden Gate Bridge to the opera house, where his old costumes were waiting. He was onstage by one o'clock, giving an electrifying performance that turned out to be his last at the San Francisco Opera.

On September 9, 1983, **Plácido Domingo** became part of San Francisco Opera legend when he leapt onto a private jet in New York and rushed cross-country to replace ailing tenor Carlo Cossutta at the opening-night performance of *Otello*. When he appeared on stage a little after 10:25 P.M. he was greeted with two tumultuous ovations; one the well-rehearsed exultation from the chorus, the second a spontaneous burst of gratitude from the audience, which had been waiting almost three hours for his arrival. The following week, he was presented with the key to the city and Mayor Dianne Feinstein announced that September 15 was "Plácido Domingo Day." Even when he arrives in more ordinary fashion, Domingo regularly thrills the audience, whether it is as a desperate Don José in *Carmen* in 1981 (left), with **Hanna Schwarz** as Carmen; as a brutal Canio in *Pagliacci* in 1976 (below), with **Noelle Rogers** as Nedda; or as the unfortunate lover in *Les Contes d'Hoffmann* in 1987 (opposite).

conversation is sung, the manly hero usually has a soaring, unnatural tenor voice, and pure sound is the ultimate expression of feeling, the audience willingly suspends its power to disbelieve. Its unreasoning rapture extends beyond the events onstage to envelop the singers who create this blend of emotion and intellect.

Although adoration of opera singers was a worldwide phenomenon in the early decades of the twentieth century, it had an added nuance in San Francisco. In a young city still conscious of its rowdy and recent beginnings, opera symbolized civilization. Opera linked San Francisco to the East Coast and Europe, at a time when San Franciscans were constantly comparing themselves with older cultures. Far into the twentieth century, the arrival of an internationally renowned singer at the train station gave the new Californians the feeling that they were not so isolated from the rest of the world.

Although the audience at the War Memorial Opera House no longer mobs the stage and the extracurricular press coverage is not as obsessively detailed as it once was, adulation of singers has not entirely disappeared. Purists may quibble about the heavily amplified, frantically hyped arias of José Carreras, Plácido Domingo, and Luciano Pavarotti at their "Three Tenors" concerts, but one has only to look at the crowds—and the sales of recordings—to know that tenors, at least, still inspire something approaching worship.

One San Francisco opera lover recalls the night before Thanksgiving, 1973, when he hesitated before going to one more *Bohème*. Nevertheless, he went—and has never forgotten it. That was the night that Spaniard **José Carreras** made his San Francisco debut as Rodolfo (opposite), with **Teresa Stratas** as Mimì, the two of them imbuing the familiar romance with a real-life intensity that was palpable to the audience. The sweet-voiced Carreras instantly became a San Francisco favorite, returning in the 1970s to give special charm to youthful, romantic roles like Nemorino in *L'Elisir d'Amore* in 1975, and Gustavo in *Un Ballo in Maschera* in 1977, and the title role in *Werther* in 1978 (above left).

Baritone **Thomas Hampson**, a native of Spokane, Washington, first came to San Francisco to participate in the Merola Opera Program for young singers. Since then, he has taken lead roles in several of the more unusual operas in the San Francisco repertoire. In 1990 he and **Frederica von Stade** made contemporary magic of one of the oldest operas in the repertoire, Monteverdi's *Il Ritorno d'Ulisse in Patria* (right), first performed in 1641 in Venice. In 1994 he returned to star again with von Stade in the world premiere of Conrad Susa and Philip Littell's *The Dangerous Liaisons*, an opera so new that some of the music was not completed until the dress rehearsal. In 1996 he sang the leading role in San Francisco's first presentation of Ambroise Thomas's *Hamlet*.

American baritone **Samuel Ramey** came to the San Francisco Opera for the first time in 1978, when he appeared as Colline in a Jean-Pierre Ponnelle production of *La Bohème*. He did not return until 1984, after several years of establishing his career in Europe. When he did, he quickly became a major box-office attraction, generally playing the bad guy. In *Mefistofele*, Boito's version of the Faust legend, his sudden appearance in a form-fitting red suit slashed to the waist and his lithe athleticism made him a stylish, supremely confident impersonation of the devil (left). He brought a similar villainous elegance to the role of Méphistophélès in Gounod's version of the legend, *Faust*, and to the title role in *Don Giovanni*.

Like most of the rest of the world, San Francisco audiences fell in love with **Luciano Pavarotti**; unlike most other fans, they were fortunate in having him onstage in most of the seasons between 1967, when he made his local debut as Rodolfo in *La Bohème* (above), and 1988. In 1984 Pavarotti said, "This is my second hometown. Musically it is my first." Pavarotti has performed many roles for the first time in San Francisco: Riccardo in *Un Ballo in Maschera* in 1971 (opposite); Fernando in *La Favorita* in 1973; Rodolfo in *Luisa Miller* in 1974; Manrico in *Il Trovatore* in 1975; Calaf in *Turandot* in 1977, where he shared the stage with **Montserrat Caballé** (right) in the title role; Enzo in *La Gioconda* in 1979; and Radames in *Aida* in 1981. In the third performance of *Aida*, the audience went wild when they discovered that Pavarotti had an unexpected costar, **Leontyne Price**, who was rehearsing for *Il Trovatore* when Kurt Herbert Adler asked her to replace ailing soprano Margaret Price at the last minute. It was considered one of Price's most vibrant portrayals of her favorite role, in which she swept Pavarotti along in her fervor.

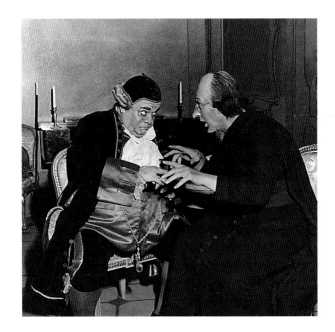

character roles

Basso buffo **Salvatore Baccaloni** was one of the greatest character actors of the century. Broad of girth but agile on stage, he appeared in San Francisco many times in roles ranging from major parts like Don Pasquale (above), Falstaff, and Dr. Bartolo in *Il Barbiere di Siviglia*, here with **Ezio Pinza** as Don Basilio (left), to memorable interpretations of small parts like the Sacristan in *Tosca*.

Ragnar Ulfung was most famous for playing villains, but he was also a master of comic roles. One of his most delightful portrayals in San Francisco came in 1984, as Alfred in Johann Strauss's cheerful *Die Fledermaus*, with **Josephine Barstow** as Rosalinda. Ulfung, a man of varied talents who was known to do cartwheels onstage, enhanced his enactment of Alfred with a little added rhythmic accompaniment in the form of spoons, clicked together like castanets.

Not all of opera's star power comes from golden-voiced tenors in heroic roles. Just below the principal roles come the secondary roles, the villains and fools, servants and henchmen, who not only help to advance the plot but add humor and realism to the drama. The roles may be as large as Dr. Bartolo in *Il Barbiere di Siviglia*, as foolish as the landlord Benoit in *La Bohème*, and as complex as Fra Melitone in *La Forza del Destino*. They share a need for acting talent and a latitude for character development. Well played, these secondary roles contribute immeasurably to the richness of opera.

As a company wedded to the concept of musical theater, the San Francisco Opera has traditionally cast in depth, paying serious attention to these roles. San Francisco audiences have been moved to laughter and tears by the likes of Salvatore Baccaloni and Ezio Pinza, major stars who played secondary as well as primary roles.

Perhaps the greatest character actor of all was Baccaloni, who sang at the San Francisco Opera almost every season from 1938 to 1962. As a boy in Rome, Baccaloni started his singing career in the Sistine Chapel Choir and continued his career at

La Scala. There he performed with Arturo Toscanini and fretted about his three-hundred-pound weight. Don't worry, Toscanini told him, "Comic roles in opera are usually sung by old men who have lost their voices. You are young and have a fine voice and a gift for comedy. Specialize in comic roles." Baccaloni took his advice and became a great *basso buffo*, bringing both vocal sensitivity and comic exaggeration to some 170 roles, ranging from the title roles in *Don Pasquale* and *Falstaff* to brief appearances as the Sacristan in *Tosca* and Benoit and Alcindoro in *La Bohème*.

Although he was known for his broad-brushed humor, Baccaloni was also a master of pathos when the situation demanded. One of his finest, most fully realized portrayals was Leporello, the talkative servant in *Don Giovanni*. Baccaloni was a master at conveying Leporello's simultaneous clumsiness and cleverness, concluding with a final scene that gave poignance to the hapless servant. In addition to histrionic skills, Baccaloni's musical talents enabled him to give each role its maximum characterization. As Dr. Bartolo in *Il Barbiere di Siviglia* he revived the second-act aria, "A un dottor della mia sorte,"

a piece of music often omitted by less talented performers of the role.

His acting ability also brought him success in the movies. He won an Academy Award as a supporting actor in *Full of Life*; his other films included *Fanny* and *The Pigeon That Took Rome*.

Another polished character actor who appeared many times in San Francisco was tenor Ragnar Ulfung, a Norwegian singer who sang principal roles at the Stockholm Opera. Ulfung began his San Francisco career in 1967 and was immediately surrounded by controversy. His first appearance was in the small role of Chuck in Schuller's *The Visitation*, an opera that was popular neither with local audiences nor with critics. His second appearance was in Verdi's familiar *Un Ballo in Maschera*. Ulfung portrayed Gustav III as a homosexual, an interpretation that he had developed in Stockholm and which accurately interpreted history. Although his portrayal had been a success in Sweden, it was less so in San Francisco, jarring both the conservative New England setting of San Francisco's production and Leontyne Price's stately version of Amelia. Ulfung offered to leave the production

Renato Capecchi was able to adapt his gestures, his way of walking, his style of sitting down, and even the timbre of his voice for each of the hundreds of roles he performed. He was a subtle and funny Dr. Bartolo in *Il Barbiere di Siviglia* (left), a sardonic Don Alfonso in *Così fan tutte* (above), and an expressive Fra Melitone in *La Forza del Destino*, one of his favorite roles.

French character tenor **Michel Sénéchal** brought a breath of fresh air to the intellectual colloquies in the 1993 production of *Capriccio*, playing the part of the prompter, Monsieur Taupe, with hilariously nearsighted confusion (right).

after a disastrous opening night, but finally stayed in a somewhat muted rendition of the part.

In spite of a difficult beginning, Ulfung returned to San Francisco often during the next ten years, winning high praise for his vigorous, individualistic characterizations. His interpretation of Števa, the rakish antihero in *Jenůfa* was world-renowned. For his first entrance, he literally cartwheeled onto the stage, using his acrobatic skills to create an impression of childish, boastful masculinity. As the opera proceeded, he made his character so real that the audience found some sympathy for the weak Števa even though he deserts Jenůfa and their son.

He performed his first Mime in the 1970 production of *Siegfried*. This, too, became the definitive portrayal, which he repeated many times around the world, including the Metropolitan Opera in New York, Covent Garden in London, and the Wagnerian shrine of shrines, Bayreuth. Ulfung, who was candid about his abilities, succinctly summed up his career in two sentences: "I never had that great tenor voice. My advantage has always been that I am an actor."

While Ulfung concentrated on villains, another

great singing actor, Italian bass Renato Capecchi, specialized in producing joy and laughter. He made his 1968 San Francisco opera debut as Dr. Bartolo, playing it quite differently than Baccaloni had. Instead of creating a clumsy dirty old man, as Baccaloni did, Capecchi offered a more subtle portrait of a clever, humorous, middle-aged man. His *recitazione* became the lightest, funniest form of patter, his stage antics hilariously funny without unnecessary exaggeration. As one observer put it, "he can do more with a flick of the finger than most singers accomplish with both arms." In addition, Capecchi could change his voice as well as his appearance and movement, so that his version of the foppish Dandini, the royal valet in *La Cenerentola*, was conveyed in unctuous tones.

Capecchi mastered an incredible 284 roles, which enabled him to step in as a last-minute replacement several times in San Francisco. If he had any regrets about his career, it was that he was stamped as a comic when he also loved serious roles like Wozzeck and Giovanni.

Since 1989, French tenor Michel Sénéchal has been one of the most prominent scene-stealers at

the War Memorial. Sénéchal, like many character actors, began his career singing leading roles, making his debut in 1950 in Brussels. For years he concentrated on Rossini, Mozart, Rameau, and the French repertoire of Paris's Opéra-Comique. He switched to character parts when, as he gracefully phrases it, "I was no longer the age to sing young lovers."

Even without portraying young lovers, he is as busy now as he has ever been, with a repertoire of about twenty-five roles such as the Gamekeeper in *Rusalka*, which he performed in San Francisco in the fall of 1995, and the valet in *Les Contes d'Hoffmann* in 1996 at the Civic Auditorium. For Sénéchal, San Francisco has been a particularly sympathetic place to perform. "I love the city. I love the climate. Most important, I love the San Francisco Opera because I find a real family there. To work in that atmosphere is a real pleasure."

THE COMPLETE ART:

chapter three ORCHESTRA, CHORUS, AND DANCE

"Is opera all about singers? I choose to disagree," says Donald Runnicles, music director of the San Francisco Opera. "I think of what Wagner called the *Gesammtkunstwerk*—opera as a complete art form in which musical, dramatic, and visual effects are interdependent. The quality of the company is not that Pavarotti and Domingo come here to sing. The quality has to do with the orchestra, the chorus, the staging."

At the San Francisco Opera, each of these is a microcosm, striving to excel in its special field, whether it be instrumental music, choral singing, ballet, or set or costume design. Each represents another layer of complexity and subtlety. Each has its own standards, but each has to compromise and blend with all the others.

Runnicles's particular microcosm is the orchestra, an element that is unjustly ignored or misunderstood by many opera-goers, who may not realize that it is the musicians half-hidden below the proscenium that make the difference between a truly moving evening at the opera and a few long hours of virtuoso singing. The conductor and his players establish the tempo, the crucial pacing that propels the music and the drama forward. Of course, in opera, the tempo does not exist in a vacuum, dependent solely on the certainty of the conductor's plan. In opera, there is always compromise in the relationship between the singer and the conductor.

Donald Runnicles, music director of the San Francisco Opera since 1992, says of the art of operatic conducting, "The singer never does it the same way twice, and the orchestra has to be flexible in the blink of an eye."

Dancers were an integral part of the San Francisco Opera's American premiere of **Michael Tippett**'s *The Midsummer Marriage*, in 1983 (opposite).

Since **Runnicles** has become music director of the company, the San Francisco Opera has begun recording. In addition to a live recording of *Hérodiade* and a studio album of *Orphée et Eurydice*, the company has recently recorded *Harvey Milk*, presented for the first time in San Francisco in the fall of 1996. Runnicles and baritone **Robert Orth**, who played Milk, relax during the taping sessions at Davies Hall.

"Conducting an opera orchestra is a synthesis of accompanying and leading," Runnicles explains. "The player is often in a slightly schizophrenic position. Should I be with the singer or with the conductor? The orchestra will wait if the singer is taking a little longer. There are countless little decisions like this being made throughout the performance. Nobody is deliberately slower or faster, but singers sometimes cannot hear the orchestra. Also, the singer has to be a little ahead of the beat, because of the delay in the sound reaching the audience from the middle of the stage. Even the opposite extremities of the orchestra itself can't hear each other, because of the long, narrow space in which they're compressed."

If there is a single element that brings the instrumentalists in the pit and the singers on the stage together, it is the human breath. Runnicles says, "A phrase, whether it's instrumental or vocal, must breathe. A pianist once said that he imagined each phrase as being sung by Enrico Caruso. This way of thinking gives the musician the sense of light and shade, of tension, which is breathing in, and of relaxation, which is breathing out. Subconsciously, the audience breathes with the music making. If the conductor doesn't end the phrase when they expect, if he drags it out a bit, there will be a little collective gasp for breath."

Arturo Toscanini, as great a conductor of opera as of symphonic music, said, "Make it legato as

In 1985, general director Terence A. McEwen appointed San Francisco Opera's first music director. He was English conductor Sir John Pritchard, who remained with the company until his death in 1989. In 1992, Scottish-born conductor Donald Runnicles was appointed to the position. **Sir Charles Mackerras** was named principal guest conductor of the company. A specialist in Handel, Mozart, and Janáček, he was the conductor for a memorable series of performances of Janáček's *Jenůfa* in 1986; here he and soprano **Leonie Rysanek**, who sang the role of Kostelnička, beamed backstage (above).

Francesco Molinari-Pradelli, a Verdi specialist, conducted most of San Francisco's Italian operas between 1957 and 1966 (below).

much as you wish, but each phrase must have its cesura which distinguishes it from the next. Surely you have never heard a person who arrives at the end of a sentence without taking a breath."

Runnicles likes to start the process of molding orchestra to singers and singers to orchestra by practicing alone with each principal singer, with him at the piano as accompanist. "At that first rehearsal, the singers bring their own ideas, and the conductor must listen. You have to build a sense of trust, because singers have to put their faith in the conductor for tempi. Sometimes singers will tell the conductor not to let them slow down, not let them be self-indulgent."

In an ideal performance one is aware, if only subconsciously, that the instrumental music provides a subtext to what is going on above onstage, highlighting and commenting, portending or reminiscing, adding exultation or sounding a note of irony, supporting or undermining the libretto. Nowhere is this truer than in Wagner, where the composer's use of motifs representing people, emotions, and places adds layers of complexity to the scene. The different sections of the orchestra may be conveying different emotions simultaneously. The brass may be playing the role of a solemn chorale, while the strings impart fluidity and softness, the woodwinds intimacy and individuality, and the percussion something elemental and rhythmic in the listener.

When Merola began to plan his first opera season at the Stanford football stadium, he turned to the San Francisco Symphony, established twelve years earlier, for players. This arrangement worked well for almost sixty years, as long as the symphony was performing in the War Memorial and its season began after the end of the opera's fall season.

When the symphony moved across Grove Street into Louise M. Davies Symphony Hall in 1980 and opened its season in September, the situation changed radically. In 1979, thirty-five of the opera's sixty-seven players also played for the symphony. In the spring of 1980, those thirty-five had to choose to play for one or the other. Twelve opted to stay with the symphony, others left for different reasons, and a nationwide search started for twenty-six new players with the talent and flexibility to deal with opera's limited rehearsal time and constant stream of guest conductors.

In the hundreds of auditions that took place, adaptability was a preeminent requirement. A musician, no matter how gifted, would not make the finals if he did not prove that he could respond to suggestions and changes. By September, the opera had its own orchestra.

For the first six decades, the company was in the hands of two men, Gaetano Merola and Kurt Herbert Adler, both of whom were conductors and cared deeply about the orchestral and choral music as well as the soloists. Merola conducted a great deal during his tenure, Adler much less, partly because board president Robert Watt Miller preferred that he devote his time to administration.

Both men brought prominent conductors to San Francisco when they could. Fritz Reiner led the orchestra several times between 1936 and 1938, and Erich Leinsdorf appeared in the pit during eight seasons from 1938 to 1957. Regulars in the middle years included Fausto Cleva, who was also active at the Metropolitan Opera; William Steinberg, a Wagner and Mozart specialist; and Francesco Molinari-Pradelli, whose conducting of Verdi was especially appreciated in San Francisco. Curiously, there seems to have been an unwritten rule that the conductor of the San Francisco Symphony did not conduct at the opera. A notable exception was in 1954, when Pierre Monteux, longtime conductor of the symphony, led the opera orchestra for performances of *Manon*, *Fidelio*, and Honegger's *Joan of Arc at the Stake*.

A few surprising names turn up on the list of conductors who have presided over the opera orchestra. Generally they made brief cameo appearances, involving a handful of operas. Among them were Sir Thomas Beecham, who conducted *Don Giovanni* and *Carmen* in 1943, and Georg Solti, who made his American debut in 1953 conducting Richard Strauss and Wagner operas. Mstislav Rostropovich, far better known as a cellist, was in the pit for *The Queen of Spades* in 1975.

In 1985 the company appointed its first permanent music director, Sir John Pritchard, who had conducted here many times. He was succeeded in 1992 by Donald Runnicles. The presence of Runnicles as permanent music director and Sir Charles Mackerras as principal guest conductor has contributed to an increased consistency of style. The opera's recent recordings of *Hérodiade*, a live performance recorded in 1994, and *Orphée et Eurydice*, recorded in the studio in 1995, have also been important milestones in the orchestra's history. In the future, Runnicles hopes, the orchestra will increasingly move out from the obscurity of the pit into the bright lights, adding instrumental-only performances to their operatic schedule.

Some of opera's greatest music, especially the gloriously exultant passages that make opera seem a substitute for religion, has been written for the chorus. This is often difficult and challenging ensemble music, but it is not enough for a chorister to sing well. The chorus must fill the stage not only with sound but with movement and color. They must play royal courtiers and peasants, soldiers and monks, often in the same opera, changing costume and dramatic personae between acts.

The women of Gaetano Merola's amateur chorus posed happily before a performance of *Madama Butterfly* in 1931 (above).

Choristers costumed as Spanish villagers added music, drama, and movement to a scene in *La Forza del Destino* in 1963 (right).

The choristers' work begins each year with three months of vocal rehearsals in the spring and two months of onstage rehearsals in the summer. Then comes the season, when they both rehearse upcoming operas and perform as often as six times a week. Many of them also act as covers and must be prepared to substitute for ailing singers in comprimario and small principal roles.

It is taxing, tiring work, rich in music and onstage time but short in glory and money. Nevertheless, singers flock to San Francisco Opera's chorus auditions, which take place locally twice a year, and in New York, Chicago, and Los Angeles annually. At a 1995 audition, 184 singers, many with music degrees, sang their hearts out for ten positions. Applicants must have four years of classical voice training, sight-reading ability, ability to sing in five languages and memorize music, and stage experience or training.

"We ask each singer to perform two arias, usually one fast, one slow," chorus director Ian Robertson explains. "I look for the quality of the voice, for rock-solid technique—because I can't go into a three-month fall season with someone whose technique is not perfect—and for flexibility of sound, so that the pianissimo is as well focused as the loud. This is important because of the large number of hushed choruses in opera."

The women of the chorus, playing the workers in the cigarette factory, give vocal and visual life to the first act of *Carmen*. They added to the taunting of the hapless Don José, played by **Barry McCauley**, in a 1991 revival. **Denyce Graves** was Carmen.

He doesn't stop there. "I watch every move they make. I watch them as they walk into the room, as they tell me what they're going to sing, even when they're getting a drink at the water fountain.

"Each member of the chorus must share a very broad musicality and a willingness to put up with the compromises that are opera. Of course, we're always looking for beautiful sound and impeccable intonation. But they're wearing hats, which cover their ears, they've got on wigs, and they've got stuck-on beards that impede their pronunciation. They can't hear the other side of the stage, and sometimes there are dozens of supernumeraries standing between them and the conductor."

To complicate choristers' work further, they are not arranged by vocal groups. Robertson says, "I like an integrated sound. I think it's more realistic than a concert-hall sound where you hear the tenors on one side, the sopranos on the other."

In the early years of the San Francisco Opera, the choristers were amateurs, who turned up after work to rehearse. In spite of their lack of experience, they were greeted with gushing enthusiasm by the local press. In youthful, boosterish California, anything that did not have to be imported from the East or from Europe was a source of wonder and pride.

Members of the **men's chorus** were active participants in the stylized action of Jean Pierre Ponnelle's production of *La Cenerentola*, seen here in a 1995 revival (overleaf).

When Kurt Herbert Adler joined the company as chorus director in 1943, he was decidedly less impressed with the caliber of the chorus's singing and, even worse, a level of discipline that allowed singers to wander in and out of rehearsals at will. He even threatened to leave, but Merola responded to the crisis with his usual charm, saying, "You don't want to leave me, after such a short time. Do whatever you want with this chorus of yours."

"With Adler you learned your music or else," recalls Eugene Lawrence, a chorus member for more than thirty years. They learned it on their own time, because choristers were not paid enough to work full-time and had to keep other jobs during the daytime, limiting rehearsals to nights and weekends. It was not until 1980, after some twenty years of discussion, that singing in the chorus was paid well enough to be a full-time job from April to December.

For some, particularly the growing number of conservatory graduates, the chorus is a step in their progression toward solo careers. For others, the chorus is a satisfactory permanent career. Jim Meyer, who has been a member since 1974, says, "What I like is participating as a necessary ingredient in such an extravagant art form. It's often quite thrilling to sing the great choruses and ensembles, and it fulfills my needs, musically."

The chorus achieved another kind of stardom in 1993, when the documentary film, *In the Shadow of the Stars*, depicting the lives and aspirations of San Francisco's choristers, won an Academy Award.

Members of the **San Francisco Opera Ballet**, predecessor of the San Francisco Ballet, performed the first production in the United States of the complete *Swan Lake* in 1940 (below).

Although the San Francisco Opera has always listed a ballet master among its personnel, dedication to dance was haphazard for the first decade. A series of part-time ballet masters came and went, rehearsal time was minimal, and a new troupe of dancers was assembled each season. By 1933, however, the opera was firmly ensconced in its impressive new home on Van Ness Avenue, and Merola decided that the company needed a ballet of its own.

As a first step, he established the San Francisco Ballet School, making San Francisco and New York the only American cities to have ballet schools as auxiliaries to their opera companies. Adolph Bolm was the first director of the school and ballet master for the company, which danced in several operas each season and occasionally performed independent, dance-only programs.

In 1938 Willam Christensen, who had organized the dance troupe's first tour the year before, became ballet master, and his brother Harold took over the school. The two Christensens, along with their brother Lew (a brilliant dancer who became director of the San Francisco Ballet in 1951), were members of a Danish family that had settled in Utah, bringing with them a European tradition of dance and music. The three came to dominate ballet in the West, with San Francisco a major focus of their effort. In 1940 they presented the first full-length performance of *Swan Lake* in the United States, and in 1944 the first complete *Nutcracker*, a Christmas tradition so successful that the San Francisco Opera must close its season in mid-December in time to allow the ballet into the War Memorial.

During World War II, the San Francisco Opera was financially strapped and had to make economies across the board. One of its most radical steps was to eliminate its financial support for the ballet. The school and the company were turned over to the Christensens in 1942. Operating independently, they continued to provide dancers and choreography to the opera on a regular basis until 1962. The opera then began hiring dancers and choreographers on a freelance basis.

Today, the opera has its own little ballet company, comprised of ballet master Lawrence Pech and eight tenured dancers, with other dancers hired as needed to fill specific needs of the repertoire.

Dancing in opera presents special problems. Former ballet mistress Victoria Morgan says, "First of all, there is the stage, which is sometimes awesomely raked. There are all sorts of different textures on the floor, from canvas to something very slick. There are singers and props and crowds of people and costumes that were not necessarily designed for dancers. Basically, we have to be squeezed into the space where the singers are not." She continues, "We are asked to be part of the scene, to participate in continuing the narrative. It's not always that we are brilliant technicians. It's more important that we look good within the framework of the opera. It's a much more theatrical approach, with a lot of depth to it. The movement reflects the historical era of the opera and the personality of the character, whether a noble or a peasant or a slave."

Morgan admits that when she came to the company from the San Francisco Ballet, she had little interest in opera itself and concentrated only on the time that the dancers were onstage. Gradually she was seduced by the complete art form and became interested in involving the dancers in the narrative. In this progression, she mimics the history of dance in opera.

In the very earliest days of opera, in the seventeenth century, ballet was not treated as an integral element of the action. Instead, dance was a separate diversion, often placed between the acts or at the end of the opera. Gradually, dance was inserted into the opera itself, although it remained a divertissement that stopped the action. Nonetheless, it was considered an essential part of the proceedings, particularly by the French, who insisted on ballet in every opera.

Then, in 1875, came Bizet's *Carmen*, the harbinger of a new trend toward greater realism in opera, later embodied by such gritty, violent dramas as Mascagni's *Cavalleria Rusticana* and Leoncavallo's *Pagliacci*. Verismo, the semblance of reality, replaced the fairy-tale world of mythology and nobility. The purely ornamental delights of formal ballet had no place in these earthy librettos or in certain grim twentieth-century operas, like Berg's *Wozzeck* and Shostakovich's *Lady Macbeth of Mtsensk*. As a result,

The choreography in *Ruslan and Lyudmila,* a coproduction of the San Francisco Opera and the Mariinsky Theater in St. Petersburg, required classical techniques from the opera's ballet corps. Russian mezzo-soprano **Elena Zaremba**, surrounded by dancers, sang the role of Ratmir.

In the San Francisco Opera's lavish 1979 production of *La Gioconda* (opposite), the first live performance televised by the company, **Gary Chryst**, at left, and **Christian Holder** were featured dancers.

dance has come to play a less integral role in opera as presented in the twentieth century.

"Now it's become the fad that if the ballet is not continuing the story, we can afford to skip it," says Morgan. "But I love seeing movement on the stage. Experienced dancers can contribute to the aliveness of the scene. When we audition now, we do some pantomime. I would like to see an in-between category, mimes, who would initiate and lead the singers in the movement onstage."

One of the ballet's triumphs came in 1995, when the opera presented Glinka's *Ruslan and Lyudmila,* in a re-creation of a historic St. Petersburg production. The work includes long segments of classical ballet that had originally been choreographed by Michel Fokine. For the San Francisco production, a choreographer and several ballerinas came from the Mariinsky Theater in St. Petersburg, and the call went out in San Francisco for additional classically trained dancers.

The result was magical. The dance segments, lengthy as they were, seemed simultaneously to stand on their own and to be essential to the whole. Like the delicate painted sets faithfully copied from the original production, the ballet was both a souvenir of the way things used to be and a reminder that dance still can add one more layer of beauty to the complicated collage called opera.

Calvin Simmons

Calvin Simmons accompanied his mentor, **Kurt Herbert Adler**, on one of the general director's ritual pre-performance tours through the opera house, including the chorus dressing room (above left).

In a serious mood, **Simmons** played the piano at a rehearsal (above right).

One of San Francisco Opera's most demanding productions, in terms of the orchestra and chorus, was the company's first presentation of Berlioz's *Les Troyens* in 1966 (opposite). French soprano **Regine Crespin**, shown here as Didon, also sang the role of Cassandra, and a compatriot, **Jean Périsson**, conducted the complicated score.

He was San Francisco Opera's Puck, its merry prankster, the man who leapt on furniture and took pratfalls just to amuse, the man who left the staff limp with laughter at his falsetto rendering of arias from *Norma*, the man who not only got away with giving imitations of Kurt Herbert Adler in his presence but was one of the few allowed to walk into Adler's sacrosanct office unannounced.

He was Calvin Simmons, a young man from San Francisco who fell in love with music at the age of seven and went on to graduate from the Curtis Institute of Music in Philadelphia and to become one of the nation's most talented young conductors. Although he worked in England, at the Glyndebourne Festival Opera, in Los Angeles, for the Philharmonic, and in Oakland,

as conductor and music director of the Oakland Symphony, his real home was backstage at the War Memorial Opera House. He came there first as a member of the San Francisco Boys Chorus and returned as a full-fledged member of the musical staff, working as a coach and assistant conductor. In 1981 Adler invited his protegé to conduct Shostakovich's *Lady Macbeth of Mtsensk*, in the original version that had been banned by Stalin. The opera was the surprise success of the season, with much of the credit going to Simmons's incisive conducting. Less than a year later, in August 1982, Calvin Simmons, then only thirty-two, died in a canoeing accident on Connery Pond in upstate New York. Fifteen years later, the opera staff still mourns him, as a person and as a musician.

chapter four KURT HERBERT ADLER

Impeccable in white tie and tails, his chest glittering with medals, Kurt Herbert Adler seemed like the prime minister of a small nation when he walked through the War Memorial Opera House on the opening night of the season. This ritual tour of his fiefdom included not only the stage-level dressing rooms of the stars but the basement chorus rooms, the prop department at stage left, and the cavernous darkness just behind the sets. It was an appropriate itinerary for a man who, as head of the San Francisco Opera from 1953 to 1981, seemed to be everywhere at once.

On a typical day, by ten in the morning he was upstairs on one of the three telephones in his office, cajoling, coaxing, threatening, and oozing Viennese-accented charm to persuade the singer or agent on the other end of the line to do his bidding. A bit later, he was downstairs at a rehearsal, sitting on the aisle, muttering comments to a note-taking secretary as long as he could stand to stay in one place, then exploding from his seat, to tear down the aisle shouting criticism.

Backstage, he would suddenly appear in the most obscure corners, to banter with propmen and stagehands. In twenty-eight years, he never failed to attend at least part of every performance. His routine began before the curtain rose, when he made visits to the principal singers in their dressing rooms. Just before the first notes of the overture sounded, he climbed a flight of stairs to his box to greet his

Kurt Herbert Adler, general director of the San Francisco Opera for almost three decades, was at his most distinguished when he walked through the lobby a few minutes before the crowds arrived for opening night of the season.

Luridly red, covered with orgiastic paintings, **Jean-Pierre Ponnelle**'s set (opposite) for the ducal chamber in his 1973 production of *Rigoletto* underlined the Duke of Mantua's perversity. Some critics felt that there was even more perversity in Ponnelle's conception of the opera as a flashback that began with Gilda already dead, lying on the floor during the Prelude.

As he did for all the artists before a performance, **Adler** went to the dressing rooms to greet Spanish soprano **Pilar Lorengar**.

carefully invited VIPs and potential donors. In the case of a first performance or a debut, he stayed in the box for the whole opera; otherwise he spent a few minutes there, then took the elevator back upstairs to work with his telephones and the handful of staff members able to keep up with his fourteen-hour day. In any case, he was ready to rush backstage at the first hint of a problem.

Kurt Herbert Adler was a complicated man. Martin Bernheimer, music critic of the *Los Angeles Times*, once described him as "the longtime, tough, ubiquitous, controversial, respected, feared, powerful, insightful, charming, rude, cantankerous, courageous managerial paterfamilias of the San Francisco Opera." Leontyne Price, interviewed by Caroline Crawford for the University of California's oral history of Adler, had a few adjectives of her own: "He is in a word at once strong, opinionated, devious, affectionate, elegant, caring, vindictive, argumentative, ruthless, determined, egomaniacal, charming, loving, sentimental and extremely successful."

Adler ran a tight ship, perhaps the tightest in the world of opera. He knew how to hire talent but was loath to delegate authority, and he took responsibility for the smallest details. He was the first to notice the chorus member wearing historically inappropriate nail polish or a wristwatch, the first to comment on everything from a tenor's baggy tights to a missed cue in the brass section of the orchestra.

His public critiques could be both scathing and demoralizing. One conductor, subjected to a lambasting at a rehearsal, took off for the airport; Adler promptly rushed after him and persuaded him to return. Lotfi Mansouri, who became general director in 1988, remembers the first production he directed in San Francisco. Adler arrived backstage with a high-volume litany of criticisms, but when Mansouri offered to quit, Adler promptly switched on the charm. "Don't be so sensitive," he said to the startled Mansouri, who eventually came to realize that the only Adler commentary that really counted was being rehired.

He was not an easy man to work for. The ebbing tide of secretaries fleeing the tension and long hours of his office was legendary. He believed firmly that the only way to run an opera company was as a dictator. He also believed in crisis and drama as management tools, and he conjured up storms just to keep everyone on their toes. Nevertheless, he also inspired great loyalty, among people like musical assistant Otto Guth, administrator Ruth Felt, production director John Priest, stage directors Matthew Farruggio and Ghita and Paul Hager, bound together for decades by Adler's insistence on excellence.

Kurt Herbert Adler was born in Vienna in 1905, the son of a comfortably well-off couple, textile manufacturer Ernst Bauer Adler and his lively wife Ida. From earliest childhood, he was steeped in music. His father was an amateur composer who played both the organ and the piano and amassed a huge collection of phonograph records. Little Kurt began piano lessons at the age of five. In his teens he attended the Music Academy and the Conservatory as well as an academic high school in Vienna. Through his uncle, a prominent politician of the Social Democratic Party, he had a regular seat in the former imperial royal box at the Staatsoper in Vienna, whose director allowed him to attend rehearsals whenever he wished. He further increased his knowledge of the classically trained voice by working occasionally as an accompanist for voice teachers.

In 1925 Adler went to work for Vienna's leading theatrical producer, Max Reinhardt, for whom he played, composed, and conducted incidental music for three years. The work brought him into contact with the leading stage directors and actors of the day. This contact with the legitimate theater had a lifelong impact, laying the groundwork for his belief that opera was musical theater, in which music alone does not carry the drama. Reinhardt himself made a profound impression on Adler, who frequently repeated his statement, "Remember, young man, in the theater, nothing is impossible."

He took his first opera job in 1928, as assistant, chorus master, and occasional conductor in Kaiserslautern, a provincial capital in southwestern Germany. He stayed there until 1932, then spent the next four years conducting, both in Italy and at the Volksoper in Vienna. In 1936, he was invited—

Adler could often be found on one of several telephones that held prominent positions, along with mementoes, coffee cups, and schedules, on his desk.

along with fellow conductors Erich Leinsdorf, Georg Solti, and Laszlo Halasz—to work at the Salzburg summer festival as Arturo Toscanini's assistant.

It was in Salzburg that he coached a young singer from Chicago, Janet Fairbank, who encouraged him to move to the United States and arranged a visa for him through a family friend, Secretary of State Cordell Hull. He stayed in Europe, however, for two more years. Although the Nazis were on the rise in Germany and politics were beginning to be felt on the cultural scene, Adler still felt safe working in Reichenberg in Sudetenland, a German-speaking region of Czechoslovakia. He finally sailed for the United States in the fall of 1938, ten days before the Nazis took over Sudetenland.

For the next five years he worked for the Chicago Opera Company, where his major achievement was to create a large new chorus of young American singers. His reputation spread. In 1942 Gaetano Merola invited Adler to San Francisco to be chorus director. Given the uncertain financial situation of the Chicago company during the war years, he accepted the job offer and arrived in California by train in June of 1943. He was met at the station by one of Merola's assistants, who whisked him off to Stern Grove to meet the man who had hired him over the telephone.

Adler's first task was to transform the chorus from an undisciplined group of enthusiastic amateurs into a more polished and professional organization. Gradually he began to take on other administrative tasks, particularly as Merola's health began to fail in the late 1940s, and was officially named assistant to the general director in 1952. When Merola fell dead at the podium at Stern Grove, Adler was kneeling at his side within seconds.

A few hours later, he was hard at work salvaging a season already plagued with cancellations. By September 2, he announced replacements for Mario Del Monaco, who had canceled his appearances in the lead roles of five operas, and the substitution of *La Bohème* and *La Traviata* for *Otello* and *Manon Lescaut*. Later in the season, another major star, Dorothy Kirsten, had to cancel several performances due to the illness of her husband, and Adler brought in longtime San Francisco favorite Licia Albanese.

Three months after Merola's death, Adler was named artistic director of the company, but rumors continued to fly about other people—conductor Fausto Cleva and stage director Armando Agnini among them—who might eventually become the company's permanent general director. By 1957, however, Adler had impressed members of the board with his competency and was given the top job permanently.

The man who convinced the board to hire him was Robert Watt Miller, president of the San Francisco Opera Association from 1937 until 1942 and from 1951 to 1966, when he became chairman of the board of the association. Miller, the president of Pacific Lighting Corporation, was supremely elegant and aristocratic. In this, he was the perfect embodiment of the relationship of San Francisco's social elite to opera, at a time when details of opening-night finery filled pages and pages of the next day's newspapers.

Nevertheless, Miller was no mere figurehead. Unlike some of his successors, he had musical training (he played both the piano and the organ) and was knowledgeable about opera around the world. He was a familiar figure during the opera season, not only during performances, dashingly dressed in a black cape and top hat, but at rehearsals, in endless conferences with Adler, at parties for artists in the Millers' jewel-box townhouse on Nob Hill, and backstage, commenting about onstage problems.

It was he who persuaded the board to make Adler head of the opera after Merola's death, working against some board members' inclination to hire someone better known, preferably from Europe. The two developed a close relationship, weathering crises from last-minute cancellations to season-threatening labor disputes and full-scale financial cataclysms. Miller took a personal interest in fund-raising, giving generously of his own money and persuading his friends to do the same. He supported the guarantor system, through which holders of certain season tickets pledged to contribute a certain amount of money if it was needed, but he was proud that he didn't have to ask for it many times.

Backstage before a performance, **Adler**, center, conferred with **Robert Watt Miller**, president of the opera's board of directors, at left, and conductor **Erich Leinsdorf**.

A Midsummer Night's Dream, by Benjamin Britten, was one of several operas that Adler introduced in the United States. In the 1961 premiere, much of the charm came from a delicately costumed Tytania played by San Francisco favorite **Mary Costa** (opposite).

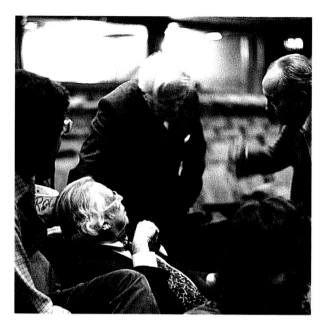

This was a familiar scene during the Adler decades: **Adler**, sitting in an aisle seat for a rehearsal, surrounded by artists and staff. In this photo, taken in 1977, he consulted with **Gianandrea Gavazzeni**, conductor of *Adriana Lecouvreur*, center, and **Janos Ferencsik**, conductor of *Ariadne auf Naxos* (top left).

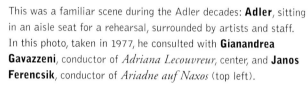

Adler literally looked up to conductor **Rafael Kubelik**, who came to San Francisco in 1977 to conduct the opera's first presentation of Janáček's *Katya Kabanova* (top center).

In 1981 **Adler** presented the San Francisco Opera Medal to **Birgit Nilsson**, at left. **Leonie Rysanek** was also at the ceremony, which took place after the two had sung a riveting performance of *Die Walküre*. Both artists had been singing with the company since 1956, when they made their American debuts in San Francisco (top right).

Adler took over a company that was well established but had the limitations of its own short history and its budgetary restrictions. In the early 1950s, the San Francisco Opera typically gave fourteen operas each season, during five weeks in San Francisco and two weeks in Los Angeles. Rehearsal time was short, and the fact that each opera was presented only once or twice meant that artists had little opportunity to polish and adapt their performances. Staging, as in many opera companies of the time, was simple, little more than decorative background for famous singers.

The repertoire was conservative, featuring constant repetitions of familiar, time-tested classics. Merola's beloved *La Bohème*, for instance, was presented for twelve years in a row from 1943 through 1954. Although Merola came to like presenting new talent from the United States and Europe, he was generally faulted for taking too many cues from the Metropolitan Opera in New York, placing the San Francisco season between Labor Day and the Met's December opening so he could use the same singers as New York.

From the start, Adler had two major problems. The first was the budget: he had substantially less money to play with than did his fellow directors in the state-subsidized houses of Europe or in the richer New York and Chicago houses. His vaunted attention to detail came partially from the need to pinch pennies at every level, from paper clips to new productions. He was famous for his lengthy negotiations about singers' fees, occasionally losing a singer in the process but most often wearing the artists down with sheer persistence. For all his scrimping, the shortage of money sometimes showed, most often in some of the minimalist sets.

His second problem was the opera house itself, handsome to look at but impractical for a resident company. There was so little office space that Adler operated out of a dressing room for many years, and the staff squeezed into closets and cubbyholes. Storage space for sets did not exist, so each set had to be stored between performances, either in an outside parking lot or in rented warehouses.

The only rehearsal space was the stage itself, so the company scattered to locations all over town—Nourse Auditorium in the Civic Center and the Armory in the Mission District among them—for run-throughs. The space problem was finally solved in two ways. In 1980, a towering addition was built onto the opera house on the Franklin Street side, to provide space for sets, offices, and rooms for coaches, chorus, and dancers. Also in 1980, the new Zellerbach Rehearsal Hall on Franklin Street, comprising one stage equal to the War Memorial stage and two smaller rehearsal rooms, eliminated the need to rehearse far from the opera house.

In spite of the limitations of money and space, Adler wasted no time reshaping the company to his own standards, presenting new talent, expanding the repertoire, and elevating the role of the stage director to emphasize the dramatic aspects of opera.

For the first time, San Francisco became a place to hear newly discovered singers, many of whom had not yet appeared in New York or Chicago. Adler found his newcomers through his omnivorous reading of opera publications, his continuous telephone calls to friends and colleagues around the world, and his trips to New York and Europe. He was tireless on these talent-hunting voyages, squeezing in performances (typically, in 1975, he attended twenty-two operas in twelve cities in three weeks), auditions, discussions about current projects and plans for future seasons, and constant checking on what was happening back in San Francisco. One of the reasons that San Francisco became the setting for many American debuts was Adler's willingness to attend performances at small provincial opera houses as well as major houses. In the smaller theaters he discovered new singers, some of them Europeans, others young Americans gaining the kind of performance experience that was then difficult to get in the United States.

The notable debuts in San Francisco began almost immediately after Adler took over. Elisabeth Schwarzkopf made her American operatic debut in 1955, singing one of her most famous roles, the Marschallin in *Der Rosenkavalier*. In 1956 Leonie Rysanek, Birgit Nilsson, Boris Christoff, and Turkish soprano Leyla Gencer sang in the United States for the first time, and Eileen Farrell made her first operatic appearance in San Francisco.

In 1957 Adler heard a young American soprano sing on the radio and recognized the kind of voice he wanted in the American premiere of Francis Poulenc's *Dialogues of the Carmelites*. He hired Leontyne Price to sing the role of Madame Lidoine, her first performance on a major operatic stage. Her success in that role was rapidly followed up by her last-minute substitution as Aida in two performances originally scheduled for Antonietta Stella.

In 1958 Adler's most important new discovery was not a singer but a designer. Jean-Pierre Ponnelle came to San Francisco for the first time, as the designer of Carl Orff's *The Wise Maiden* and *Carmina Burana*. It was the start of a long and controversial career, in which he became both designer and director of some of the most interesting productions that ever took place at the War Memorial. These included the United States premiere of Strauss's *Die Frau ohne Schatten* in 1959, a vociferously disputed *Rigoletto*, and an equally debated *Der Fliegende Holländer*, as well as a charmingly stylized *La Cenerentola*.

It was a relationship of which Adler was extraordinarily proud. Ponnelle, although highly musical, shared his conception of opera as musical theater, in which sets, costumes, acting, and music were integrated. Ponnelle was brilliant, imaginative, difficult, and fearless. Reviewers and members of the audience argued heatedly about his ideas, and Adler was delighted.

Adler also began to expand the company's repertoire beyond Merola's classics, introducing works new to San Francisco and sometimes new to the United States. After the 1959 *Die Frau ohne Schatten* came the West Coast premiere of Alban Berg's *Wozzeck* in 1960. In 1961 San Francisco audiences saw two contemporary pieces, the world premiere of Norman Dello Joio's *Blood Moon*, never presented again, and the United States premiere of Benjamin Britten's *A Midsummer Night's Dream*, which had greater success. The year 1962 brought Stravinsky's *The Rake's Progress* for the first time in San Francisco, and 1963 both Tchaikovsky's *Queen of Spades* and Strauss's *Capriccio*.

At the same time that he was getting his regular audience accustomed to unfamiliar music and drama, Adler began the paradoxical tasks of lengthening the season and reducing the number of operas presented each year. Merola's practice had been to offer as many as fourteen operas in a five week season, often giving an opera only once. Adler realized that it made economic sense to schedule more performances of fewer works, thus amortizing production costs, and he believed that the potential audiences were large enough to support the additional performances.

In 1976 Adler's favorite director, Jean-Pierre Ponnelle, created new productions for *Cavalleria Rusticana* and *Pagliacci*. **Plácido Domingo** sang the role of Canio in *Pagliacci* (above) and also the role of Turiddu in *Cavalleria* on the same evening.

By the mid-1960s the San Francisco Opera offered a ten-week season with four performances each of a dozen operas, starting in early September and ending just before Thanksgiving, when the symphony and the ballet took over the War Memorial. Filling the seats meant building new audiences beyond the social elite that had traditionally filled the boxes of the Golden Horseshoe and the front-row seats of the orchestra. Adler was tireless in his efforts to expose more people to opera and to provide training and experience to youthful singers.

He founded the Merola Opera Program in 1957, as the company's first formal effort to find and develop young voices through a summer training program that included voice coaching, acting, and performances onstage. The program, which has nurtured such artists as Carol Vaness, Ruth Ann Swenson, Thomas Hampson, and Dolora Zajick, is considered the finest in the United States.

Spring Opera, founded in 1961, was his response to the closing of Cosmopolitan Opera, a competing company that had been presenting a traditional repertoire of operas at the War Memorial, sometimes hiring singers at fees much higher than the San Francisco Opera was paying. Cosmopolitan's scheme of top singers, little rehearsal time, and a standard repertoire worked until 1960, when the company's angel, Campbell MacGregor, decided that he was no longer willing to write his annual check for the deficit.

Adler took the opportunity to create a spring season, initially presenting traditional repertoire in the opera house. Later, Spring Opera evolved into a showcase for young singers and unfamiliar repertoire in the more intimate setting of the Curran Theater. Adler was able to fill the house with opera goers who were interested in contemporary and offbeat works, a different group of people than the fall-season audience. Spring Opera provided opportunities for young singers whose voices and dramatic abilities were not yet ready for the cavernous expanses of the War Memorial. Frederica von Stade, James King, Maria Ewing, Marilyn Horne, and Barry McCauley were among those who bloomed in Spring Opera.

In 1966 Adler created Western Opera Theater, a touring company whose young singers, plus a truckful of scenery, went to small towns across the West to present opera to audiences that otherwise might never have had any contact with the art form. Like Spring Opera, it provided opportunities for young singers, conductors, and designers, some of whom had trained in the Merola summer program. From Alaska to Arizona, they exposed people to opera for the first time. Locally, young singers got more performance experience in Brown Bag Opera, in which they sang to lunch-hour audiences in the downtown area.

In 1971 Adler began Opera in the Park, the annual outdoor concert that attracts many thousands of people to Golden Gate Park on the Sunday after the opening night of the season. The singers usually include some of the stars of the season's early operas, augmented by young singers in the opera's training programs.

Many of Adler's achievements could be measured in terms of longer seasons, more performances, better box office, and more premieres and debuts. The stature and professionalism that he brought to the San Francisco Opera are more difficult to quantify but are at least as important.

Singers, conductors, directors, and designers came back season after season, even when Adler paid them less than they could get elsewhere. They came because Adler made the San Francisco Opera an internationally respected company that ran at a high level of professionalism and offered them interesting things to do in a warm and supportive atmosphere. For baritone Geraint Evans, for example, it was the chance to sing the title role in *Wozzeck* for the first time, developing a part that he ultimately repeated around the world. To Leontyne Price and Luciano Pavarotti, Adler offered the opportunity to perform a number of roles for the first time in what was considered a performer-friendly house with a sympathetic audience. For soprano Carol Vaness, Adler meant not only the Merola Opera Program for young singers but a knowledgeable mentor who gave her good advice on choosing roles appropriate to her voice.

Actress **Hermione Gingold** agreed to perform a cameo role in *The Daughters of the Regiment* if Adler would send a man on a white horse to meet her. When she arrived at the station in the fall of 1974, Adler's assistant, **Dana Huffmann**, suited in armor and riding a brown horse, was there to greet her.

Artists also came because San Francisco and the War Memorial Opera House were pleasant places to be. In spite of Adler's bursts of ferocity, the opera company acquired a reputation for its strong family feeling and eagerness to make visiting performers feel at home. Dramatic soprano Anja Silja said about working in San Francisco, "Here things are friendly, easygoing. If things collapsed, I could call on people for help." Meeting singers at the airport, finding attractive apartments rather than hotel rooms, giving opening-night dinners for the cast and staff after performances, and arranging a bit of social life were important priorities in a company far from other operatic capitals.

Sometimes Adler went far beyond routine courtesy. While he was trying to persuade actress Hermione Gingold to perform the cameo speaking role of the Duchess of Krakenthorp in the 1974 production of *The Daughter of the Regiment*, Gingold said, "I'll come if you send a knight in armor on a horse to meet me." When the appointed day came, Adler suited up one of his assistants in clanking metal and sent him, along with a horse, to greet her at the train station.

His courtesy often paid off. The great soprano Birgit Nilsson did not sing in the United States for four years between 1975 and 1979, due to disagreements with the Internal Revenue Service. When the matter was settled, she promptly called Adler, explaining later, "Kurt Herbert Adler was the only one in America who called me through all those years and asked if there was any chance I could sing here. He even phoned me to wish me good luck when I performed in Vienna and Munich. He was the first one I called when I knew I would be back."

On a less glamorous but no less essential level, Adler managed to get along well with the myriad unions involved in opera production because he made it clear that he respected their work and he developed personal relationships with the union representatives. Nevertheless, there were crises. In 1964, contract negotiations dragged into September, the season was briefly canceled, and the final settlement was only achieved in the office of Mayor John Shelley. In 1980 a last-minute request for parking places delayed the signing of the new contract so long that the orchestra members were late getting

In 1974 **Joan Sutherland** and **Adler** conferred on the set of
Esclarmonde.

into the pit on opening night. Generally, however, relations were fairly smooth, and one of the opera's treasured traditions during the Adler years was the annual "Crab Feed," an onstage lunch given by the stagehands for the staff at the end of the season.

Although ironhanded discipline and hard work were the essentials of Adler's success, luck also played a role. San Francisco could not always afford to hire covers to understudy major roles, and its geographical isolation from other opera houses made it difficult to fly in replacements at the last minute. Most of the time he was able to coax and cajole ailing or nervous singers onstage, but occasionally there were full-blown catastrophes. The solutions were sometimes ingenious and risky. Operagoers remember Mary Costa miming onstage while Sheila Marks, standing offstage, sang the role of Zerlina in *Fra Diavolo* in 1968. A similar situation occurred in 1989, when William Johns sang the title role in *Lohengrin* from behind a scrim while scheduled tenor Paul Frey played the part on stage. In 1979, the audience applauded warmly for an almost unknown local singer, Ellen Kerrigan, with almost no performance experience on the opera stage, who stepped in for Montserrat Caballé after the first performance of Bellini's *Roberto Devereux*, but local critics complained about the lack of a more experienced cover.

Two of Adler's most spectacular saves came during his final season in 1981. Leontyne Price, in town for *Il Trovatore*, took over as Aida, giving a radiant performance to Luciano Pavarotti's first Radames. Later in the season, local resident Jess Thomas, one of the world's greatest Wagnerian tenors, sped across the Golden Gate Bridge on an hour's notice to replace James King as Siegmund in *Die Walküre*.

Adler's final day in charge came on December 13, 1981, when he conducted the season-closing matinee performance of *Carmen*. It was a day of pain and sadness for the man who had spent thirty-eight of his working years at the San Francisco Opera. During the curtain calls, as a grateful audience stood and applauded for several minutes, he appeared before the golden curtain, grim-faced, as if shocked that the moment had finally come.

Afterward, at a party for the whole company onstage, the mood lightened slightly. Adler smiled graciously as Plácido Domingo, the Don José of the day, assumed the role of master of ceremonies, placing the Meistersinger's insignia around Adler's neck. The supernumeraries presented him with the first "Order of the Silver Spear," and the chorus sang a medley of excerpts with special words. Finally, the company presented him with a grand piano, which rose on a platform from the pit, with prompter Philip Eisenberg, tricked out as Liberace, playing the waltz from *Der Rosenkavalier*.

Once retired, Adler enjoyed his family, especially delighting in his young daughter, Sabrina, and son, Roman. He did some conducting, both at the San Francisco Opera and elsewhere. He fretted about what was going on in his erstwhile kingdom at the War Memorial. When, on February 8, 1988, Terence McEwen, Adler's successor, announced his resignation as general director, Adler mused to a friend that he would be willing to step in as temporary director if needed. This never came to pass, because on the following afternoon, Adler died of a heart attack at his house in Marin County. He was eighty-two.

Renata Tebaldi, who made her American debut in San Francisco in 1950, greeted **Kurt Herbert Adler** at a rehearsal of *Aida*.

Coloratura soprano **Joan Sutherland** made her San Francisco Opera debut in the title role in *Lucia di Lammermoor* in 1961 (opposite).

Heroines

chapter five HEROINES

In the intricate conjuring act known as operatic scheduling, which comes first, the opera or the singer?

Sometimes, it's the opera: the decision to present Wagner's four-opera *Ring* cycle in its extravagant, seventeen-hour entirety must be taken wholeheartedly before the casting of dozens of roles begins. At other times, the general director is filling in the season with operatic bread and butter, works that the audience likes to hear and a reasonable choice of artists that the audience likes to hear sing.

Often, however, individual singers shape the repertoire, in San Francisco and elsewhere around the world. Great singers are a rarity, and even more rare is the singer with the breadth of, say, Birgit Nilsson or Leonie Rysanek, who mastered both the Italian and the German repertoires. In most cases, a singer has a much more limited area of specialization, which depends on voice type and dramatic abilities.

A few superstars can dictate exactly what opera they would like to do next. Most artists, slightly less brilliant in the firmament, weigh various options. For a singer, learning a new role is an investment of time and money in hopes that offers will roll in from many opera houses. For the general director, an opera that shows off a singer's strengths or the promise of a new production is a way to lure major artists to the company.

A single diva dominated the first two seasons of the San Francisco Opera. **Bianca Saroya** sang all three of the lead soprano roles at the Stanford University football stadium in the summer of 1922 and returned the following year to sing not only the title role in *Tosca* but leading roles in seven other operas. Saroya was born in Pennsylvania, where she was discovered by Leopold Stokowski at the age of seventeen, but she mastered the art of playing the diva as well as any European: she never revealed either her real name or her age. In appropriately romantic style, she met her husband, Romanian tenor Dimitri Onofrei, onstage in Boston when she was rushed in to perform Marguerite in *Faust* without rehearsal or even a chance to meet the cast. Although she never sang again with the San Francisco Opera, she came to the city frequently in the 1930s with the touring San Carlo Opera Company, where her spinto soprano was most often heard in *Aida*. In 1967 she and her husband moved to the city, where she lived in the Richmond District until her death in 1981.

French soprano **Lily Pons** had a twenty-year San Francisco career in which she often played Gilda in *Rigoletto* (above), here with **Robert Weede** as her father, and the title roles in Donizetti's *Lucia di Lammermoor* and Léo Delibes's *Lakmé*, an opera that was wildly popular through the mid-1940s and then dropped off the operatic map. Pons had a unique touch in each opera; she sang a high F in the Mad Scene in *Lucia*, and she wore a jewel in her bared navel as the Indian princess, Lakmé. Her biggest audiences came during World War II, when she traveled around the world to sing for American troops (above, right), once giving a concert in Cologne twenty-four hours after the Germans had been driven out. At the end of the war, she sang the French national anthem, "La Marseillaise," to 250,000 Frenchmen massed in the Place de L'Opéra in Paris after the liberation of France in 1944. She received the Order of the Legion of Honor from Charles de Gaulle and was decorated by the United States, of which she had become a citizen in 1941.

German soprano **Elisabeth Rethberg** was the San Francisco Opera's most versatile soprano in the 1930s. Her radiant high notes soared in operas ranging from Puccini to Wagner, with many Verdi heroines in between, such as Aida, Amelia in *Un Ballo in Maschera*, and Desdemona in *Otello* (right) with **Lauritz Melchior** in his only United States performance as Otello. It was an impressive schedule, but only a small portion of the 128 roles she mastered during her twenty-eight-year career.

The great Wagnerian soprano **Kirsten Flagstad** sang for the first time in San Francisco in 1935, as Brünnhilde in the company's—and her own—first complete production of Wagner's *Ring of the Nibelung*. Her most memorable performance in San Francisco came much later, in 1949, in the midst of controversy about her activities during World War II. Flagstad had returned to her native Norway at the start of the war to be with her husband. After the war, New York columnist Walter Winchell fanned the flames of scandal around her by falsely accusing her of anti-Semitism and performing for the Nazis, creating an atmosphere that made some American opera companies afraid to hire her. When San Francisco Opera engaged her for *Tristan und Isolde* (left) and *Die Walküre*, the veterans on the War Memorial board of trustees tried to prevent her from appearing. The opera's board of directors responded that they would cancel the season if Flagstad were not allowed to sing. The veterans finally changed their minds and voted in favor of Flagstad. On September 30, the opening night of *Tristan und Isolde*, security was so tight at the opera house that Flagstad herself had to present identification at the stage door. The atmosphere in the house was emotional, and when Flagstad appeared onstage, the audience leapt to its feet, shouting their welcome. Ironically, Flagstad's closest friend in the United States was Caroline Esberg, member of a prominent Jewish family in San Francisco.

Ohio-born mezzo-soprano **Blanche Thebom** had never had a music lesson when, at the age of nineteen, she was heard by Marian Anderson's accompanist, who encouraged her to pursue a singing career. She came to San Francisco frequently in the 1950s, singing everything from Cherubino in *Le Nozze di Figaro* to Brangäne in *Tristan und Isolde* (below). Thebom, a great beauty, had dark, shining, floor-length hair and rarely needed a wig. She usually wore it braided, but she let it loose for an appearance as Lady Godiva on a white horse at the Fol de Rol, an annual fund-raising event for the opera.

This mating dance has been particularly important to San Francisco, which has had to persuade the world's artists to travel thousands of miles from the opera capitals of Europe. The company has succeeded by offering singers interesting opportunities, particularly the chance to perform new roles for the first time in a theater known for its professionalism and confidence-building atmosphere.

The influence of singers on the repertoire has been especially significant when several singers of a certain vocal or dramatic type have flourished around the same time. For instance, the presence of a flock of coloratura sopranos capable of producing bel canto trills is good reason for an opera director to start scheduling not just one Rossini opera but several. In addition, the existence of several singers who can perform a certain role may make it possible to find a replacement in case of a cancellation. The trend becomes a worldwide phenomenon, as international opera houses around the globe make use of the same talent.

To today's audiences, Gaetano Merola's repertoire, basically a tour of opera's greatest hits, may seem limited. To some extent, his choices reflected the conservatism of San Francisco's—and America's—opera-going public and Merola's own Italian background and his talent as a conductor of Italian opera. Significantly, Merola's repertoire also reflected the extraordinarily rich supply of Puccini singers available to him.

Swedish soprano **Birgit Nilsson** has been called the world's greatest Turandot (opposite), as well as the world's greatest Brünnhilde and Sieglinde. She sang all these roles and many more in San Francisco, where she made her American debut in 1956, as Brünnhilde in *Die Walküre*. Her close relationship with Kurt Herbert Adler led to her returning first to San Francisco after a four-year period from 1975 to 1979 when she refused to come to the United States due to a disagreement with the Internal Revenue Service. Whatever the language, and she was dominant in both German and Italian repertoires, she delivered her notes with more power than any other woman onstage, perhaps in the history of opera. If she didn't drown everyone out, it was only because she was polite to her colleagues.

It seems that soprano **Dorothy Kirsten** was fated to have a long and successful operatic career in San Francisco. Her great-aunt was Catherine Hayes, an Irish-born singer who braved the chaos of the gold rush to give several operatic concerts in San Francisco in 1852 and 1854. Kirsten and Merola, both Puccini specialists, formed a mutual admiration society, and she sang her way through *Madama Butterfly*, *Manon Lescaut*, *Tosca* and Minnie in *La Fanciulla del West* (right), one of her favorite roles. She was not limited to Puccini but did several contemporary operas in San Francisco, including Poulenc's *Dialogues of the Carmelites*; Charpentier's *Louise* (above), with tenor **Brian Sullivan** and for which she trained with the composer; and William Walton's *Troilus and Cressida*. Kirsten lived in southern California, and her proximity to the Bay Area allowed her to make several last-minute saves, including two opening-of-the-season *Tosca*s. She was the first performer to celebrate twenty-five years with the San Francisco Opera. She said on that anniversary, "I have special affection for San Francisco because I've had more debuts and broken in more major roles here than anywhere else. I've opened the season—planned and unplanned—many times. This is my home. The audience is my family."

Lyric soprano **Queena Mario** was an exception to the rule that prevailed in the earliest years of San Francisco Opera, that principal singers should have already had Metropolitan Opera experience. Mario, born in Ohio of Greek-American parents, made her San Francisco debut in 1923 as Mimì (above), in the opening-night performance of *La Bohème* at the Civic Auditorium. She developed an enthusiastic following in San Francisco, singing frequently through 1932. She was a woman of many facets: before establishing herself as an opera singer, she had worked as a reporter for several New York newspapers, where her journalistic efforts included a column called "Hints for Mothers," written when she was sixteen. Her operatic career got a boost when Enrico Caruso heard her audition for the San Carlo Opera Company and persuaded impresario Fortune Gallo to hire her, promising to pay her salary if she did not succeed.

"I'm not a singer but an operatic performer. I have a natural sense of the stage," said Australian soprano **Marie Collier**, who took on some of the least familiar operas in the 1960s. She made her San Francisco debut in 1964 in the United States premiere of Shostakovich's *Katerina Ismailova*. She returned two years later for another premiere of an unfamiliar modern opera, playing the three-hundred-year-old heroine, Emilia Marty, in Janáček's eerie *The Makropulos Case* (right). In 1968 she played the only part in Schoenberg's *Erwartung*; her fifteen curtain calls, some said, took longer than the twenty-seven-minute opera.

The list of the singers who played two of Puccini's heroines, the title role in *Tosca* and Mimì in *La Bohème*, for the San Francisco Opera is a tour of the history of opera in the United States in the twentieth century. In the first thirty years of the San Francisco Opera, the role of Tosca was taken by Bianca Saroya, Claudia Muzio, Maria Jeritza, Lotte Lehmann, and Dorothy Kirsten, among others. Their interpretations were not alike: there was a world of difference between Maria Jeritza's histrionic intensity and Lotte Lehmann's more introverted characterization. Nevertheless, each soprano was a good reason to go to one more presentation of this often-repeated opera. Similarly, Puccini's fragile seamstress, Mimì, was given life by many of the leading singers of the time, including Claudia Muzio, Queena Mario, Elisabeth Rethberg, Lucrezia Bori, Bidú Sayão, and Licia Albanese.

The male side was equally impressive. The adored Giovanni Martinelli was San Francisco Opera's first Rodolfo and first Cavaradossi. As the decades went on, the roles of Puccini's tenor heroes were taken by the likes of Beniamino Gigli, Jussi Bjoerling, Mario Del Monaco, and Jan Peerce, all internationally recognized for their interpretations. Scarpia, the villainous baritone in *Tosca*, was given all the wickedness the role deserved by Giuseppe De Luca, Lawrence Tibbett, Robert Weede, Ramon Vinay, Tito Gobbi, and Ingvar Wixell, among others. Even the medium-sized role of Colline in *La Bohème*,

German soprano **Lotte Lehmann** was one of many European artists who fled the Nazis in the late 1930s, to the benefit of American opera houses. When Nazi leader Hermann Göring asked Lehmann to confine her singing to Germany, she went first to Vienna, then in 1938 to Santa Barbara, California, where she lived for the rest of her life. Lehmann had already performed at the San Francisco Opera in 1934 as Tosca and Cio-Cio-San in *Madama Butterfly* and in 1936 in one of her greatest roles, Sieglinde in *Die Walküre*, this time sharing the stage with Kirsten Flagstad as Brünnhilde. Lehmann was known for her warm, honeyed voice and for the intelligent humanity she brought to her roles. She came to San Francisco often in the 1940s, usually to perform another of her definitive roles, the Marschallin in *Der Rosenkavalier*. Here, dressed for the part, she sits on stage and chats with **Robert Watt Miller**, president of the opera's board of directors, at left, and stage director **Armando Agnini**. She sang her final Marschallin with the company in 1946. Upon retiring from opera, she went on to teach at the Music Academy of the West, write several books, and paint well enough to have several solo shows in southern California.

Is it possible to rise from the ranks of the chorus and three-line comprimario roles to the peaks of operatic stardom? A number of Bay Area singers did so. **Claramae Turner**, born in Dinuba, California, abandoned singing when she married at the age of nineteen but took up a musical career again when her husband was serving in World War II. She moved up through the ranks and was a company regular from 1942 to 1974, usually in supporting mezzo roles.

Soprano **Dorothy Warenskjold** grew up comfortably in Piedmont, attended Mills College, and sang around the Bay Area, in concerts and on the radio, where Merola heard her. Thanks to her experience, she did not have to start in the chorus, and she made her debut in 1948 as a last-minute replacement for Licia Albanese as Nanetta in *Falstaff*. Among her other roles, she was Liù in *Turandot* in a 1953 production (above).

One of the most successful local talents was **Janis Martin**, a Sacramento mezzo-soprano who made her San Francisco Opera debut in 1960 as a servant in *Simon Boccanegra* and played some twenty-five other roles in the next five years. From 1966 on, she was a major star, whose repertoire included Venus in *Tannhäuser*, Marie in *Wozzeck*, Brünnhilde in the *Ring*, Elektra, and Tosca (above, left), with tenor **Giacomo Aragall** as Cavaradossi.

Two dramatic singing actresses, **Sena Jurinac** and **Elisabeth Söderström**, appearing in the 1980 production of Janáček's *Jenůfa*, convinced San Francisco audiences that this violent, dramatic twentieth-century opera belonged in the standard repertoire. Jurinac, who played the stern stepmother Kostelnička with terrifying dignity (opposite, top), had previously sung the title role in *Madama Butterfly*, Eva in *Die Meistersinger*, the Composer in *Ariadne auf Naxos*, and the Marschallin in *Der Rosenkavalier* (opposite, left), with **Christa Ludwig** as Octavian. Söderström (opposite, bottom), as Jenůfa, made her local debut in 1977 in a deeply moving performance of the title role of another Janáček opera, *Katya Kabanova*.

Licia Albanese holds the record for most leading roles performed with the San Francisco Opera, hardly surprising considering her particular talent for Puccini's heroines. She was adored not only for her voice but for the intensity of her dramatic portrayals, in which she used her hands, her eyes, and her gestures to embellish the words and music. Speaking of one of her favorite heroines, Madama Butterfly, she said, "Take the words in 'Un bel dì.' You must dramatize each one, from the noise of the ships, the calm of the harbor...you must reach the public with gestures and eyes and elegance but as if you are talking, not directing traffic." She made her debut in San Francisco in 1941 as Madama Butterfly and ended her career with the company in 1961, singing the same role in a Los Angeles performance. In 1973 she came back to sing with Luciano Pavarotti at one of the first annual Opera in the Park events in Golden Gate Park. Among her numerous roles was Liù in *Turandot* (above), with **Nicola Moscona** as Timur, center, and **Eugene Tobin** as Calaf, in 1957, and Violetta in *La Traviata* in 1947 (above, right).

which consists of some lively ensemble music and a single aria, got star treatment in San Francisco, where Ezio Pinza sang the part in almost every performance of the opera between 1927 and 1945.

A dramatic example of singers transforming the repertoire came in the 1950s, when soprano Maria Callas revived the art of bel canto (literally, "beautiful singing"), a style of singing in which the singer—usually a woman—ornaments the notes on the page with additional trills, roulades, and cadenzas of her own devising. This kind of vocal embellishment had been wildly popular in the nineteenth century, when the operas of Italian bel canto composers Bellini, Donizetti, and Rossini dominated the repertoire.

Around the turn of the century, the vocal acrobatics began to seem excessively decorative and contrary to the trend toward greater realism in opera. Conductors, notably Arturo Toscanini, began to discourage florid additions to the score, and the bel canto operas practically disappeared from the stage, in San Francisco and elsewhere in the operatic world.

Bellini's *La Sonnambula*, a prime example of the genre, was the first opera ever presented in San Francisco, in 1851, and was frequently performed during the next five decades. It, along with two other Bellini bel canto masterpieces, *Norma* and *I Puritani*, abruptly vanished from the repertoire around the

Claudia Muzio, possessor of one of the most distinctive soprano voices of the century, was born in Pavia, Italy, in 1889, the illegitimate daughter of an assistant stage manager who later worked at the Metropolitan in New York and at Covent Garden in London. His daughter literally grew up in the theater, watching singers rehearse and taking naps in the wings. She made her American debut at the Met in 1916, as Tosca. The following year, her father died, and after that she and her silent, fanatically religious mother led an increasingly reclusive life, declining even to dine with the rest of the company when on tour. Her loneliness and the pain of brief, secret love affairs seemed to come out when she went onstage, where her singing was called "one long, tragic cry." She made her San Francisco debut in 1924, as Maddalena in *Andrea Chénier*, followed by *Tosca* and *La Traviata* (below). On several occasions Merola had to reschedule performances for Muzio, who seemed to have a talent for being caught in storms at sea en route from Buenos Aires, where she was a regular at the Teatro Colón.

Tiny, delicate **Bidú Sayão** came from Rio de Janeiro, the daughter of a rich Brazilian family that sent her to Paris to study singing. She was discovered by Toscanini in New York where she sang with the New York Philharmonic. Her San Francisco debut came as Massenet's Manon in 1939 (left), when she replaced one of the many Italian artists who canceled that year due to Mussolini's restrictive travel laws. Her Chevalier des Grieux in 1939 was the great **Tito Schipa**, of whom she later said, "Schipa was wonderful. He was a great, great singer—small voice, but great singer. I had a small voice, too, so our voices blend together. I am five three or five two . . . he was more or less my size, a bit taller. . . . We were a handsome pair." Sayão protected her small soprano voice throughout her career, favoring roles like Juliette in Gounod's *Roméo et Juliette*, Mimì in *La Bohème*, and Mélisande in *Pelléas et Mélisande* (left). In her last season in San Francisco, 1952, she tried two new roles, Margherita in *Mefistofele* and Nedda in *Pagliacci*, on the grounds that she was about to retire and could afford to push her voice a bit.

In 1956 Austrian soprano **Leonie Rysanek** made her San Francisco and American debut as Senta in *Der Fliegende Holländer.* The following year, she proved herself both versatile and indispensable to the company by singing not only her own scheduled roles in *Turandot* and *Ariadne auf Naxos,* but the principal soprano roles in Verdi's *Macbeth,* replacing Maria Callas, and in one performance each of *Un Ballo in Maschera* and *Aida,* replacing the scheduled Antonietta Stella. It was the start of a thirty-seven-year relationship with the company, a lengthy run that was interrupted only by her decision in 1980 not to perform the role of Santuzza in Jean-Pierre Ponnelle's contro-versial production of *Cavalleria Rusticana.* One of her most suc-cessful roles was the Empress in *Die Frau ohne Schatten* (right), which she sang in 1960, 1976, and 1980. Her final role in San Francisco came in 1993, when she left local audiences with the vivid memory of her dying scream as the Old Countess in *The Queen of Spades.*

Soprano **Elisabeth Schwarzkopf**, one of many German singers who made their American operatic debuts in San Francisco, first appeared soon after Kurt Herbert Adler heard her in concert at the Hollywood Bowl. Her debut role in 1955—the Marschallin in *Der Rosenkavalier* (left)—was one of her most definitive roles. **Kerstin Meyer** was Octavian. Another of Schwarzkopf's appearances was as a fetching Mistress Ford in *Falstaff* in 1956 (above). She became a frequent visitor to San Francisco during the next decade, not only at the opera but also as a recitalist and, later, as a teacher of master classes in the Merola Opera Program.

Coloratura soprano **Joan Sutherland** firmly established the bel canto repertoire in San Francisco, beginning with her debut performance in *Lucia di Lammermoor* in 1961. Among her many successes were the title roles in *Esclarmonde* in 1974 (above) and *La Sonnambula* in 1963. *Sonnambula* was one of the first productions that current general director Lotfi Mansouri directed for the San Francisco Opera, and signaled the start of a long professional relationship between the two, in which he ultimately directed her in nearly a dozen roles over two decades. She was also close to former general director Terence McEwen, who, as head of the classical music division of London Records, enthusiastically supported her decision to concentrate on Italian bel canto operas and was responsible for many of her recordings.

start of the twentieth century. In the first fifty years of its history, San Francisco Opera presented *Norma* only once, in 1937, then in 1972 returned it to the regular repertoire. *La Sonnambula* was given for the first time in 1960, and *I Puritani* reached the War Memorial stage for the first time in 1966.

Donizetti, another composer of bel canto operas, did a little better, with *La Fille du Régiment*, *L'Elisir d'Amore*, *Don Pasquale*, and *Lucia di Lammermoor* turning up with fair frequency, but many other Donizetti operas, such as his pseudohistorical dramas, *Maria Stuarda*, *Anna Bolena*, and *Roberto Devereux*, were not heard until much later. With the single exception of his comic opera, *Il Barbiere di Siviglia*, Rossini's vast output was almost completely unknown to San Francisco audiences until the 1960s.

The special art of bel canto was in danger of oblivion until Maria Callas took it up again. Significantly, she was an intensely theatrical artist who brought humanity and vulnerability to the stage, in sharp contrast to the birdlike earlier coloraturas and their shallow, decorative interpretations.

Callas, incidentally, never sang at the San Francisco Opera. In the mid-1940s, the story goes, she auditioned for the company. When she was advised to come back again after building up a name for herself, she was quick to say, "When I make a name I shall not want you." In 1957 she was scheduled to

Italian soprano **Renata Tebaldi**'s warm voice was first heard in the United States in 1950, when she made her American debut as Aida at the San Francisco Opera. The performance, which also featured tenor Mario Del Monaco making his United States debut as Radames, was one of Gaetano Merola's greatest coups. It took place near the end of Merola's long reign and marked a sharp contrast to the early years, when singers who had not appeared at the Metropolitan Opera in New York were rarely hired by San Francisco. The supposed rivalry between Tebaldi and Maria Callas fueled opera gossip for many years, pitting Tebaldi's lyric-dramatic soprano, serene disposition, and spun-out high notes and pianissimi against Callas's dramatic coloratura and tempestuous personality. In 1956, Tebaldi sang her first Amelia in *Simon Boccanegra* (left).

sing the roles of Lady Macbeth and Lucia di Lammermoor, starting in late September. When, as the season got under way, she began to hedge, offering to come in mid-October, weeks after her first scheduled performances, Adler fired her and filed a complaint with the American Guild of Musical Artists, which eventually issued a reprimand, stating that Callas was not justified in refusing to fulfill her contract. Callas did appear in San Francisco a few years later, in a concert billed as a "triumphant return." Even with illustrious tenor Giuseppe di Stefano onstage with her, the event was a humiliating failure for Callas, whose voice was an unpleasant shadow of what it once had been.

As Callas's career was fading in the late 1950s, another great bel canto voice, that of Australian soprano Joan Sutherland, came along in time to continue the revival. Although she lacked Callas's dramatic intensity, she, like Callas, was anything but chirpy. She had a huge voice and had begun her career aspiring to Verdi and Wagner roles. After seven years at Covent Garden in London, Sutherland finally became a so-called overnight success when she sang her first Lucia di Lammermoor, electrifying the audience with the power and flexibility of her voice in the demanding Mad Scene, in which the blood-drenched heroine wanders the stage after slaying her bridegroom. Encouraged by her husband, pianist/conductor Richard Bonynge, she put aside Verdi and Wagner and began to concentrate on bel canto.

Soprano **Beverly Sills**'s San Francisco career began with a couple of catastrophes. She came to the city for the first time in late August 1953; when no one met her, she made her way to Merola's house, where she learned that he had just died. Penniless, she spent the next weeks in a Market Street hotel, heating up her food on the radiator, and at the opera house, playing roles that ranged from a maidservant in *Elektra* to Donna Elvira in *Don Giovanni*. That same season, while she played a Valkyrie, her helmet fell off and she rushed to pick it up instead of ignoring the mishap. Kurt Herbert Adler was furious and asked if she were drunk. She did not return to San Francisco Opera until 1971, when she sang the title role in *Manon* on the opening night of the 1971 season. When she arrived in her dressing room, she found the same helmet filled with orchids and a welcoming note from Adler. Peace restored, she returned to San Francisco many times, reinforcing the bel canto revival with operas like *Lucia* and *I Puritani* and excelling in both comic and tragic roles, from *The Daughter of the Regiment* (above) to *La Traviata* and *Manon* (right), with **Nicolai Gedda** as Chevalier des Grieux. She and Adler became great friends, and she often asked his advice when she became head of New York City Opera. "He gave me the best advice. He told me to run an autonomous company and don't delegate authority."

Mezzo-soprano **Frederica von Stade** began her career with the San Francisco Opera in 1971. Her debut role was Sesto in the Spring Opera production of *Titus*, the English-language version of Mozart's *La Clemenza di Tito*. A year later von Stade was on the War Memorial stage as Cherubino in *Le Nozze di Figaro*. Audiences fell in love with her delicate looks and pure and refined tone. She has had triumphant successes in several San Francisco premieres, including Monteverdi's *Il Ritorno d'Ulisse in Patria* and the world premiere of Conrad Susa and Philip Littell's *Dangerous Liaisons* (left), with **Thomas Hampson**. A Bay Area resident, von Stade has been active locally, appearing with the San Francisco Symphony, giving recitals, and singing for AIDS benefits.

One of the most eagerly anticipated new productions of 1977 was *Turandot*, because the title role was sung by Spanish soprano **Montserrat Caballé**, making her company debut in her first encounter with the role of the autocratic princess (opposite) with **Giorgio Tozzi** as Timur. She shared the stage with another superstar, Luciano Pavarotti, who was singing the part of her successful suitor Calaf for the first time. Jean-Pierre Ponnelle's sets, dominated by a giant statue of a female figure, were much criticized, but Caballé's powerful, effortless singing of the demanding title role was greeted with standing ovations.

Regina Resnik essentially made two debuts in San Francisco, the first as a soprano in the 1940s, singing Leonore in *Fidelio* and Mistress Ford in *Falstaff*, and again in the 1960s, when she returned as a mezzo-soprano and a powerful actress, giving roles like Carmen, Clair in *The Visit of the Old Lady* (right), the Countess in *The Queen of Spades*, and Klytemnestra in *Elektra* (above) the full force of her dramatic abilities and her willingness to look ugly and to sing in an ugly way when her interpretation required it. "You must depend on your voice as an instrument, but then you must set it aside and use your voice as an actress," she said. She was still singing in San Francisco more than forty years after her debut, this time as Fräulein Schneider in the musical *Cabaret*, explaining, "Fräulein Schneider is a musical role that seemed made for me. She's hard, joyous, sentimental, romantic, practical, cynical, guilty, partly cowardly and partly courageous."

San Francisco's own bel canto revival began in 1960, when Kurt Herbert Adler brought Anna Moffo in to star as Amina, the sleepwalking heroine of *La Sonnambula*. Sutherland's own debut came the following year, as Lucia. Two years later, she returned as Amina, then, in 1966 she introduced local audiences to *I Puritani* and in 1972 reintroduced them to *Norma*.

The bel canto repertoire might still have been a short-lived novelty, in San Francisco and elsewhere in the opera world, had not other coloraturas come along around the same time. Beverly Sills, the ebullient soprano from Brooklyn, had a different style than Sutherland's but triumphed in some of the same roles. In San Francisco, her bel canto turns included *Lucia di Lammermoor*, *The Daughter of the Regiment*, and *I Puritani* in the 1970s. Marilyn Horne, who was that rarity of operatic birds, a coloratura mezzo-soprano, mastered the trouser roles, the male parts written for female voices. As she phrased it, "I'm always either the girl who doesn't get the guy—or the guy." Teamed up with Sutherland or Montserrat Caballé, she helped revive Rossini's noncomic operas, including *Semiramide*, *Tancredi*, and *Maometto II*, in San Francisco. Two other comic operas of Rossini, *La Cenerentola* and *L'Italiana in Algeri*, returned to the San Francisco Opera or Spring Opera schedules in the 1960s.

Not long after the vocal delights of bel canto took hold, a quite different sort of artist came along to

Mezzo-soprano **Tatiana Troyanos** made a specialty of trouser roles, male parts written for female singers, such as the Composer in *Ariadne auf Naxos,* which she sang in San Francisco in 1977. In her appearances in San Francisco, she was most often in lavishly feminine costumes, starting with her debut in the title role of Monteverdi's *L'Incoronazione di Poppea* in 1975. Her final operatic appearances came in 1993 in San Francisco during the summer Strauss Festival. She sang the role of the actress Clairon in Strauss's *Capriccio,* wearing extravagant new costumes by designer Thierry Bosquet (right). Kiri Te Kanawa sang the role of the Countess. Troyanos's unexpected death two months later shocked the opera world.

Teresa Berganza's career in San Francisco began in the late 1960s with delectable, girlish roles—Rosina in *Il Barbiere di Siviglia* (above), with **Pietro Bottazzo** as Almaviva; Cinderella in *La Cenerentola;* Dorabella in *Così fan tutte*—well suited to her coloratura mezzo-soprano and flirtatious stage presence. In 1981 she returned as an earthier seductress, the Gypsy Carmen, in the production of Bizet's opera conducted by Kurt Herbert Adler during his final season. For authenticity, she had spent days observing the Gypsies in her native Spain.

The Countess in *Le Nozze di Figaro*, the Marschallin in *Der Rosenkavalier*, the title role in *Arabella*, yet another Countess in *Capriccio*: these roles, each a beautiful heroine filled with questions about herself, were the specialty of soprano **Kiri Te Kanawa**, whose lush looks matched her radiant voice. Te Kanawa, the daughter of a Maori father and a European mother, began singing in her native New Zealand and made her San Francisco debut in 1972 as the Countess in *Le Nozze di Figaro* (left).

Born in Harlem, **Reri Grist** began studying dance at the age of six and later spent a year in the role of Consuelo in the original production of *West Side Story*. She made her San Francisco Opera debut in 1963 and quickly became a regular fixture at the company, specializing in light soprano roles such as Rosina in *Il Barbiere di Siviglia*, Zerbinetta in *Ariadne auf Naxos*, and Sophie in *Der Rosenkavalier*. "Oh yes," she once told an interviewer, "the roles are all the same, but then I have the same two vocal cords I've always had. I would love to do Desdemona or Salome, but I'm limited by the little instrument I have." She was persuaded by Kurt Herbert Adler to return in a new role, Manon in the Massenet opera (above), for his final season as general director of the San Francisco Opera in 1981.

When soprano **Anja Silja** came to the San Francisco Opera for the first time at the age of twenty-eight, she already had a vivid reputation that led one music critic to describe her as "femme fatale and living legend." She confirmed both descriptions in her debut performance in 1968 as Salome, a role that she had already done more than two hundred times while living with opera director Wieland Wagner, grandson of the composer and head of the Bayreuth Festival. One of her most memorable portrayals in San Francisco came in 1981, when she sang and vividly acted the title role in Shostakovich's *Lady Macbeth of Mtsensk* in a performance conducted by the late Calvin Simmons. Here she is yet another sex symbol, Alban Berg's lustful Lulu.

expand the standard repertoire in another direction. This was the singing actress, the performer willing to sacrifice prettiness of tone and appearance for a more intense and realistic interpretation. The idea was not entirely new, of course. One of the most notable examples was Maria Jeritza, who, along with Caruso, was probably the most worshiped operatic artist of the early part of the twentieth century. Jeritza came to San Francisco Opera for the first time in 1928, when she sang the title roles in *Tosca*, *Turandot*, *Fedora*, and *Carmen*. She was back in 1930, when her roles ranged from raw sensuality in *Salome* to saintliness as Elisabeth in *Tannhäuser*.

Whether she was saint or sinner, the audience and the critics were entranced. Of her Salome, one critic wrote, "Jeritza does not hesitate to make her despicable and vulgar. She sang as well as she ever does, which is well enough for anyone. There are some glorious tones in her voice and when she sacrifices quality it is not for the sake of quantity, but for the sake of the dramatic effect . . . Friday night's performance was sufficiently provocative to make it the talk of the town." After *Tannhäuser*, another critic said, "Her Elisabeth is no pallid ascetic, but a saint of the overwhelming intensity of a Santa Teresa. . . . Voice is only part of the endowment of a prima donna. Jeritza has it in glorious richness; but she has the rarer boon of a personality that sweeps all before it like a tide."

Schooled by the legendary Viennese theatrical director Max Reinhardt, Kurt Herbert Adler wanted opera to be powerfully dramatic as well as musical. To do this, he needed singers who could do more than stand in place against a pretty background. He achieved his goal with the help of a number of powerful singing actresses who turned up on the operatic scene in the 1960s and 1970s.

One of his allies was Regina Resnik, who essentially had two separate careers with the company. In the 1940s, she came to San Francisco as a soprano, singing Leonora in Beethoven's *Fidelio* and the title role in the company's first production of Ponchielli's *La Gioconda*. In the 1960s and 1970s she returned to the company as a mezzo-soprano and as a formidable actress. She stamped her identity, ferocious

and unforgettable, on roles like the old Countess in Tchaikovsky's *Queen of Spades* and the evil Klytemnestra in Strauss's *Elektra*.

Several other singing actresses helped Adler introduce twentieth-century verismo operas from Germany and Czechoslovakia to San Francisco audiences. Soprano Sena Jurinac, who had triumphed in 1971 as a touching Marschallin in *Der Rosenkavalier*, came back in 1980 to play a stern and terrifying Kostelnička in a mesmerizing performance of Janáček's *Jenůfa*, which starred another great actress, Elisabeth Söderström, in the title role.

Evelyn Lear was an American dramatic soprano who thrilled San Francisco audiences. Her husband, Thomas Stewart, was also a riveting actor who was a regular at the San Francisco Opera. One of Lear's most devastating performances was her "frantically erotic" interpretation of the wanton heroine of the company's first presentation of Alban Berg's *Lulu* in 1965. According to a critic, "If an occasional strident edge—even a squeak—crept in her vocalism, it almost enhanced the characterization. After all, she was not singing Lucia."

Another specialist in operatic sex objects was Anja Silja, who arrived in San Francisco in 1968 with a colorful reputation as the protégée and mistress of Wieland Wagner, grandson of Richard Wagner and head of the annual Wagner festival in Bayreuth. She did not disappoint local audiences, who literally gasped at the unabashedly amoral females she played in *Salome* in 1968, *Lulu* in 1971, and *Lady Macbeth of Mtsensk* in 1981.

Performances like hers changed people's expectations of opera, appealing to a younger and more intellectual audience and making it possible to expand the company's repertoire beyond the routine and familiar. *Madama Butterfly* and *La Traviata* will always sell tickets, but in San Francisco so do *The Queen of Spades* and *Lady Macbeth of Mtsensk*, thanks to this synchronicity of dramatic artists and the company's willingness to use them.

American soprano **Evelyn Lear** was San Francisco Opera's first *Lulu*, in 1965 (above right), with **Ramon Vinay** as Dr. Schön, her obsessed admirer. She threw herself into the role of Alban Berg's wanton heroine with gusto, both vocally and dramatically. The role was a huge success for Lear, who subsequently performed it at opera houses around the world.

Leontyne Price

For **Leontyne Price**, the most personally meaningful role in her repertoire was the role of the Ethiopian slave Aida. She sang the Verdi role for the first time during her first season in San Francisco, in 1957, and in her last, in 1984 (above, left), as well as many times in between. In 1959, her Amneris (above, center) was with one of San Francisco Opera's favorite mezzo-sopranos, **Irene Dalis**. In 1958, she sang the first Leonora of her career in Verdi's *Il Trovatore*; in her dressing room, she watched carefully as a company hairdresser prepared her hair for the role (above, right). In 1963, she performed another Leonora for the first time, this time the heroine of *La Forza del Destino* (opposite, left), a role she repeated in 1965 and 1979. For many members of the San Francisco audience, her "Pace, pace, mio Dio" was the ultimate Price experience.

September 27, 1957. The headlines screamed of hatred and confrontation. In Little Rock, Arkansas, shrieking crowds massed outside Central High School that hot autumn morning, their faces distorted with loathing for the black teenagers who were attempting to integrate the school. Governor Orval Faubus had called in the National Guard to prevent them from entering the building. President Eisenhower was about to send in the 101st Airborne Division of the United States Army to force the integration of the school.

That same week, in San Francisco, Leontyne Price had made her first appearance on a major operatic stage, singing the role of the young nun, Mme. Lidoine, in the company's American presentation of Poulenc's *Dialogues of the Carmelites*. A cordial audience applauded her debut with enthusiasm. The reviews that appeared on the following days were favorable.

The two events could not have been more disparate, yet there was a connection that reverberated through the long career of San Francisco's most worshiped diva. Price was not the first black artist to sing at the San Francisco Opera, where Mattiwilda Dobbs had broken the color barrier as the Queen of Shemakha in *Le Coq d'Or* in 1955. Nor was she the first black woman to sing at the Metropolitan; Marian Anderson had sung there near the end of her career. Leontyne Price was a different phenomenon. She was possessed of a talent so obvious that it could not be denied, and she appeared on the scene at a historic moment, as indomitable a force as the civil rights movement that surged around her.

A few weeks after Price's San Francisco debut, Italian soprano Antonietta Stella, scheduled to sing Aida, had to cancel because of appendicitis. Price, who had been scheduled to sing her first Aida the following year in Vienna, stepped into the role that came to define her, not only professionally but personally. The Friday-night audi-

ence, usually considered phlegmatic, stomped and screamed its enthusiasm.

Many years later, Price said, "I can't tell you what a joy that role can be to a black woman: the skin tone, the duskiness of the voice—all those clinical things that give incredible freedom. Coupled with that the role afforded me the opportunity to say what I had to say, the pioneer that I was on the operatic scene. It was my warrior part. . . . It enabled me to say what should have been said for all of us at that time: oppression, civil rights, the opening of doors, the beginning of equal opportunity. Aida was my sword. I will always, always love her for that."

From the first, San Francisco audiences recognized her as someone extraordinary in the history of opera and paid her unique and moving tributes. One of the most unusual accolades came in 1958, when she returned to sing her first Leonora in *Il Trovatore*. As she concluded her fourth-act aria, "D'amor sull'ali rosee," the audience burst

into prolonged applause. So, too, did the conductor, Georges Sebastian, who paid her the extraordinary compliment of putting down his baton to clap along with the audience.

Price went on to many more firsts in San Francisco, including her debuts as Donna Elvira in *Don Giovanni*, Amelia in *Un Ballo in Maschera*, Giorgetta in *Il Tabarro*, the title roles in *Ariadne auf Naxos* and *Manon Lescaut*, and another Leonora, in *La Forza del Destino*. She developed a close relationship with general director Kurt Herbert Adler, noting that he had given her roles pretty much in the order that she herself would have chosen them.

"I have always regarded San Francisco as my home company. . . . The company always reaches for the maximum effort, even in the smallest details—a very thoughtful, thorough group that still makes it seem easy. It's the captain at the helm," she said in 1977.

Her success in San Francisco was so complete and unalloyed that it is easy to forget what it was like to be Leontyne Price in the 1950s and 1960s. As writer Vincent Sheean expressed it in 1964, "The opera public has known Leontyne Price for several years in several countries and has, I think, not altogether recovered from its astonishment that this superb voice and sovereign technique come from the throat of an American Negro born in the state of Mississippi."

Even her own publicity releases in the early years of her career seem to reflect this surprise, with delicately phrased sentences like, "It is only in recent years that Negroes have been admitted to the operatic stage at all, and then only in about a dozen roles that are dark-skinned or non-European."

She was simultaneously proud and uncomfortable about the extracurricular role that she had to play as a token black in the era of the civil rights movement. She said later, "Whenever there was any copy about me, what I was as an artist, what I had as ability, got shoveled under because all the attention was on racial connotations." Admittedly thin-skinned, she had to face both racial slights and the criticism of black leaders who complained that she was insufficiently outspoken on the subject of civil rights.

San Franciscans were anything but critical whenever she appeared on the opera stage or in the concert hall, where standing ovations of five minutes or more were not unusual. Were they for her gloriously unique voice or for her dignified presence in the history of the American civil rights movement? It does not take anything away from her overwhelming talent to say that it was both.

...action

THE CURTAIN RISES:

chapter six

SETS, COSTUMES, LIGHTS...ACTION

The notes of the overture die away, and the audience settles into their seats in the darkness. The golden curtain rises, its sinuous, silken folds rising and moving outward. The audience, collectively and unconsciously, takes an inward breath as the first-act scenery is revealed. At this moment, opera is a visual experience, a coalescence of colors, shapes, light, and movement that defines what is to come and transports the viewers into another world.

Unlike the singers on the stage and the players in the orchestra pit, whose tools and techniques have not changed in hundreds of years, the physical presence of the opera is in a continual state of flux, reflecting changing aesthetics, evolving concepts, and revolutionary technology. All of these have influenced production at the San Francisco Opera during its seventy-five year history.

In September 1997, when San Franciscans entered the War Memorial Opera House for the first time since December 1995, when seismic reconstruction and extensive cosmetic refurbishing began, the scene was little different than it was when the theater opened in October 1932.

The crowds milled around the lobby under a newly gilded coffered ceiling. The elite walked upstairs to the semicircle of spacious boxes known as the Golden Horseshoe, designed so that the box-holders could both see and be seen. Downstairs, people took their places in seats newly covered with

General Director **Lotfi Mansouri** and designer **Michael Yeargan** used a scale model of the Civic Auditorium to visualize the set that Yeargan designed for the 1996–1997 season's production of *Carmen* (above).

Artist David Hockney took a painterly approach to Puccini's ferocious fairy tale *Turandot* (opposite) in 1993, conjuring up brilliantly colored cartoon-like sets that seemed to express the opera's exaggerated exoticism.

The creation of a new production starts years before the curtain rises with detailed sketches (above). The next step is a model (right), such as the one on the table in front of **John Priest**, the opera's technical director from 1966 to 1995. The design then goes to the scene shop, where carpenters begin to build the set (opposite, left); here **Pierre Cayard**, head of the opera's scene shop, helps relate model and sketch to the carpenter building the scenery. Finally, the finished product moves to the stage of the opera house (opposite, right), where stagehands raise it for the first time.

red velvet, although the new chairs lack the wire tophat holders they had in 1932. Less well-off opera aficionados staked out standing-room space behind the back rows of the orchestra and upper levels, although they paid more than the dollar charged in 1932.

There was history onstage as well. The new curtain is an exact reproduction of the original 1932 curtain; it was woven of two thousand yards of gold organzine silk on a computerized loom that operated for two shifts a day for two months. Following the opening gala concert, the first production of the San Francisco Opera's seventy-fifth year was *Tosca*, presented in designer Thierry Bosquet's re-creation of the original 1932 sets. The church of Sant' Andrea della Valle was created entirely of beautifully painted canvas drops, a tribute to the time when scenery painting was considered an art worthy of great artists.

Those early scenery painters had special skills. Like a Monet water lily, a painted canvas makes little sense when one examines it from a foot away. Only distance transforms the splashes of paint into a recognizable subject. Scenery painters also had to be masters of perspective, so that buildings seemed to diminish in size toward the back of the stage to give a sense of depth. They created further illusions of three-dimensionality by painting shadows on the canvas.

These techniques, refined as they were, had some limitations. The painted perspective meant that singers moving toward the back of the stage seemed larger and larger in relationship to their surroundings. Painted shadows were visually confusing when a singer cast a shadow in the opposite direction. Audiences, accustomed to the quirks of painted sets, did not complain.

Designer **Thierry Bosquet** designed lush scenery for the San Francisco Opera's new production of *Pelléas et Mélisande* in the 1997–1998 season.

This quaint village of half-timbered houses (below) was expected to do multiple duty in the early decades of the San Francisco Opera. Here, in 1938, it was onstage for a performance of *Martha*, but it also served as the setting for *La Juive* and other operas requiring a small-town atmosphere.

Designer **Beni Montresor**'s evocative watercolors, enhanced with gilded paper, for the 1974 production of Massenet's *Esclarmonde* accurately suggested the rich and brilliant colorations of the sets.

Nor did they expect new settings for familiar operas. In any case, there was no chance that they would receive such novelties. In San Francisco, Merola often ordered traditional sets from Italy or had them painted by a handful of talented scenery artists in the United States. The sets were usually copies of the opera's original sets or whatever the Metropolitan Opera was putting onstage in New York. The New York link was strong in San Francisco, where Gaetano Merola's cousin, Armando Agnini, who had worked at the Metropolitan, was responsible for the physical setting of almost every performance staged by the San Francisco Opera from 1923 to 1953.

In those days, there were neither directors nor new productions in the modern sense of the terms. The look of a production was created by the conductor working with the stage director and the master electrician. With a few exceptions, instead of designing sets specifically for a particular opera, Agnini worked with generic bits of scenery—a country village, the steps of a church, a palatial interior—which he endlessly assembled and reassembled. Opera buffs, noting a grille from *Il Barbiere di Siviglia*, a chaise longue from *Der Rosenkavalier*, or a painted drop from the first production of *Mefistofele*, claim to have identified from eighteen to fifty-five previous productions represented in a single act.

If the productions lacked individuality, the painted drops had the advantage of portability. Each canvas had to be folded in a precise way, so that fold marks would be indistinct the next time the scenery was hung, or areas painted with metallic gold paint would not touch each other and cause flaking. An entire opera could be stored in a trunk, an indispensable bonus in a theater with the limited backstage space of the War Memorial. Matthew Farruggio, stage director for the company for some thirty-five years, recalls, "As soon as the symphony season ended, we brought in the scenery for the whole season, which was sometimes fifteen operas. You could store a season's worth in the alcoves at the back of the stage."

Space was a problem from the day the War Memorial opened. For all the splendor of the front of the house, the building had not been designed to meet the demands of a permanent opera company. Almost no backstage space had been allotted for offices or workshops. Sets had to be painted on the stage, where there were hanging facilities for only two drops at a time. The carpentry shop was crowded

The set model (below) was one of the early steps in presenting *Carmen* at the Civic Auditorium during the 1996–1997 season. The production took advantage of the thrust stage and the placement of the orchestra behind the stage to bring the fourth-act parade of toreadors close to the audience (left).

For many years, each light change onstage required the carefully choreographed movements of up to nine stagehands, who simultaneously raised and lowered the handles on the light board (right) located a few feet from the right edge of the stage. Gradually computers and so-called smart lights made the process a matter of pushing a button at the right moment in the score, enabling lighting designers to program hundreds of lighting cues in a single opera.

Designer **Michael Stennett** is responsible for some of the most beautiful depictions of the costumes he designed for productions such as *Idomeneo*, presented in San Francisco in 1989.

into a small third-floor space, and office space was almost nonexistent. Farruggio, who came to the company in 1956, remembers, "Mr. Adler operated out of a broom closet for years. Then he moved into a dressing room, and I took the broom closet. I covered the sink with a board to have a desk."

In 1932 the War Memorial Opera House boasted that it was the most technically advanced theater in the United States, with up-to-date lighting and the newest versions of wind and cloud machines. By today's standards, the equipment was primitive, and productions looked quite different than they do today.

Performances took place on a flat stage; raked platforms came along much later. Lighting, too, was relatively flat, with most of the general illumination onstage coming from carbon arc spotlights, which hissed when they were turned on and emitted clouds of soot. Resistance dimmers, contraptions involving oiled plates, became dangerously hot as they lowered the stage lights. Each change of lighting, cued by the prompter, required the carefully choreographed teamwork of up to nine stagehands, pulling and pushing the controls at the light board.

Given these limitations, an opera typically would have only eight to ten lighting changes, rather than the hundreds now made possible by computers. Instead of employing follow spots to isolate individual artists or different areas of the stage as is done in today's productions, the lighting served only to create a general atmosphere. Wattage was limited, so the illumination was often murky, both on the stage and in the orchestra pit, where the players squinted at their scores with the help of puny twenty-five-watt bulbs.

Like the sets, the costumes for a production were cobbled together from stock. For its first six decades, the company did not have its own costume shop and depended on the redoubtable Goldstein and Company, a private costume-rental firm. Everyone in town knew the place, from the teenager in

Costume designer **Carl Toms** created swaggering costumes for *Lucia di Lammermoor*, such as this heavily ornamented outfit for the character of Arturo (above). **Jean-Pierre Ponnelle**, who designed costumes as well as sets for many of his productions, painted a romantic costume for Desdemona in the 1970 production of Verdi's *Otello* (above, right).

Artist **David Hockney** created cartoon-bright costumes for his 1993 production of *Turandot*; the costume for Ping (opposite) was executed in heavy felt with gold trim.

search of a costume for a school play to the society matron invited to a Mardi Gras ball. It was a dizzying experience to squeeze down the narrow aisles, pushing aside stiff petticoats and braid-trimmed military tunics. That the costumes were also worn onstage at the opera house made the experience more thrilling, although most of the private clients probably never appreciated that the Goldsteins' formidable collection included costumes sent by the Metropolitan Opera to San Francisco after the 1906 earthquake and fire.

The opera had the same choices as the society matron. When it came time to produce *Carmen*, someone from the opera went off to Goldstein's to pick out anything that looked vaguely Spanish. The procedure was so routine that if the opera was a revival, Merola often dispensed with the dress rehearsal. Later, as Adler gradually moved to more coherent productions, Goldstein's would make—or "build" in operatic terminology—costumes designed for specific productions. According to contract, these designs could not be rented out to the public for five years.

Perhaps in self-defense, principal singers often brought their own costumes. Soprano Claudia Muzio's beautifully embroidered dresses for *Tosca* were lavish re-creations of the mode of Napoleonic

France, sewn by the prestigious haute couture house of Worth in Paris. (Sometimes, of course, the prima donna's costumes were less faithful to the traditions of the production and stood in marked contrast to what everyone else onstage was wearing.) Lily Pons, Bidú Sayão, and Licia Albanese were famed for the expensive, custom-made costumes they wore in their most-performed roles. Nor was it only the women who dressed themselves according to their own notions of what was flattering; Ezio Pinza's costume for the title role in *Boris Godunov* was lavished with pearls and beads. More recently, both Joan Sutherland and Montserrat Caballé, conscious of their figures, insisted on bringing their own costumes or having the designs built in the ateliers of their choice.

By today's standards, this way of putting together productions seems careless and haphazard. Miraculously, this hodgepodge of diverse elements often managed to create magical evenings in the opera house. It helped that the singers often worked together, in Europe and in the small number of opera houses that existed in the United States in the first half of this century, so that they were able to come together as an ensemble without lengthy rehearsals. It helped, too, that the audience was expecting traditional productions, not three-dimensional realism or innovative reinterpretations of the familiar repertoire. They were there for a vocal treat, presented against familiar backgrounds.

After World War II, the situation began to change, in San Francisco and elsewhere in the opera world. The trend emerging from postwar German theater, particularly Bayreuth under the direction of Wagner's grandsons Wieland and Wolfgang, was toward abstraction and three-dimensionality. Romanticized German landscapes and singers dressed in helmets and breast-plates, with their overtones of German nationalism, were gone, replaced by abstract structures, artful lighting effects, and unspecific, vaguely classical costumes.

In San Francisco, Adler, who had close ties to the German operatic community, was quick to respond. In 1954 he brought Paul Hager from Germany to act as stage director for the company. As Armando Agnini had been during the Merola years, Hager, often working with his wife Ghita, was responsible for most of the productions for the next twenty years. He was a master of minimalism, which represented not only a dramatic change of style but a way for the eternally cash-strapped company to save money and to deal with its limited space.

Sets were constructed in the opera house's crowded carpentry shop until 1966. When the proposed set was too large—as in Leo Kerz's 1956 *Francesca da Rimini* featuring a giant bridge across the stage—it was built in Los Angeles.

In the 1960s and 1970s, designers Wolfram Skalicki and Leni Bauer-Ecsy helped to introduce audiences to modernism and abstraction. Skalicki's *Fidelio*, with its huge black grille symbolizing prison, has stood the test of time for longer than anyone probably intended. Bauer-Ecsy was responsible for most of the new productions required by Adler's expanding repertoire of twentieth-century operas; her designs included the company's premieres of *Wozzeck*, *Capriccio*, *Lulu*, *The Makropulos Case*, and *Jenůfa*.

In 1958 a young Frenchman came to San Francisco to design the American premiere of Carl Orff's *The Wise Maiden* and the first fully staged version of *Carmina Burana* in the United States. The following year he was two-thirds of the way through the design for both the sets and the costumes for *Die Frau ohne Schatten* when he was drafted by the French government for the war in Algeria.

His name was Jean-Pierre Ponnelle, and the San Francisco Opera has never been the same since. Following his military service, he decided that he wished to be director as well as designer in order to create a unity between the visual, musical, and theatrical aspects of the production. Although the trend toward opera with a unifying concept had been developing in fits and starts since World War II, Ponnelle and fellow director/designer Franco Zeffirelli are credited with elaborating this approach in the world's opera houses.

Well educated and fluent in several languages, Ponnelle began each new production by studying the sources of an opera, whether literature or myth, and the context in which it was written, searching for details and nuances to enrich his productions. In addition to possessing a remarkable visual imagination, he was one of surprisingly few directors who could look at the score of an opera and hear every note of every instrument. It was an ability that enabled him to match each bit of stage action, from the turn of a head to a freeze of the chorus, to a specific note of music.

His talents led to a close relationship with Kurt Herbert Adler, who ultimately treated him like a son. Each was a man who disdained the abilities of most other people but had infinite respect for the other. Both were men who valued detail, and their communications, written and spoken, about every fine point of an upcoming production were lengthy. Marian Lever, Adler's secretary during the 1970s, recalls that there were five folders of communications on the choice of an edition of *Carmen* for the 1981 production.

Ponnelle's influence on the way opera was staged, in San Francisco and elsewhere, can hardly be overstated. He was not afraid to be controversial. His 1973 *Rigoletto*, presented in lurid, violently red sets, was treated as a flashback, with Gilda lying dead onstage during the overture and her father reliving the tragedy in a series of erotic scenes that sometimes suggested an incestuous relationship between the crippled jester and his doomed daughter. It caused a sensation, with some critics and members of the audience howling in dismay.

Two years later Ponnelle stirred up more frenzy with his rethinking of *Der Fliegende Holländer*, in which he combined the roles of Erik and the Steersman, with Erik emerging as the protagonist in the sleeping Steersman's dreams. Skeletons floating from the ship's ropes were just one detail of the ghoulish decor. After stirring up arguments in San Francisco, the production traveled to the Metropolitan Opera in New York, where it was violently booed by the audience and loathed by the critics.

Ponnelle and Adler were delighted with the furor. After all, weren't people talking about opera as vital contemporary theater rather than vocal high-wire act and historical revival? Besides, not all of Ponnelle's productions were so intellectually demanding. His cartoonlike 1969 *Cenerentola*, enhanced by the conducting of Sir Charles Mackerras and the talents of Spanish mezzo Teresa Berganza and comic actors Renato Capecchi and Paolo Montarsolo, was pure delight, filled with the witty details and lightning timing that were classic Ponnelle. When the curtain rose on his 1981 *Carmen*, its first-act stone wall covered with graffiti instantly established a mood of hard-edged realism that cut through the familiarity of one of opera's most-performed works.

One of the most dramatically modern sets of the opera's second decade was this austere suggestion of the prison in Beethoven's *Fidelio*. The set, designed by **Herbert Graf** in 1937, was one of the few designed specifically for a single opera in the early decades of the San Francisco Opera.

Brilliantly patterned costumes, such as these worn by tenor **Joseph Frank** in the role of the Emperor Altoum, and his servant (opposite), made **David Hockney**'s production of *Turandot* a ravishing spectacle.

During a rehearsal on the opera house stage for Wagner's *Der Fliegende Holländer*, **Jean-Pierre Ponnelle** instructed the chorus underneath the tattered sails of Daland's ship. His version of Wagner's opera, presented in San Francisco for the first time in 1975, was one of his most controversial productions. It was not so much the eerie setting that caused the furor but the fact that Ponnelle had merged the characters of Erik and the Steersman, presenting the entire opera as the Steersman's dream.

Ponnelle's fanatical attention to detail extended beyond the physical production. He played an active role in casting his productions, choosing principals not only for their vocal abilities but for their willingness to develop and reveal the motivations of their characters. Even the lowliest supernumerary was expected to rise to the Ponnelle standard. He liked to choose every super, looking not only for size and looks but for the ability to play a distinctive, if nonspeaking, role in his crowd scenes. Under his guidance, the members of the chorus became much more than costumed voices; he gave them individual personalities, massed them for dramatic visual effects, and demanded precisely choreographed movement. Rehearsals with Ponnelle were always intense and often physical, but the choristers boasted of their bruises and wept when they heard of his unexpected death, at fifty-six, in 1988.

He died only a few months after Kurt Herbert Adler, further marking the end of an era. Although some of Ponnelle's productions, including the spirited *Cenerentola*, have been successfully revived, the presence of the master, controlling every flicker of movement onstage, is sometimes noticeably absent. Nevertheless, his work has had a lasting effect on the San Francisco Opera, establishing the preeminence of the director and the importance of a unified theatrical vision.

Ponnelle also made technical demands on the backstage activities of the company. After decades of

"I love *Wozzeck*, because it's such a marriage of music and text," says Lotfi Mansouri. The Berg opera was given a dramatic new production in 1990, designed by **Michael Levine** (above).

A giant, gilded lion was the central feature of designer **Gerard Howland**'s 1994 production of Rossini's *Otello*. Computer drawn models (below) were the first step in creating the massive beast, which dominated the stage. Tenor **Chris Merritt** (above) played the Moor in this unfamiliar version of the Shakespeare drama.

murkiness, he wanted glaring brilliance. Instead of painted flats, he wanted three-dimensional sets strong enough for the artists to stand on. As a result, the scene shop moved to a building south of Market Street big enough for the construction of several productions at a time. Carpentry and sculpture became crucial skills. Materials changed, with the traditional canvas and wood supplanted by plastic, Styrofoam, and steel.

Similarly, the costume shop moved to a building of its own and began to build all the costumes for San Francisco Opera productions, from Renaissance dresses and peasant costumes to armor and thigh-high boots. Sewing techniques may not have changed much in the last three hundred years, but the fabrics are different, due to innovations in manmade fibers and greater access to fabric suppliers all over the world.

"We rarely buy one hundred percent wool any more," costume shop director Jenny Green explains. In part, that's for reasons of economy, since blends of synthetic and natural fibers generally cost a bit less and require less ironing. More important to the performers, the new costumes, particularly the underpinnings, are lighter and more flexible. In response to directors' demands for more natural movement onstage, designers have had to become more aware of the needs of the performers inside. "Some old costumes were so heavy," recalls costume shop manager Walter Mahoney, "you wonder how the artists could possibly sing. You could hardly lift the costumes off the racks. [Joan] Sutherland's costumes were so structured and stiff that she had to have them completely remade when she developed back trouble."

One thing hasn't changed. Each costume, whether for a principal or a supernumerary, is constructed so that it will last twenty-five years and stand up to endless remodeling and resizing. In heavily subsidized European houses, the money is available to build new costumes for a given opera and keep them intact and together. San Francisco's costume shop is more like a frugal housewife, changing the trim on a blouse, adding braid to a skirt, and dyeing a group of soldiers' tunics to suit an upcoming production. After enough of this, the costume may end up in "rag stock," to be used whenever an opera requires peasants, paupers, or proletariat. Practically nothing is thrown away.

While scenery and costumes changed gradually and continued to depend on some traditional skills, the arts of lighting and sound have been transformed dramatically by new technology. Audiences in the 1932 War Memorial Opera House never saw anything like the seamless change from blue-green night to radiantly red day as Calaf awakes in the third act of *Turandot*, nor the smaller subtleties of light and shadow that highlight an individual artist at crucial moments of the plot.

In the early 1970s, the opera appointed its first fulltime lighting designer, a position now held by Thomas Munn, who recalls, "As directors became more important, there came to be a need for a specialist to work with them fulltime. They needed someone with an artistic bent. I came here around the time that the first major computer to control lighting was installed in 1976.

"The first thing that I did was to relight *Die Walküre*. Mr. Adler kept saying it was too bright and that you could see too much. But the critics wrote that it was the first time that they had ever been able to see Wagner as well as hear him in San Francisco."

The newly remodeled War Memorial Opera House is in the forefront of theatrical design, as it was in 1932. The Committee to Restore the Opera House, a group of local citizens who raised funds for improvements to the War Memorial, raised enough to enable the company to spend more than ten million dollars on new lighting systems. New hardware and software were developed by theatrical consultants Auerback + Associates to control the stage lights, many of which are so-called intelligent lights, able to change colors and focus at the push of a button. Lighting bridges, the structures that suspend the lights over the stage, have been motorized, eliminating much of the hand operations of the past. Electrical wires are safely installed in conduits, and illegal bundles of wires no longer run across the floor.

The audience, of course, never thinks of any of this. When the overture is finished and the curtain is rising, the magic of theatrical production will entrance them once more.

Designer **Leni Bauer-Ecsy** created the costumes for the 1963 production of Strauss's *Capriccio*, including a colorful, caped dress for the Italian Singer.

On June 7, 1979, Kurt Herbert Adler made a formal announcement at a meeting of the San Francisco Opera board of trustees that he was going to retire in 1981, after twenty-eight years as general director of the company. His handpicked successor was Terence A. McEwen, vice-president of London Records. In the clubby world of opera, where artists and administrators are constantly crossing paths at the various opera houses of the world, Adler and McEwen were old friends. Most important, McEwen was one of the few people whom Adler truly respected for his knowledge of voices and emerging talent around the operatic world. Staff members remember their endless telephone conversations and their huddled, whispering conferences whenever McEwen sailed into town.

For McEwen, the new job was the culmination of a dream that had begun when he was a young boy growing up in Canada. Later in life, he was quick to recall his first opera recording—Dusolina Giannini singing "Casta diva" from *Norma* and the love duet from *Madama Butterfly*. His mother, whom he liked to describe as a kind of "Risë Stevens mezzo," sang in church and encouraged his interest in music. He began listening to the radio, particularly to the Metropolitan Opera's Saturday afternoon broadcasts.

The office of **Terence McEwen**, third general director of the San Francisco Opera, was filled with photographs of his favorite singers. Among them was a picture of Brazilian soprano Bidú Sayão, whose touching rendition of "Adieu, notre petite table" from Massenet's *Manon* caused him to fall permanently in love with opera when he was a teenager growing up in Montreal.

In *Das Rheingold*, the first opera of McEwen's *Ring* cycle, **James Morris** (opposite) led the gods toward Valhalla.

One of the most memorable productions during the McEwen era was *Don Carlos* in 1986. For the first time in San Francisco Opera history, the Verdi opera was performed in the original French rather than the more familiar Italian. The role of Elisabeth was sung by Spanish soprano **Pilar Lorengar** (above, right), with **Stefania Toczyska** (above) as Eboli.

The Midsummer Marriage, a three-act opera by twentieth-century English composer Michael Tippett, was given its American premiere by the San Francisco Opera in 1983 (opposite). The ballet played a constant role in the love story; here dancers surround soprano **Mary Jane Johnson**, portraying Jenifer.

McEwen was known for the confidence he placed in young singers. One of these was soprano **Cheryl Parrish**, who emerged from the opera's training programs to have a smash success as the delectable Sophie in the 1985 production of *Der Rosenkavalier.*

McEwen, who was known in the music world as Terry, was born in Thunder Bay, Ontario, in 1929. When the McEwen family moved to Montreal in the 1930s, he met a friend who was equally wild about opera, Irving Guttman, now a leading opera director in Canada. Together they became convinced that they could run the Metropolitan Opera better than Edward Johnson, then the general director, could. They scribbled down perfect casts and perfect seasons in the back pages of their schoolbooks. When they were fourteen, they took the money they had saved from summer jobs and went to New York after Christmas to experience the Met for themselves. Their hotel was inexpensive, but the operas were fantastic: In a single week, the two starstruck boys saw Lauritz Melchior and Blanche Thebom in *Tannhäuser*; Jussi Bjoerling, Bidú Sayão, and Leonard Warren in *Rigoletto*; Licia Albanese and Jan Peerce in *La Traviata*; and Mario Del Monaco and Renata Tebaldi in *Andrea Chénier.*

The defining moment in McEwen's love affair with opera came in a Montreal performance of *Manon*, with Bidú Sayão in the title role. When the delicate soprano fell to her knees to sing, "Adieu, notre petite table," a touching farewell to love, the teenaged McEwen began to weep. For days after, he haunted her hotel lobby in hopes of seeing his new idol. From then on, opera was the most important thing in his life. As a student, he worked in a record store and studied voice with a cantor, making his first and last stage appearance in the small role of Lillas Pastia in *Carmen*, with Regina Resnik in the title role. Although he quickly realized that his light tenor voice would never lead to a real operatic career, he later said that the experience of studying contributed greatly to his understanding of the human voice.

In 1950 McEwen headed for Europe, with notions of studying music in Italy. He got as far as England, where he stepped off the ship in Liverpool and headed directly to the opera house at Covent Garden. McEwen never forgets a performance or a cast, and that night in London he saw a Scala production of *Otello* with Ramon Vinay and Renata Tebaldi.

When he learned that he would not be able to obtain a work permit in Italy, he stayed in London, taking a job as a warehouseman for Decca Records. Thanks to his encyclopedic knowledge of music, he rapidly entered the executive ranks and rose to positions that required him to live in both London and Paris.

He moved to New York in 1959, with the charge of developing the classical division of London Records, Decca's American subsidiary. In the next twenty years, McEwen made London the leading classical record label in the United States, raising its artistic levels to new heights. Although he was technically in marketing, he used his influence and prodigious knowledge to influence the choice of artists, developing a reputation for assembling fabulous casts, with excellent conductors, recorded for the best possible sound.

He was a genius at promotion, transforming singers into superstars recognized beyond the world of opera. He had a major influence on the careers of Joan Sutherland, Régine Crespin, Renata Tebaldi, Marilyn Horne, and Luciano Pavarotti. Although his first love was opera, he did not limit himself to singers: pianists Vladimir Ashkenazy and Alicia de Larrocha and conductor Georg Solti were among the artists in his impressive stable. He lavished attention on his favorites, specializing quite literally in the care and feeding of artists. His six-figure expense account, much of which went for entertaining, was a legend in the industry.

So, too, was his personal collection of recordings, which included some eight-thousand long-playing records. John Copley, opera director at Covent Garden, remembered the years when McEwen lived in London and invited friends to his apartment to listen to music. "We listened to people like Ponselle and Tebaldi and were absolutely mad about them all. I remember piles and piles of records in white sleeves; there was never enough time to hear them."

In the late 1970s Decca was sold to Polygram, a Dutch conglomerate, and McEwen began to think about getting out of the record business. When Adler mentioned the San Francisco job to him, he reacted first with disbelief that his friend would ever leave the job and then leapt at the opportunity, moving out to San Francisco in late 1980 and spending two fall seasons learning the complexities of putting an actual opera onstage and planning for his own seasons. It was no secret that it was a difficult transition, during which his old friend Adler essentially ignored him, but in January of 1982 McEwen was finally in full charge of the company.

By this time, he was far more than an impassioned opera groupie, far more than the brightest guy on the Texaco opera quiz on Saturdays. He had become one of the world's greatest authorities on the operatic voice. Once he had heard a voice, or a recording of one, he never forgot it, and he was as familiar with the great voices of the past as he was with his contemporaries. He not only remembered voices but heard their potential. He was able to hear a young singer in a small role like the Forest Bird in *Siegfried* and recognize there was something in that unpolished sound that could be developed.

Ebullient, articulate, and optimistic, McEwen gave numerous interviews on the impact he hoped to have on the San Francisco Opera. While paying homage to the achievements of Adler, he had some ideas of his own. Specifically, he wanted to present more French opera, a natural outgrowth of his childhood in French-speaking Montreal, and he wanted to introduce San Francisco audiences to Russian works. His tastes in operatic production, he said, were more conservative than his predecessor's. He denied rumors that he was going to throw out all of Ponnelle's controversial productions, but said that the company had a few too many in stock and that he would probably not hire Ponnelle as much as Adler had. After three decades of Adler's emphasis on opera as musical theater, McEwen wanted to emphasize voices, shaping the seasons around singers rather than repertory.

Above all, McEwen made clear, opera should be glamorous, otherworldly, and beautiful, both to see and to hear.

The most ambitious statement of his philosophy was an entirely new production of Wagner's four operas comprising *The Ring of the Nibelung*. This was to be neither a *Ring* cycle in the starkly minimalist style of Wagner's grandson, Wieland Wagner, nor a *Ring* updated into modern industrial society. Instead, said McEwen, "My *Ring* has to be a colorful, romantic, beautiful *Ring*. I want Wotan to have the biggest feathers on his hat you've ever seen. The music is full of color and the stage should be full of color as well. I'm sick of 'Star Wars' *Rings* and I think the whole world is, too." Director Nikolaus Lehnhoff and designer John Conklin came up with a production inspired by the paintings of German Romantic painter Caspar David Friedrich and the neoclassical architecture of Karl Friedrich Schinkel.

The first two operas of the cycle, *Das Rheingold* and *Die Walküre*, were presented during the summer season of 1983, the third, *Siegfried*, in the summer of 1984. With the addition of the final opera, *Götterdämmerung*, all four were presented in sequence in June 1985, with former San Francisco Symphony conductor Edo de Waart in the pit. The presentation of any *Ring* cycle is always newsworthy, and this one was particularly so, because of the importance of the company and because it was essentially McEwen's first and biggest chance to show what he could do. Appropriately, the music critics of North America chose the month of June in San Francisco for their annual meeting, so press coverage was lavish.

Although reaction to any given *Ring* is never unanimous, the critics were generally warm in their praise for the richly detailed sets. They were even more enthusiastic about the musical aspects of the production. As soon as he had arrived in San Francisco, McEwen had gone to work to hire the world's finest Wagnerians for his *Ring*.

McEwen's most notable casting choice, though, was not known as a singer of Wagner. This was American bass-baritone James Morris, whose associates tried to persuade him that singing Wagner

McEwen, a self-described "canary fancier" who was especially loyal to a number of experienced female singers, persuaded one of his favorites, Italian soprano **Mirella Freni**, to sing the title roles in Puccini's *Manon Lescaut* (above) and Cilea's *Adriana Lecouvreur* for the first time in her career.

McEwen attracted the attention of Wagner lovers around the world when he presented the *Ring* cycle in its entirety in the summer of 1985. Directed by Nikolaus Lehnhoff, with sets and costumes by John Conklin, McEwen's *Ring* was a spectacle of classical and romantic motifs. In the first presentation of *Die Walküre*, in the summer season of 1983, the roles of Sieglinde and Siegmund were taken by **Jeannine Altmeyer** and **Peter Hofmann** (above). In the third opera of the cycle, *Siegfried*, the title role was sung by **René Kollo**, who confronted a brightly hued dragon (left) and awakened Brünnhilde (opposite, left), sung by **Eva Marton**. **William Lewis** (opposite, right) was Loge, observed by the giants.

would be bad for his voice. McEwen thought otherwise, convincing Morris that Wagner's music, though long and challenging, was written for the voice. Thanks to his persuasive abilities, Morris's interpretation of Wotan was a triumph in San Francisco and led him to sing the role in opera houses around the world.

The discovery and development of young voices were perhaps McEwen's greatest achievements in his years at the San Francisco Opera. Faced with a deficit and concerned about the quality of the program, McEwen quickly took the step in 1982 of canceling Spring Opera Theater, the company's most conspicuous showcase for young talent.

Simultaneously, however, he began to reorganize the company's other programs for young singers under a single umbrella organization to be named the San Francisco Opera Center. Previously, the four programs—Merola Opera Program, Brown Bag Opera, Western Opera Theater, and Affiliate Artists program for more advanced singers—each had its own administration and its own audition. McEwen realigned them so that a new talent moved from the Merola program, a ten-week summer training program, through Brown Bag Opera and Western Opera Theater, for experience onstage, on to the Adler Fellowship Program, which offered the opportunity to perform in the fall season.

McEwen gave the young people more than a coherent pathway for training. He loved introducing artists to the great singers of the past, and he often gave a young artist tapes from his vast record collection. He made a number of changes designed to bring the neophytes into contact with experienced singers; he opened rehearsals to them, invited them to opening-night cast parties, and gave them tickets to performances. He encouraged them to make appointments to talk to him about everything from diets to career decisions, and he treated them as an affectionate, exigent father might have.

Most important, he believed in them. As Christine Bullin, administrator of the Opera Center, said, "He really encouraged them in a very knowledgeable way. If they fell down, they got to get up again." He tried to use them as much as possible, as covers and in comprimario roles, and he believed that all the participants in the whole program should have a chance to come back in the fall season at least once.

When he had confidence in a voice, no matter how young, he didn't worry that the audience was paying as much as one hundred dollars a ticket to hear someone who was not a big name. When Ruth Ann Swenson was cast as Despina in *Così fan tutte* and Cheryl Parrish was Sophie in *Der Rosenkavalier*, they enchanted the audiences and justified his confidence.

Another of McEwen's success stories was Dolora Zajick, a young Nevadan with a huge, Verdian mezzo-soprano voice. McEwen recalled his first experiences with her. "Back then, Dolora walked onstage like a truck driver and just stood there and sang. But in my career I haven't run into a voice like that since Stignani. Betsy [Crittenden, a New York agent] and I agreed that Dolora needed to go undercover for a few years at the Center, above all to work on her acting. Sure, Dolora could have even made an Azucena debut at the Met in 1982. But she would have sung one performance, fallen flat on her face, and then retired or spent the rest of her career recovering from it."

Instead Zajick spent three years, from 1983 to 1986, at the Opera Center. Only then did McEwen feel that she was ready for the demanding role of the ancient Gypsy crone Azucena, one of opera's most dramatic personages. She sang her first Azucena in a Nevada State Opera production of *Il Trovatore* that had been created for her. She then sang the role with an international cast in San Francisco's summer season of 1986. McEwen recalled with pride, "We put Dolora next to established international stars so that everyone could see that she's as good as they are, and she walked off with the show." As he had planned, her San Francisco debut made her a star, and opera houses around the world got in line to hire her.

After his fledglings were launched, he continued to keep in touch, advising them on roles that would enhance rather than destroy their emerging voices. In this he was acting as artists' managers had in the past, when they were knowledgeable enough to develop an artist's potential through a carefully chosen series of roles. This kind of intelligent nurturing has faded in the modern opera world, today singers are apt to rush into demanding parts, learning them in months rather than the years that older singers used to spend to understand a character and to complete that mysterious process known as getting the role into the voice.

In a rushed, jet-age world, McEwen wanted to act within the continuum of operatic history. He wanted to retain some of the traditions of the past, particularly as far as repertoire and productions were concerned. At the same time, he was imaginative and energetic in his development of the voices of the future. Although he was criticized in San Francisco for some of his flashy productions, he was universally lauded for his incubation of young artists.

On February 8, 1988, McEwen announced his retirement, citing his declining health and explaining his need to have a more routine schedule in order to manage his diabetes. The next day, his predecessor, Kurt Herbert Adler, died of a stroke. The stage was set for the company's fourth general director, who turned out to be one of San Francisco Opera's oldest friends.

During 1982, McEwen's first year as general director, the summer season included a production of Stravinsky's *The Rake's Progress*. During a rehearsal for the opera, **McEwen** chatted with **Jonathan Green**, costumed for the role of Sellem.

When Terence McEwen decided to present Offenbach's light-hearted confection, *La Grande Duchesse de Gérolstein*, as part of the 1983 season, there was no doubt as to the perfect soprano for the title role. **Régine Crespin** made an impressive San Francisco debut in 1960 singing both Dido and Cassandre in Berlioz's *Les Troyens*, repeating this tour de force in 1966, and singing such other heavyweight roles as Sieglinde and Tosca in later years. Offenbach, however, requires a lightness of touch and an understanding of French style, and Crespin proved herself the mistress of both, bringing vocal agility and piquant humor to the title role.

In McEwen's presentation of the final opera, *Götterdämmerung* (following pages), the epic came to an end in a setting washed with the blue light of twilight. **René Kollo** was the dying Siegfried.

the future

chapter eight VOICES OF THE FUTURE

Around the opera house, they are known fondly as the Merolini. They're the winners of the annual Merola Opera Program auditions, participating in the first phase of San Francisco's highly regarded training program for young singers and musicians.

In 1996 there were twenty-six of them, ranging in age from twenty to thirty-four, from as close as Fresno and San Diego and as far as St. Petersburg, Seoul, and Athens. Eleven were from the United States, fifteen from around the world. They had been selected from more than six hundred applicants who had auditioned for the program in several cities in the United States and in the Far East. For their auditions, they had each sung six arias chosen to measure their ability to sing in different languages and musical styles. Applicants for the positions of apprentice coaches, the pianists who play for rehearsals and do individual coachings with the singers, had equally taxing auditions, starting by playing and singing all the parts in the first act of *La Bohème*.

They vied for places in San Francisco's Merola program because it is one of the few operatic training programs that, at least for some of them, lead to roles on the main stage. The summer session is the first step in a series of programs operated by the San Francisco Opera Center.

Three members of San Francisco's Merola Opera Program, bass **Kevin Langan**, soprano **Carol Vaness**, and tenor **Barry McCauley**, from left to right, sang to a large audience in San Francisco's Sigmund Stern Grove in 1981.

Adler Fellows, the most advanced members of San Francisco Opera's training programs for young singers, regularly go to local schools to perform. In 1995, **Chester Patton** (above) explained opera to a group of elementary school children and encouraged them to write their own musical drama. At another school performance, Adler Fellows **Elizabeth Bishop**, **David Okerlund**, **Claudia Waite**, and **Alfredo Portilla** (opposite from left to right) performed one of the student-designed operas, with chorus director **Ian Robertson** conducting an ensemble of musicians.

San Francisco's training programs emphasize acting and ensemble singing and offer varied opportunities to perform. In ten weeks, the Merola students present two operas, one in English at Stern Grove and one in the original language at Villa Montalvo's outdoor theater in Saratoga, and perform in a final concert before a large audience. In the summer of 1996, the first opera was Donizetti's *L'Elisir d'Amore*, and the second, Rossini's *Il Barbiere di Siviglia*.

Following their introductory meeting on the second Monday in June, they immediately began musical coaching, fittings for costumes, and staging rehearsals. They participated in master classes, including a week of sessions with retired French soprano Régine Crespin. When they weren't involved with the productions, they were taking classes in movement, posture, nutrition, acting, language, diction, and sword fighting. This last is no joke, because onstage swords are deadly weapons. One year, during a Merola performance of *Don Giovanni*, an inexperienced Commendatore lunged forward with his sword and cut the Don's forehead. Suddenly real blood and fake blood (hidden in a little bag) gushed everywhere. A member of the orchestra fainted, someone in the audience collapsed, the performance came to a halt, and the shaken bass stood paralyzed, wringing his hands and repeating, "I'm sorry, I'm sorry."

When the cast of *L'Elisir* began rehearsing on the stage of Stern Grove a week before the performance, their gestures were small and imprecise, their ability to project a character tentative, and their

voices strained by nerves. Four weeks later, when the cast of *Il Barbiere di Siviglia* took the stage at Villa Montalvo, the impact of classes and rehearsals was obvious. Gestures had the right balance between precision and exaggeration, characterizations were more fully formed, and there was a sense of teamwork. The singers were more confident vocally, and by opening night, they had learned the difficult skill of making people laugh.

The final event in the ten-week program is the Grand Finale concert, a program of arias and ensembles with a full orchestra. It is an emotional experience for the young singers, blending a sense of celebration, a nostalgia for their ten-week experience together, and the cool edge of competition. Agents are listening in the audience, and more than a half-dozen major cash prizes are awarded at the end.

For more than half the students, the next step was to take *Il Barbiere di Siviglia* on the road for two months in the fall, under the aegis of Western Opera Theater (WOT). WOT was founded in 1966 by Kurt Herbert Adler, who wanted to take opera to places where it had never been seen and to provide performance experience for young artists. His idea appealed to the National Endowment for the Humanities, which awarded WOT the first NEH grant to a touring troupe. In the thirty years since, WOT has brought opera to small towns and college campuses all over the United States. On an early trip to Alaska, the troupe traveled by bush plane and dogsled to small towns near the Arctic Circle, performing for audiences that also traveled long distances and sometimes outnumbered the population of the villages.

In 1987 Western Opera Theater became the first professional opera company to perform Western-style opera in China, when the troupe took *La Bohème* there. The following year the company returned to present *Tosca* for the first time in China, sharing the stage with Chinese artists singing in Chinese. The performances continued a relationship with China that had begun several years before when Adler went to Shanghai to give master classes. In 1991 WOT went to Japan for the first time, just one of a number of trips designed to discover and encourage Asian singers.

For many years, Western Opera Theater toured for six months a year, performing several operas and presenting educational programs on the side. The program has since been compressed into an intense, exhausting nine-week tour, during which three casts perform one opera six times a week. The artists still travel from coast to coast by bus, accompanied by a truckload of costumes and scenery. They are expected to sing a lead role one night and then participate in the chorus the next. If they get to a theater that does not have dressing rooms, they dress and put on their makeup in the truck. If the scenery does not fit the stage, they improvise a new staging. If they are exhausted from the day-after-day performances, they go right on stage anyway.

One sweltering evening in a badly ventilated old vaudeville house in Sandpoint, Idaho, the theater staff opened the front doors during a performance of *La Traviata*. A poodle poked its nose in, sauntered down the center aisle, sniffed curiously at the conductor, and leapt onstage to join the party scene in the first act. A young woman singing the chorus leaned down, scooped up the dog, and continued to sing without missing a note or allowing the animal to disturb the proceedings.

The ability to come up with this kind of improvisation lasts a lifetime. After months on the road, Western Opera Theater veterans can be counted on to cope with emergencies onstage, whether picking up a stray handkerchief or putting on a colleague's fallen hat with an unscripted kiss so graceful that it seems to have been rehearsed for weeks. The length of the WOT marathon also gives singers a chance to sing arias in a different way or to change the nuances of characterization. The weeks on the road offer an opportunity for personal growth as well, a time to learn to work with colleagues and a time to see more of the world. Soprano Patricia Racette, who went on the WOT tour in 1988, said, "For me, that's where a hobby became a profession."

During the fall, four or five of the Merola students are chosen to continue at the San Francisco Opera as Adler Fellows. This is the most advanced stage of the company's artist-development programs and is offered to singers who are both vocally and emotionally ready for the exposure of a career in an international opera house.

For two years, each Adler Fellow sings everywhere from kindergarten classrooms to the main stage of the War Memorial. As part of Brown Bag Opera, the singers give hour-long concerts at downtown locations at lunchtime. As participants in the company's extensive educational programs, they frequently perform in the city's schools. They go on ocean cruises, giving recitals every day and learning what it's like to be in the limelight, offstage and on, for days at a time. They sing at events for donors, and they present benefit concerts as far away as Micronesia. In the summer they are stars in the Showcase, an annual presentation of an unfamiliar opera; in 1996 the opera was Dominick Argento's *The Aspern Papers*, presented at the Center for the Arts at Yerba Buena Gardens. They are featured in the annual Opera in the Park concert in Golden Gate Park in September, and a few of them perform more introspective works in the Schwabacher Debut Recitals. In 1996 the Adler Fellows had some additional engagements. Nineteen of the twenty-four singers in the company's twenty-eight-day series of *La Bohème* at the Orpheum Theater were past or present Adler Fellows. In addition, the 1996 class of Adler Fellows sang a dozen performances of *Hansel and Gretel* during the Christmas season.

Of all their audiences, the toughest are the schools, where they introduce an unfamiliar art form to students from kindergarten through high school, acting both as role players and as role models. It takes élan to pull off the program called Interactive Opera! for an audience of elementary students sitting on

One of the highlights of the Merola Opera Program is the sword-fighting class. Until his retirement, stage director **Matthew Farruggio** was in charge of teaching young artists the fine art of onstage clashes.

One of the Merola Opera Program's most successful graduates is **Ruth Ann Swenson**, who traveled with Western Opera Theater and was an Adler Fellow in 1983 and 1984. After establishing herself in lighter roles, such as Susanna in *Le Nozze de Figaro* and Adina in *L'Elisir d'Amore*, Swenson thrilled local fans with her dramatic power in the title role of *Lucia di Lammermoor* in 1994 (left). She returned as another madwoman, Ophélie, in Ambroise Thomas's *Hamlet* in the fall of 1996.

Carol Vaness, who began her San Francisco career in the Merola Opera Program and continued in Spring Opera, is now a favorite on the main stage. In 1993, she took the role of Elena in Verdi's *I Vespri Siciliani*.

Countless Bay Area residents remember their first operatic experience at the War Memorial, where the only thing more riveting than the performance was wondering whether the giant chandelier would fall on them. This vivid introduction to grand opera came about thanks to the San Francisco Opera Guild, a volunteer organization that presented its first student matinee *(Madama Butterfly)* in 1939 and has been introducing Bay Area youth to opera ever since.

Each year, more than six thousand students come to the opera house to see a full performance of a popular opera. In addition, some ten thousand more young people see operas in condensed one-hour versions performed in their own schools, thanks to the Opera Guild's Opera à la Carte program. Another of the Guild's educational programs is Opera Inside Out, a presentation designed to introduce people to the technical aspects of presenting opera.

The Guild's outreach activities also include tours of the opera house and seminars and publications to familiarize adult audiences with each season's repertoire. Hundreds of volunteers help out in various departments of the company. Financing for these activities comes from several benefits, particularly the Opera Ball, an opening night festivity that follows the performance.

the floor of an all-purpose room. Interactive Opera! lets the youngsters create their own opera. The artists begin by introducing themselves and their vocal types and explaining the kinds of characters associated with different voices. They offer examples of the kind of music associated with different plots and give the children a choice of typical operatic situations, such as falling in love, engaging in treachery, and saying extended farewells. Finally, they ask the students whether they want their opera to be a comedy or a tragedy by choosing a happy or sad ending.

They create the children's opera from a preselected menu of arias, duets, and ensembles that represent archetypal operatic situations. The plot's twists and turns are explained in recitatives that the singers make up on the spot. The fact that the words of the arias don't really have anything to do with the plot doesn't matter, since the children have been told to listen to the music and watch the action to know what's happening.

It is exhausting work, and the reviews are frank and instantaneous. A fifth-grader does not hesitate to point out that the mezzo-soprano wasn't as evil as she had promised to be or that the tenor sang too loud. Frequently the whole group protests loudly if a kiss is part of the impromptu action. The frivolity has a serious purpose. The program, which is free to the schools, is a response to the lack of music education in the public schools.

Another of the company's outreach programs is Opera Inside Out, an hour-long introduction to opera that starts with the setting of the stage and ends with a performance of one act, complete with orchestra, chorus, and costumes. In 1996 the opera was the ever-popular *La Bohème*, presented in June at the Orpheum Theater. Master of ceremonies Clifford Cranna, the opera's musical administrator, introduced various members of the backstage crew. The stage manager showed off the movements of the set, the lighting technician illustrated the workings of the spots that highlight the artists, and the propmen had a snowball fight with spheres of Styrofoam. The stagehands revealed how to make snow fall gently onstage. One member of the orchestra reacted with surprise, saying, "Thirty years with this orchestra, and I never knew how they made it snow." Once the stage was set, artists, chorus, and supernumeraries filled the stage to give a lively performance of the Café Momus scene.

The Adler Fellows learn up to seven roles for the fall season. They have been chosen with specific reference to the company's casting needs, to fill small and medium-sized roles, and to cover for larger ones. As understudies, they learn not only the words and the music but the staging as well, and they attend rehearsals and observe the work of experienced artists.

Although covering major roles is regarded mainly as a learning experience, it has happened that Adler Fellows have been rushed onstage at the last minute. In 1994 baritone Eduardo del Campo was just sitting down to dinner in a restaurant with his sponsors when a telephone call came from the opera's rehearsal department. The curtain was about to rise on *Il Trovatore*, and there was no Count di Luna. The young man rushed to the opera house, threw on his *Lucia di Lammermoor* costume, and sang a triumphant performance. In 1995, a second-year Adler Fellow, Zheng Cao, replaced a former Adler Fellow, Susan Quittmeyer, as Siebel in *Faust*. The change was so last-minute that Samuel Ramey, in the role of Mephistophélès, gaped in surprise when he saw an unfamiliar face onstage.

The company has shown increasing confidence in its young artists, casting them in major roles. Terence McEwen, who was responsible for the reorganization of the various programs, did not hesitate to cast a very young Ruth Ann Swenson as Despina in *Così fan tutte* in 1983 nor to give the role of Sophie in *Der Rosenkavalier* to an equally young Cheryl Parrish in 1985. After three years as an Adler Fellow, mezzo Dolora Zajick had a major success when she sang Azucena in *Il Trovatore* in 1986. The list of singers who began their careers in San Francisco Opera's training programs and went on to have major international careers is impressive. To name only a few, Jess Thomas, one of the earliest participants in the Merola Opera Program, became one of the world's leading Wagnerian tenors. Soprano Carol Vaness and tenor Barry McCauley were members of the 1981 Merola class. Thomas Hampson

Patricia Racette, who toured the country with Western Opera Theater, made her debut on the main stage as Freia in *Das Rheingold* (above) in 1990, while she was an Adler Fellow. Her career has since become worldwide, with 1996 appearances in Santa Fe, New York, and Paris, as well as in San Francisco, where she sang the role of Mimì in the June *La Bohème* and returned in the fall to sing Antonia in *Les Contes d'Hoffmann*.

Deborah Voigt, a graduate of the San Francisco Opera's highly regarded training program for young singers, was acclaimed in 1994 for her performance as Elisabeth in *Tannhäuser*.

General director Terence McEwen guided the early career of **Dolora Zajick**, who made her main stage debut in San Francisco as Azucena in *Il Trovatore*. In 1994 she took on the title role in *Hérodiade* (opposite).

spent a year training in San Francisco before going on to stardom in both opera and recitals. Deborah Voigt, whose colleagues treasure the memory of her singing the Supremes' "Stop in the Name of Love" with Nancy Gustafson and Cathy Cowdrick at a benefit, is now a world-renowned opera heroine, onstage and in recordings.

The Opera Center program is often praised as the best training program in the world, and it has been copied by other opera companies. Christine Bullin, former head of the Opera Center, was invited by the Paris Opera to set up a similar program there. She points out that in the 1996–97 Paris season, eleven former Adler Fellows were scheduled to sing. She says, "American singers are now the workhorses of the opera world. They're on time, they do what they're told, they have a work ethic, and they don't think that they already know everything. In San Francisco, we were hard on them, and we got them disciplined."

Neil **Rosenshein**, Herb **Foster**, and Maria **Ewing** were members of the cast of Jacques Offenbach's satirical *La Périchole,* presented in a Spring Opera production in 1976.

spring opera

One of Spring Opera's most unusual productions was a staged version of Bach's *The Passion According to St. Matthew,* presented in 1973 and 1976.

During the first four decades of its history, the San Francisco Opera had competition from touring troupes like the San Carlo Opera Company and a series of local companies that changed names and locations every few years. The Pacific Coast Opera Company became the Pacific Opera Company and then the New Pacific Opera Company, presenting performances in theaters ranging from the War Memorial Opera House to Fugazi Hall in North Beach.

The goal was to present popular operas at popular prices, as low as a dollar a ticket in 1948. Patrons got no more than they paid for. In 1929 music critic Redfern Mason mentioned that many of the artists appeared for free. The chorus, he wrote, consisted of "four waiters, a Southern Pacific mechanic, three fishermen, a salesman, teamster, painter, carpenter, druggist, ironworker, sheet metal worker, bookkeeper, electrician and insurance collector." Even as late as 1954, the demanding title role in Donizetti's

Lucia di Lammermoor was sung by a sixteen-year-old Oakland girl who had never performed it before.

The last of these competing companies to appear in San Francisco was the Cosmopolitan Opera Company, the success of which depended on presenting a spring season of tried-and-true repertoire, briefly rehearsed but with the drawing card of a few well-paid, big-name stars. The Cosmopolitan had the financial support of a local man, Campbell McGregor, who was willing to erase the inevitable deficit by writing a large personal check. This situation continued until 1960, when he delivered the death blow to the Cosmopolitan by announcing that he would no longer subsidize it.

One of the Cosmopolitan's most loyal supporters, Mrs. Leon Cuenin, would not let the idea of a spring season die. She persuaded Kurt Herbert Adler to sponsor a spring season, using the opera's facilities, including sets and costumes,

personnel, and location. Adler agreed, and Spring Opera became a reality in May 1961.

Like the Cosmopolitan, Spring Opera was based on low ticket prices—four dollars was the magic figure—that would attract new young audiences. Unlike the Cosmopolitan, the new organization would not use big-name, big-fee stars but would rely on an ensemble of young singers. The repertoire would differ from the fall season's by emphasizing lesser-known works, including new operas by American composers. Many operas would be performed in English translations.

During the next twenty years, Spring Opera patrons had the chance to see dozens of unusual operas, including Ravel's *The Spanish Hour,* Bartok's *Bluebeard's Castle,* Menotti's *The Consul,* Britten's *The Turn of the Screw* and *Death in Venice,* Donizetti's *Viva la Mamma,* and Carlisle Floyd's *Susannah* and *Of Mice and Men.*

Controversial concepts, imaginatively and inex-

Soprano **Leona Mitchell** sang the role of Suzel and tenor **Vinson Cole** was Fritz in Spring Opera's 1976 production of Mascagni's *L'Amico Fritz*, an opera first presented in San Francisco in 1909 by a touring opera company, with San Francisco Opera founder Gaetano Merola as the conductor.

Spring Opera's repertoire varied from intensely serious to riotously comic. Definitely comic was Donizetti's *Viva La Mamma*, presented in 1975 and 1977, starring countertenor **John Ferrante** as an unforgettable Mother (above).

pensively produced, became easier after Spring Opera moved from the opera house to the Curran Theater in 1971. Two years before Jean-Pierre Ponnelle's controversial 1973 production of *Rigoletto*, theater director Gilbert Moses gave the same work a racy Spring Opera production that featured an orgiastic opening scene, the Duke of Mantua in hippie dress, and Gilda's garden surrounded by a Cyclone fence.

Spring Opera introduced many young singers who went on to real stardom. In the first season, the title role in *Carmen* was sung by a young mezzo named Marilyn Horne, and the Don José was James King, who became a San Francisco Opera regular and a world-renowned Wagnerian tenor. Maria Ewing appeared several times in the early 1970s, starting in 1973 in the small role of Mercédès in *Carmen* and moving on by 1976 to the title role in Offenbach's *La Périchole*. Frederica von Stade made her first San Francisco appearance in 1971 in the spring production of

Mozart's seldom-seen *Titus*. Leona Mitchell is remembered for her Micaëla in a 1973 *Carmen* and as Suzel in Mascagni's *L'Amico Fritz* in 1976, also featuring Vinson Cole as Fritz.

Many other singers made their mark in Spring Opera before going on to international houses. Allan Monk, Alan Titus, Ariel Bybee, Carmen Balstrode, Neil Rosenshein, Frederick Burchinal, Simon Estes, and Carol Vaness were among the reasons that Spring Opera attracted a fiercely loyal group of devotees.

Unfortunately, there were never quite enough patrons to ensure the necessary attendance and financial support, particularly in the face of rising costs. From its first decade, Spring Opera had trouble meeting all its goals. By 1969 the price of a ticket had risen from $4 to $5.50, a change that sounds insignificant today but intimidated some of the intended audience. In order to attract larger audiences, the company had to hire better-known singers, a step that raised costs, diluted

the goal of encouraging younger artists, and invited unfortunate comparisons with the fall season.

Kurt Herbert Adler never had the heart to discontinue Spring Opera. That became the task of his successor, Terry McEwen, who announced at his first press conference as general director that there would be no Spring Opera season in 1982. He left the door open to the possibility that the spring season might be revived later, but it never happened. In addition to struggling with the San Francisco Opera's first significant deficits, McEwen was trying to turn the summer season into a moneymaker. Some people never forgave him for closing down Spring Opera. Even those who accepted the financial realities still mourn the loss of one of the liveliest chapters in San Francisco Opera history.

chapter nine LOTFI MANSOURI

One instant he's the loutish sergeant Morales; the next he's the naive country girl Micaëla, simultane- ously feigning girlish fear and giving instructions out of the side of his mouth to the chorus. It's the first staging rehearsal of the first act of *Carmen*, the fifty-eighth production that Lotfi Mansouri has directed at the San Francisco Opera.

On this particular August evening, the opera is familiar to everyone but the location is new. This is the first rehearsal to take place in the Civic Auditorium, temporary home for the company for the 1996 fall season, due to the remodeling of the War Memorial Opera House. Mansouri is introducing the chorus and supernumeraries to the challenges of an entirely new kind of production.

When it became apparent that the opera would have to move, Mansouri decided to take a bold approach to the relocation. Instead of putting on a cautious, low-budget season of semistaged and cos- tumed concert performances, he decided to do an entire season of productions specifically designed for the 4,177-seat Civic Auditorium, setting for seven of the season's operas, and the 2,500-seat Orpheum Theater, location for three others.

The solution to the barnlike space of the Civic Auditorium was a semicircular stage, with the audi- ence seated in a larger semicircle around it. The orchestra pit was located above and in back of the stage, an arrangement that brought the audience closer to the singers.

Lotfi Mansouri came to California from his native Iran to study medicine at the University of California at Los Angeles, but it was not long before he dropped his science classes to devote himself to opera—as a singer (very briefly), a director, and a general director.

Berg's *Wozzeck* was given a dramatic new production designed by **Michael Levine** in 1990. **Stuart Kale** as the Captain and **Siegfried Vogel** as the Doctor met on a long staircase that cut across the stage.

Mansouri's first new production at the San Francisco Opera was designer **Robert Darling**'s charming interpretation of Donizetti's *L'Elisir d'Amore*. The production, complete with potion-peddler Dulcamara's wagon drawn by an animated, stuffed horse, is still in use, as in this 1984 revival.

On the first night of *Carmen* rehearsals, Mansouri, who had directed in a similar theater in Stratford, Ontario, was explaining to the chorus the subtleties of performing in a semisurround theater. "It's a big theater, so I'm going to keep you together in vocal groups, so that you will have the security of hearing each other, but you must remember to project to the whole theater," he pointed out. "Your acting style should be as if you were acting for a camera, without any exaggerated operatic grand gestures."

Pointing out the video screens around the curved edge of the stage, which would show the conductor during the performance, he said, "You must learn to see where the monitors are, because they are your orchestra." In a final tip, he warned that the dressing rooms are farther from the stage than they are in the War Memorial and that the chorus would have to adjust their timing to be able to arrive on stage on time.

Mansouri, general director of the San Francisco Opera, has less time for directing these days, but he put himself in charge of *Carmen* and scheduled chorus rehearsals in August in order to be the first to work in the Civic Auditorium. He commented during a break in the rehearsal, "I did this on purpose so that when the visiting directors come to me and complain, I can say, 'Well, I managed.'"

Mansouri's hands-on familiarity with every aspect of the company was one reason that the San Francisco Opera's board of directors chose him as the company's fourth general director in the spring of 1988. Mansouri, then head of the Canadian Opera Company in Toronto, was an old friend who already knew everyone from choristers and propmen to prima donnas and stage directors.

His involvement with the San Francisco Opera had begun more than thirty years earlier. Mansouri, born in Iran to an aristocratic and cultured family, fell in love with American movies and music when he was very young. His father insisted that he study medicine but allowed him to go to the University of California in Los Angeles to do so. Although he dutifully signed up for biology and physics, music was also part of his new life in America.

He enrolled in a course in choral singing and discovered that he was a tenor who could hit high C. He began to perform in musical comedies, and one of his singing partners, Carol Burnett, became a lifelong friend. He began spending more time with UCLA's Opera Workshop, singing in operas from *Così fan tutte* to *Jenůfa*. Gradually he realized that he lacked the temperament for a singing career and was more interested in theater in general.

The first entire opera he ever saw was *Madama Butterfly*, with Eleanor Steber in the title role. That night at the Hollywood Bowl was the end of any lingering thoughts about a medical career. He began spending his money on records, and he volunteered to be a supernumerary every time the San Francisco Opera came to Los Angeles for its season at the Shrine Auditorium. If there were no supering roles, he ushered, to make sure that he saw as many productions as possible.

When his father discovered that young Lotfi had given up his premed studies for the theater, a calling that ranked just above prostitution in the esteem of aristocratic Iranians, he tried to force his son back to Iran by sending him a one-way ticket and stopping his allowance. Lotfi chose to stay with America and with music, supporting himself for the next few years by packing groceries, selling wallpaper, moving furniture, teaching in a junior high school, and starring as Enrico Caruso in a forgettable movie called *The Day I Met Caruso*.

"At that time Los Angeles City College had an opera workshop that was run by refugees from Nazi Germany," he recalls. "They offered me my first full production. It was *Così fan tutte*, and I got a salary of $150. It was the first time I had ever been paid to direct an opera." His salary was only $45 for one of his next directing jobs, a version of Puccini's *Il Tabarro*, with the swimming pool of the Biltmore Hotel representing the Seine. In the audience that night was Kurt Herbert Adler, a man who would change his life.

"Afterward, I wrote Mr. Adler a fuzzy, humble letter, asking if I could attend rehearsals in San Francisco as an observer. I never got an answer from him," says Mansouri. Turning down an offer to become a house director at the Metropolitan Opera, he went to work as resident stage director at the Zurich Opera, then headed by Dr. Herbert Graf, whom he had known at the Music Academy of the West in Santa Barbara. The next few years were a time to attend operas all over Europe, to work in Italy as well as Zurich, and to build his own reputation. Word of his talent filtered back to Iran, and the government of the Shah began to pressure him to return. After a first trip in which his American passport was taken away at the airport, he turned down many offers to become head of the Tehran Opera and consented only to come occasionally to direct. Each time, he feared that he would not be allowed to leave.

In 1962 Adler came to Zurich to observe Mansouri's dress rehearsal of Meyerbeer's cumbersome *Le Prophète*. Afterward, he discussed directing jobs for three operas in San Francisco that fall. "Dr. Graf refused to release me," Mansouri remembers ruefully. "I was so haughty and arrogant that I threatened to quit if he would not allow me to go to San Francisco. He finally said yes, and then I got a one-line telegram from Mr. Adler, saying 'Your services are no longer required.' I was devastated. I was so ashamed. Fortunately, Dr. Graf, who was a great man, forgave me and never mentioned it again."

The following year San Francisco's resident stage director, Paul Hager, came to Zurich and made Adler's offer: six operas for 1963. Since then Mansouri has conducted sixty productions for the San Francisco Opera, as well as countless others for opera houses all over the world.

One of his favorite productions came in the first season in San Francisco, when he directed Joan Sutherland in *La Sonnambula*. The two not only worked well together but became fast friends. It was the first of many productions in which Mansouri developed his reputation for working well with superstars, most of whom are far more temperamental and difficult than Sutherland.

He also has fond memories of the 1967 production of Donizetti's comic *L'Elisir d'Amore*, blessed with a bubbly Reri Grist as Adina, Alfredo Kraus as Nemorino, Ingvar Wixell as Belcore, and Sesto

Mansouri's relationship with the San Francisco Opera began during the Adler years. In 1979 **Adler** visited the set of *La Gioconda*, which Mansouri was directing.

Bruscantini as Dulcamara, plus a lovable plush horse. "It was my first new production in San Francisco. We had these wonderful new sets by Robert Darling. I think they cost something like $13,500, and we're still using them. We had a gorgeous cast and everything came together. We had a standing ovation at the end."

In 1975 Mansouri was named general director of the Canadian Opera Company in Toronto. At the time the company had fewer than ten thousand regular subscribers and an annual fund-raising potential thought to be only $300,000. Mansouri, accustomed to European theaters with generous government subsidies, appraised the situation and promptly started studying fund-raising and marketing.

Within six years, the subscriber list was up to nineteen thousand, and fund-raising goals were extended to $4 million. He established an independent orchestra for the opera and the company's first training program for young singers. He began to expand the repertoire beyond the usual standards, adding *Lulu* and *Jenůfa* and *Les Contes d'Hoffmann*. Most important, in his view, he started to develop new audiences in a city where the opera had always ranked far below the symphony and the ballet in

One of Mansouri's first decisions was to introduce San Francisco Opera audiences to Rossini's epic *Guillaume Tell*, which was presented for the first time at the War Memorial Opera House in 1992. Soprano **Carol Vaness**, a graduate of the opera's Merola program for young singers, sang the role of Mathilde. Soprano **Janet Williams**, kneeling at left, played the role of William Tell's son Jemmy.

stature. To introduce younger audiences to opera, he began a number of school programs. In the summer he attracted audiences of all ages to the one-hour operatic programs staged in a tent set up in Toronto's Harbourfront, an area of parks and development on Lake Ontario.

Also, in Toronto, Mansouri came up with an idea that has influenced opera around the world. Supertitles (originally known as surtitles), the projected translations that appear on a screen above the stage as the singers perform in the original language, made their debut in 1983 at a Canadian Opera Company performance of *Elektra*. The idea came to Mansouri one night when he and his wife were watching a videotape of the controversial *Ring* operas directed by Patrice Chéreau at Bayreuth. He recalls, "Midge didn't really like Wagner, but with the subtitles, she really began to get involved and finally said, 'This is really interesting.' I suddenly thought, 'If they can do it on television, why not in the theater?'"

For artists, the titles mean that they no longer have to overact in order to semaphore where they are in the plot. Their acting style can be far more realistic and detailed. In addition, the artists can feel the response of the audience, which not only knows what is going on but can appreciate the subtlety and the humor of the libretto. "In the days before titles, the audience was always an outsider, watching

through a pane," Mansouri says. "Now they're right in the midst of it in terms of their involvement." He also believes that the titles took the exclusivity out of opera, making it accessible to everyone, rather than a few experts. For the general director of an opera company, the titles made it far easier to introduce new and unfamiliar repertoire.

Beverly Sills, then head of New York City Opera, flew to Toronto to take a look at Mansouri's new invention and promptly installed supertitles in her opera house. Terry McEwen was also enthusiastic and began using them in San Francisco. Not everyone agreed. Some called the supertitles "the plague from Canada," and the Metropolitan Opera's music director, James Levine, swore they would never be used at the Met. (Projected translations finally made it to the Met in 1995, seen on small screens in front of each seat.) Stage director Jean-Pierre Ponnelle loathed the idea of supertitles because they took people's eyes away from the stage, distracting them from his precisely choreographed motions.

The audience, however, responded favorably, and supertitles are now a fact of life at almost every major opera house in the world.

Even after four decades in the opera business, Mansouri has a passion for opera that remains undiminished. Asked to choose the operas that he would include in an imaginary, ideal season, he answers the banal question with a burst of words.

One of Mansouri's favorite prima donnas is **Joan Sutherland**, whom he first directed in San Francisco's 1963 production of *La Sonnambula*. In 1981 he was the director for *The Merry Widow*, in which Sutherland played the title role. She gave her all to one of the *Merry Widow* rehearsals, wearing a deliciously ruffled dress even though the men onstage were not in costume.

In 1989, Berg's *Lulu* was one of the highlights of the fall season. In the title role was **Ann Panagulias**, an Adler fellow in her first major role. Also in the cast was the great Wagnerian bass **Hans Hotter**, whose roles in San Francisco included the title role in *Der Fliegende Holländer* in 1954 and 1956. More than three decades later he returned to sing the part of the old man, Schigolch. In between these long-separated appearances, he came to San Francisco several times to teach young singers in the Merola Opera Program.

"My interests are very varied. If you asked me what one opera I would have to have on a desert island, I wouldn't be able to answer. I would have to have a minimum of ten, or twenty. For Mozart, for example, I wouldn't know whether to choose *Marriage of Figaro* or *Così*. I get chills every time I think of the second act of *Marriage of Figaro*. Then I would have to have *Bohème*. And *Carmen*, because it's such a perfect marriage of drama and music. There's good reason that people like these operas. As far as Wagner, I don't know whether I'd choose *Tristan und Isolde* or *Meistersinger*. *Meistersinger* I love because of the subject of art and beauty, but *Tristan und Isolde* is something where you just wallow in the sound."

His imaginary season would continue with either *Otello* or *Falstaff* from Verdi and *Pelléas et Mélisande*, "because it's perfection." *Wozzeck* would definitely be on the schedule, "because it's such a marriage of music and text, and it's like a hot blast." Another Berg opera, *Lulu*, might also make the list. Mansouri smiles wickedly as he says, "I love it for its perversity. I like the spectrum of human experience from the exalted to the gutter. It's wonderful to be able to deal with Jack the Ripper. That's the joy of this profession. Look at the gamut, from *L'Incoronazione di Poppea* to *Lulu*. How can you choose between these jewels?"

Mansouri acknowledges the influence of Kurt Herbert Adler in creating an audience willing to try out the whole spectrum. "Our audiences are much more sophisticated and more aware of theatrical totality. Look at their reaction to *Fiery Angel* and to *Ruslan and Lyudmila*. We could have sold three more *Ruslan*s, because there was so much interest in it. The San Francisco audience is interested in novelty and appreciates newness. My job is to balance the unknown, the less known, and the familiar each season."

Additions to the repertoire since Mansouri's arrival in San Francisco have ranged from lavish productions of Rossini's *Guillaume Tell* in 1992 and Verdi's *I Vespri Siciliani* in 1993 to contemporary novelties like Hans Werner Henze's *Das Verratene Meer* in 1991, a showcase for San Francisco countertenor Brian Asawa, and the co-commissioning of John Adams's *The Death of Klinghoffer* in 1992. Some of the most striking of the unfamiliar operas have been Russian, starting with Prokofiev's giant *War and Peace* in 1991.

The performance of *War and Peace*, which has thirteen scenes and more than sixty solo performers, was possible because of the carefully forged link between the San Francisco Opera and the Kirov Opera of St. Petersburg. The relationship started when Mansouri, who had decided to do *War and Peace*, heard of a dynamic young conductor, Valery Gergiev, from St. Petersburg. Mansouri flew to London to have dinner with him.

"It was love at first sight. I loved his energy and his ideas. We had a little affinity, because part of my family came originally from Georgia, where he is from. But the main thing is that he is one of the few conductors who really excites me. At the time he was working on a co-production of *War and Peace* with Covent Garden, which didn't work out too well. I suggested that we do a new production here and collaborate on the casting. We brought thirteen singers from the Kirov."

For Gergiev, *War and Peace* in San Francisco was his operatic conducting debut in the United States. For some of the singers, it was the first time that they had left Russia. On the day that they began rehearsing the burning of Moscow, a conservative putsch attempted to unseat Mikhail Gorbachev. "It was an incredible coincidence," Mansouri recalls. "They were all so nervous, not knowing what was going on in Russia, what was going to happen to their families. We set up television

One of the most thrilling operatic events in recent years was the 1991 production of Sergei Prokofiev's massive *War and Peace*, a collaboration between the Kirov Opera of St. Petersburg and the San Francisco Opera. The Opera's thirteen scenes included the Battle of Moscow and a view of the city's domes and spires (above). Although many of the major roles were filled by singers from the Kirov, the part of the romantic heroine Natasha was sung by **Ann Panagulias**, a young graduate of the San Francisco Opera's training programs for young singers. In one of the opera's most romantic moments, she waltzed with Russian baritone **Dimitri Kharitonov**, who played Prince Andrei Bolkonsky (left).

monitors at the rehearsals so that they could watch CNN between scenes."

Other collaborations followed. Mussorgsky's *Boris Godunov* in 1992 was followed by Prokofiev's *The Fiery Angel* in 1994. In 1995 the two companies worked together on *Ruslan and Lyudmila*, a favorite of both Mansouri and Gergiev. Mansouri directed the production, both in St. Petersburg and in San Francisco. San Francisco audiences have responded enthusiastically to Russian opera, and Mansouri would like to have one Russian opera each season, a luxury that can only be afforded by major companies. "Russian opera is so big, and it always requires ballet and extra chorus," Mansouri says. "Without the Kirov, we could not have done *Ruslan* or *War and Peace*."

As interesting as it is to re-create old productions, such as the Kirov's *Ruslan and Lyudmila* and San Francisco's own 1932 *Tosca*, which opened the season in 1997, Mansouri spends much of his time thinking ahead. "My responsibility is to work for the future of this company," he says seriously. That means developing new talent, new repertoire, and new audiences.

He wants to expand the training programs to include young conductors, designers, stage directors, and administrators as well as singers and coaches. He also wants to make good use of the participants in the program, especially the Adler Fellows, both during the two years of their fellowship and afterward. "The Adler Fellows are the core artists of this company," he comments. "You have to have this kind of ensemble, trained by your artistic standards, and then you bring in major stars, because you owe that, too, to your audience in a house like this."

He also feels strongly that an important opera company like San Francisco has an obligation to foster new repertoire and would eventually like to commission a new opera every year. The company commissioned Conrad Susa and Philip Littell to turn French novelist Choderlos de Laclos's *Les Liaisons Dangereuses* into an opera. The world premiere in the fall of 1994 had a star-studded cast, with Renée Fleming, Frederica von Stade, and Thomas Hampson in the lead roles.

For more than a decade, Mansouri had been talking about turning Tennessee Williams's *A Streetcar Named Desire* into an opera. At a press conference in early 1996, he was clearly delighted when he announced that the project was under way, with composer/conductor André Previn contracted to write the score and Phillip Littell the libretto. The opera's world premiere is planned for the fall of 1998. The following year, the premiere will be an opera with music by the multitalented Bobby McFerrin and libretto by Tony Kushner, playwright of *Angels in America*.

Mansouri's close relationship to the Kirov Opera in St. Petersburg led to the first San Francisco performance of Glinka's fabulous fairy tale, *Ruslan and Lyudmila*, based on a poem by Pushkin. The two opera companies collaborated on the elaborate production, sharing both singers and technical facilities. The sets were exact replicas of a historic Russian production, and the ballet re-created the original choreography of Michel Fokine. The costumes, seen above in the opening scene, were built in Russian workshops, using fabrics purchased around the world.

Sergei Prokofiev's *The Fiery Angel*, presented in 1994, was one of the results of the collaboration between the San Francisco Opera and the Kirov Opera. The production was notable for its fine Russian voices, including **Galina Gorchakova** as the demented Renata and **Sergei Leiferkus** as Ruprecht (opposite).

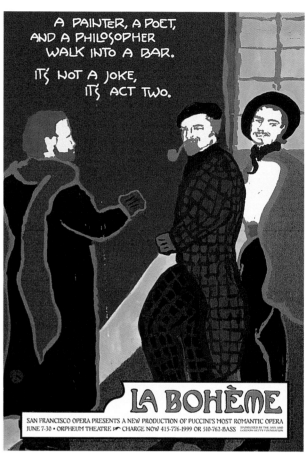

Mansouri, articulate and extroverted, is continually looking for new ways to involve more people with the opera. It may be a small thing, like advertising for supernumeraries for *Carmen* in both the English and the Spanish-language newspapers of the city. More than 250 people, some of them veteran supers but others first-time aspirants, turned up for the casting call.

On a larger scale, San Francisco Opera tried an intriguing experiment in June, 1996, presenting *La Bohème* like musical comedy, twenty-four nights in a row in the Orpheum Theatre. Witty, decorative posters popped up all over town, and prices were kept much lower than for performances in the War Memorial. A young and attractive cast consisting mostly of past and present Adler Fellows and clever, realistic scenery made the opera a particularly believable piece of theater.

As Mansouri and sponsor Gordon Getty had hoped, a whole new crowd turned up. The sight of couples embracing during the most romantic moments of the opera was proof that *Bohème* was attracting a younger, more informal group of patrons than come to the regular fall season. Indeed, of the forty-two thousand people who bought tickets to *Bohème*, eighty percent were not fall season subscribers.

Mansouri was delighted not only by the number of new patrons but by their enthusiasm for a traditional art form. *La Bohème* was presented exactly as it was written, without cuts and without amplification.

"I didn't cheat on *Bohème*," said Mansouri, in a statement that sums up many of his activities as general director. "I want to excite the new generation about opera as an art form, but I don't ever want to demean the art form or to lower our standards."

On October 17, 1989, the Loma Prieta earthquake shook the Bay Area, canceling not only the first game of the World Series at Candlestick Park but that evening's performance of Mozart's *Idomeneo* at the War Memorial Opera House. At the end of the 1995 fall season, the opera house was closed for seismic reconstruction, repairs of the damage from the earthquake, and extensive renovation. As a result, the company had to look for new locations for the 1996–97 season, the first to extend beyond Christmas. General director Lotfi Mansouri chose the Bill Graham Civic Auditorium and the Orpheum Theater on Market Street.

Each theater presented special challenges to the production and musical staffs. The Orpheum had an extraordinarily shallow stage, with the orchestra pit tucked underneath. For the Orpheum's productions, the company created two new productions—for *Hamlet* and *Harvey Milk*— and radically adapted pieces of an existing set for *Il Barbiere di Siviglia*. The Civic Auditorium presented problems due to its cavernous size and

mediocre acoustics—problems that Gaetano Merola had faced when he first presented opera there in the 1920s.

Unlike Merola, who created a proscenium stage within the Civic, Mansouri chose a solution much more foreign to San Francisco Opera subscribers: a huge semicircular stage that jutted out into the audience. The performances were spectacular because of the scale of the stage and the 4,100-seat auditorium, but they were also curiously intimate because the orchestra was placed in back of the stage, thus narrowing the space between singers and audience. There was no curtain, so opera fans were able to watch scene changes effected by crew members dressed in black. To the dismay of singers unsure of their words, there was no prompter, as there were neither wings nor a prompter's box. The effect of the productions was often thrilling, as directors used huge numbers of choristers and supernumeraries on towering, multilevel sets to fill the space.

The 1996–1997 season was divided between the wide open spaces of the Bill Graham Civic Auditorium and the intimate stage of the Orpheum Theater. In the Orpheum, audiences at *Harvey Milk* relived a painfully familiar chapter in San Francisco's history, including the dramatic moment when Dan White, played by **Raymond Very**, fired the fatal shot at Harvey Milk, sung by **Robert Orth** (opposite). At the Civic, the operas included *Les Contes d'Hoffmann* in a stylized set featuring a giant pen soaring over tenor **Jerry Hadley** in the title role (left), *Lohengrin*, with **Karita Mattila** as Elsa and **Ben Heppner** in the title role (below, left), and *Carmen*, in which Russian mezzo-soprano **Olga Borodina** (below) sang the title role for the first time in her career

All San Francisco performances took place at the War Memorial Opera House, except as noted and:
1923–1927; 1930–1931: Civic Auditorium
1928–1929: Dreamland Auditorium

Performed in the original language, unless otherwise indicated
** U.S. premiere; U.S. opera debut
*** World premiere

1923

Puccini, *La Bohème*
Queena Mario (Mimi),
Anna Young (Musetta);
Giovanni Martinelli (Rodolfo),
Alfredo Gandolfi (Marcello),
Adamo Didur (Colline)
Gaetano Merola
Sept. 26, 29

Giordano, *Andrea Chénier*
Bianca Saroya (Maddalena);
Beniamino Gigli (Chénier),
Giuseppe De Luca/
Alfredo Gandolfi (Gérard)
Gaetano Merola
Sept. 27, Oct. 6

Puccini, *Il Tabarro*
Bianca Saroya (Giorgetta);
Armand Tokatyan (Luigi),
Alfredo Gandolfi (Michele)
Gaetano Merola
and
Puccini, *Suor Angelica*
Bianca Saroya (Angelica),
Doria Fernanda (Princess)
Gaetano Merola
and
Puccini, *Gianni Schicchi*
Merle Epton (Lauretta);
Giuseppe De Luca (Schicchi),
Armand Tokatyan (Rinuccio)
Gaetano Merola
Sept. 29m

Boito, *Mefistofele*
Bianca Saroya (Margherita,
Elena); Adamo
Didur (Mefistofele),
Beniamino Gigli (Faust)
Gaetano Merola
Oct. 1

Puccini, *Tosca*
Bianca Saroya (Tosca);
Giovanni Martinelli
(Cavaradossi), Giuseppe
De Luca (Scarpia)
Gaetano Merola
Oct. 2

Gounod, *Roméo et Juliette*
Queena Mario (Juliette);
Beniamino Gigli (Roméo),
Giuseppe De Luca (Mercutio),
Louis D'Angelo (Laurence)
Gaetano Merola
Oct. 4

Puccini, *Gianni Schicchi*
Merle Epton (Lauretta);
Giuseppe De Luca (Schicchi),
Giordano Paltrinieri
(Rinuccio)
and
Leoncavallo, *Pagliacci*
Queena Mario (Nedda);
Giovanni Martinelli (Canio),
Giuseppe De Luca (Tonio),
Alfredo Gandolfi (Silvio)
Gaetano Merola
Oct. 6m

Verdi, *Rigoletto*
Queena Mario (Gilda),
Doria Fernanda (Maddalena);
Giuseppe De Luca
(Rigoletto), Beniamino
Gigli (Duke), Adamo
Didur (Sparafucile)
Gaetano Merola
Oct. 8

1924

Giordano, *Andrea Chénier*
Claudia Muzio (Maddalena);
Beniamino Gigli (Chénier),
Giuseppe De Luca (Gérard)
Gaetano Merola
Sept. 22

Puccini, *La Bohème*
Queena Mario/Myrtle
Donnelly (Mimi), Anna
Young (Musetta); Beniamino
Gigli/José Mojica (Rodolfo),
Millo Picco (Marcello),
Francesco Seri (Colline)
Gaetano Merola
Sept. 24, 28m

Puccini, *Madama Butterfly*
Thalia Sabanieeva
(Cio-Cio-San), Irene
Marlowe (Suzuki);
José Mojica (Pinkerton),
Millo Picco (Sharpless)
Gaetano Merola
Sept. 26

Verdi, *Rigoletto*
Queena Mario (Gilda),
Margareta Bruntsch
(Maddalena); Giuseppe
De Luca (Rigoletto),
Beniamino Gigli (Duke),
Francesco Seri (Sparafucile)
Gaetano Merola
Sept. 27

Massenet, *Manon*
Thalia Sabanieeva (Manon);
Tito Schipa (des Grieux),
Millo Picco (Lescaut)
Gaetano Merola
Sept. 29

Puccini, *Tosca*
Claudia Muzio (Tosca);
Beniamino Gigli
(Cavaradossi), Giuseppe
De Luca (Scarpia)
Gaetano Merola
Sept. 30

Mascagni, *L'Amico Fritz*
Thalia Sabanieeva (Suzel);
Tito Schipa (Fritz),
Giuseppe De Luca (Rabbi)
Gaetano Merola
and
Puccini, *Gianni Schicchi*
Myrtle Donnelly (Lauretta);
Giuseppe De Luca (Schicchi),
José Mojica (Rinuccio)
Gaetano Merola
Oct. 2

**Testimonial for
Gaetano Merola**
Madama Butterfly (Love
Duet); *Manon* (Act II); *Tosca*
(Act III); *Gianni Schicchi*

(Complete). Same casts.
Gaetano Merola
Oct. 3

Verdi, *La Traviata*
Claudia Muzio (Violetta);
Tito Schipa (Alfredo),
Giuseppe De Luca (Germont)
Gaetano Merola
Oct. 4

1925

Massenet, *Manon*
Rosina Torri** (Manon);
Tito Schipa (des Grieux),
Antonio Nicolich (Lescaut)
Gaetano Merola
Sept. 19, Oct.3m

Saint-Saëns,
Samson et Dalila
Marguerite D'Alvarez
(Dalila); Fernand
Ansseau (Samson),
Marcel Journet (Priest)
Pietro Cimini
Sept. 21, 26

Rossini,
Il Barbiere di Siviglia
Elvira De Hidalgo (Rosina);
Riccardo Stracciari (Figaro),
Tito Schipa (Almaviva),
Marcel Journet (Basilio),
Vittorio Trevisan (Bartolo)
Pietro Cimini
Sept. 24, Oct. 1

Vittadini, *Anima Allegra*
Rosina Torri (Consuelo);
Antonio Cortis (Pedro),
Vittorio Trevisan (Don Eligio)
Gaetano Merola
Sept 26m

Verdi, *La Traviata*
Elvira De Hidalgo (Violetta);
Tito Schipa (Alfredo),
Riccardo Stracciari
(Germont)
Gaetano Merola
Sept. 28

Flotow, *Martha*
(in Italian)
Elvira De Hidalgo
(Lady Harriet),
Elinor Marlo (Nancy);
Tito Schipa (Lionel),
Marcel Journet (Plunkett)
Pietro Cimini
Sept. 30

Montemezzi,
L'Amore dei Tre Re
Rosina Torri (Fiora); Fernand
Ansseau (Avito), Riccardo
Stracciari (Manfredo),
Marcel Journet (Archibaldo)
Gaetano Merola
Oct. 2

Verdi, *Aida*
Claudia Muzio (Aida),
Marguerite
D'Alvarez (Amneris);
Antonio Cortis (Radames),
Cesare Formichi (Amonasro)
Gaetano Merola
Oct. 3

Puccini, *Tosca*
Claudia Muzio (Tosca);
Fernand Ansseau
(Cavaradossi), Riccardo
Stracciari (Scarpia)
Gaetano Merola
Oct. 4m

1926

Flotow, *Martha*
(in Italian)
Florence Macbeth
(Lady Harriet),
Elinor Marlo (Nancy);
Tito Schipa (Lionel),
Marcel Journet (Plunkett)
Pietro Cimini
Sept. 21

Gounod, *Faust*
Myrtle Donnelly
(Marguerite), Flossita
Badger (Siebel);
Paul Althouse (Faust),

Desiré Defrère (Valentin),
Marcel Journet
(Méphisthophélès)
Gaetano Merola
Sept. 23

Rossini,
Il Barbiere di Siviglia
Florence Macbeth (Rosina);
Richard Bonelli (Figaro),
Tito Schipa (Almaviva),
Marcel Journet (Basilio),
Vittorio Trevisan (Bartolo)
Pietro Cimini
Sept. 25

Saint-Saëns,
Samson et Dalila
Louise Homer (Dalila);
Charles Marshall (Samson),
Marcel Journet (Priest)
Pietro Cimini
Sept. 27

Puccini, *Manon Lescaut*
Claudia Muzio (Manon);
Antonio Cortis (des Grieux),
Desiré Defrère (Lescaut)
Gaetano Merola
Sept. 28

Verdi, *Rigoletto*
Luella Melius (Gilda),
Elinor Marlo (Maddalena);
Richard Bonelli (Rigoletto),
Tito Schipa (Duke), Marcel
Journet (Sparafucile)
Pietro Cimini
Sept. 29

Verdi, *Aida*
Claudia Muzio (Aida),
Kathryn Meisle (Amneris);
Antonio Cortis (Radames),
Richard Bonelli (Amonasro)
Gaetano Merola
Oct. 1

Auber, *Fra Diavolo*
(in Italian)
Florence Macbeth (Zerlina),
Elinor Marlo (Lady Pamela);
Tito Schipa (Fra Diavolo),

Vittorio Trevisan
(Lord Richburg)
Pietro Cimini
Oct. 2

Puccini, *La Bohème*
Claudia Muzio (Mimì),
Myrtle Donnelly (Musetta);
Antonio Cortis (Rodolfo),
Richard Bonelli (Marcello),
Marcel Journet (Colline)
Gaetano Merola
Oct. 3m

Puccini, *Tosca*
Claudia Muzio (Tosca);
Antonio Cortis (Cavaradossi),
Marcel Journet (Scarpia)
Gaetano Merola
Oct. 4

Donizetti,
Lucia di Lammermoor
Luella Melius (Lucia);
Tito Schipa (Edgardo),
Richard Bonelli (Enrico),
Antonio Nicolich (Raimondo)
Pietro Cimini
Oct. 5

Verdi, *Il Trovatore*
Claudia Muzio (Leonora),
Kathryn Meisle (Azucena);
Aroldo Lindi (Manrico),
Richard Bonelli
(Count Di Luna)
Gaetano Merola
Oct. 6

1927

Puccini, *Manon Lescaut*
Frances Peralta (Manon);
Giovanni Martinelli
(des Grieux), Antonio
Scotti (Lescaut)
Gaetano Merola
Sept. 15

Wagner, *Tristan und Isolde*
Elsa Alsen (Isolde),
Kathryn Meisle (Brangäne);
Rudolf Laubenthal (Tristan),

Pasquale Amato (Kurwenal),
Fred Patton (King Marke)
Alfred Hertz
Sept. 16, 25m

Puccini, *Tosca*
Anne Roselle (Tosca); Mario
Chamlee (Cavaradossi),
Antonio Scotti (Scarpia)
Gaetano Merola
Sept. 17

Puccini, *Turandot*
Anne Roselle (Turandot),
Myrtle Donnelly (Liù),
Armand Tokatyan (Calaf),
Ezio Pinza (Timur)
Gaetano Merola
Sept. 19, Oct. 2m

Gounod,
Roméo et Juliette
Florence Macbeth (Juliette);
Mario Chamlee (Roméo),
Desiré Defrère (Mercutio),
Ezio Pinza (Laurence)
Gaetano Merola
Sept. 20

Verdi, *Il Trovatore*
Anne Roselle (Leonora),
Kathryn Meisle (Azucena);
Giovanni Martinelli
(Manrico), Millo Picco
(Count Di Luna)
Pietro Cimini
Sept. 22

Mascagni,
Cavalleria Rusticana
Frances Peralta (Santuzza);
Mario Chamlee (Turiddu),
Pasquale Amato (Alfio)
Pietro Cimini
and
Leoncavallo, *Pagliacci*
Anne Roselle (Nedda);
Giovanni Martinelli (Canio),
Pasquale Amato (Tonio),
Millo Picco (Silvio)
Pietro Cimini
Sept. 24

Verdi, *Falstaff*
Frances Peralta (Alice),
Myrtle Donnelly (Nannetta),
Ina Bourskaya (Quickly),
Elinor Marlo (Meg);
Antonio Scotti (Falstaff),
Armand Tokatyan (Fenton),
Lawrence Tibbett (Ford)
Gaetano Merola
Sept. 27

Verdi, *Aida*
Anne Roselle (Aida),
Ina Bourskaya (Amneris);
Giovanni Martinelli
(Radames), Pasquale
Amato (Amonasro)
Pietro Cimini
Sept. 28

Giordano,
La Cena Delle Beffe
Frances Peralta (Ginevra),
Myrtle Donnelly (Lisabetta);
Lawrence Tibbett (Neri),

Armand Tokatyan (Giannetto)
Pietro Cimini
Sept. 29

Puccini, *La Bohème*
Florence Macbeth (Mimì),
Katherine Seymour
(Musetta);
Mario Chamlee (Rodolfo),
Millo Picco (Marcello),
Ezio Pinza (Colline)
Pietro Cimini
Sept. 30

Bizet, *Carmen*
Ina Bourskaya (Carmen),
Myrtle Donnelly (Micaëla);
Giovanni Martinelli
(Don José), Desiré
Defrère (Escamillo)
Gaetano Merola
Oct. 1

1928

Verdi, *Aida*
Elisabeth Rethberg (Aida),
Marion Telva (Amneris);
Edward Johnson (Radames),
Lawrence Tibbett (Amonasro)
Gaetano Merola
Sept. 15

Giordano,
La Cena Delle Beffe
Elda Vettori (Ginevra),
Myrtle Donnelly (Lisabetta);
Lawrence Tibbett (Neri),
Armand Tokatyan (Giannetto)
Pietro Cimini
Sept. 17

Puccini, *Tosca*
Maria Jeritza (Tosca);
Armand Tokatyan/Gennaro
Barra** (Cavaradossi),
Lawrence Tibbett/Giuseppe
Danise (Scarpia)
Gaetano Merola
Sept. 19, 29m

Puccini, *Madama Butterfly*
Elisabeth Rethberg (Cio-Cio-
San), Marion Telva (Suzuki);
Gennaro Barra (Pinkerton),
Millo Picco (Sharpless)
Pietro Cimini
Sept. 21

Puccini, *Turandot*
Maria Jeritza (Turandot),
Elda Vettori (Liù); Armand
Tokatyan (Calaf), Louis
D'Angelo (Timur)
Gaetano Merola
Sept. 22

Montemezzi,
L'Amore dei Tre Re
Elda Vettori (Fiora); Edward
Johnson (Avito), Lawrence
Tibbett (Manfredo),
Ezio Pinza (Archibaldo)
Wilfred Pelletier
Sept. 24

Giordano, *Fedora*
Maria Jeritza (Fedora),
Myrtle Donnelly (Olga);

Edward Johnson (Loris),
Giuseppe Danise (De Siriex),
Louis D'Angelo (Grech)
Gaetano Merola
Sept. 25

Giordano, *Andrea Chénier*
Elisabeth Rethberg
(Maddalena); Gennaro
Barra (Chénier), Giuseppe
Danise (Gérard)
Gaetano Merola
Sept. 27

Gounod, *Faust*
Elisabeth Rethberg
(Marguerite), Rose
Florence (Siebel);
Armand Tokatyan (Faust),
Millo Picco (Valentin),
Ezio Pinza (Méphistophélès)
Pietro Cimini
Sept. 29

Bizet, *Carmen*
Maria Jeritza (Carmen),
Myrtle Donnelly (Micaëla);
Armand Tokatyan (Don José),
Ezio Pinza (Escamillo)
Wilfred Pelletier
Oct. 1

Mascagni,
Cavalleria Rusticana
Elda Vettori (Santuzza);
Gennaro Barra (Turiddu),
José Mercado (Alfio)
Pietro Cimini
and
Leoncavallo, *Pagliacci*
Elda Vettori (Nedda);
Edward Johnson (Canio),
Lawrence Tibbett (Tonio),
José Mercado (Silvio)
Pietro Cimini
Oct. 3

1929

Verdi, *Rigoletto*
Queena Mario (Gilda),
Eva Gruninger (Maddalena);
Giuseppe De Luca
(Rigoletto), Giacomo
Lauri-Volpi (Duke),
Léon Rothier (Sparafucile)
Gaetano Merola
Sept. 12

Humperdinck,
Hänsel und Gretel
Lenore Ivey (Hänsel),
Queena Mario (Gretel),
Kathryn Meisle (Witch),
Eva Gruninger (Gertrude);
Eugenio Sandrini (Peter)
Karl Riedel
Sept. 14m

Donizetti, *L'Elisir d'Amore*
Nina Morgana (Adina); Tito
Schipa (Nemorino), Millo
Picco (Belcore), Pompilio
Malatesta (Dulcamara)
Pietro Cimini
Sept. 14

Verdi, *Il Trovatore*
Elisabeth Rethberg
(Leonora), Kathryn Meisle
(Azucena); Giacomo Lauri-
Volpi (Manrico), Giuseppe
Danise (Count Di Luna)
Gaetano Merola
Sept. 16

Rossini,
Il Barbiere di Siviglia
Nina Morgana (Rosina);
Giuseppe De Luca (Figaro);
Tito Schipa (Almaviva),
Léon Rothier (Basilio),
Pompilio Malatesta (Bartolo)
Pietro Cimini
Sept. 18

Puccini, *La Bohème*
Elisabeth Rethberg (Mimì),
Anna Young (Musetta);
Gennaro Barra (Rodolfo),
Giuseppe Danise (Marcello),
Léon Rothier (Colline)
Pietro Cimini
Sept. 20

Puccini, *Gianni Schicchi*
Nina Morgana (Lauretta);
Giuseppe De Luca (Schicchi),
Gennaro Barra (Rinuccio)
Gaetano Merola
and
Leoncavallo, *Pagliacci*
Nina Morgana (Nedda);
Giacomo Lauri-Volpi (Canio),
Giuseppe De Luca (Tonio),
Millo Picco (Silvio)
Pietro Cimini
Sept. 21

Flotow, *Martha* (in Italian)
Queena Mario (Lady Harriet),
Lenore Ivey (Nancy);
Tito Schipa (Lionel),
Giuseppe De Luca (Plunkett)
Karl Riedel
Sept. 23

Verdi, *Aida*
Elisabeth Rethberg (Aida),
Kathryn Meisle (Amneris);
Giacomo Lauri-Volpi
(Radames), Giuseppe
Danise (Amonasro)
Gaetano Merola
Sept. 25

Donizetti, *Don Pasquale*
Nina Morgana (Norina);
Pompilio Malatesta
(Pasquale), Tito
Schipa (Ernesto), Giuseppe
De Luca (Malatesta)
Antonio Dell'Orefice
Sept. 27

Gounod, *Faust*
Elisabeth Rethberg
(Marguerite), Suzanne
Torres (Siebel); Giacomo
Lauri-Volpi (Faust), Giuseppe
Danise (Valentin), Léon
Rothier (Méphistophélès)
Wilfred Pelletier
Sept. 28

Massenet, *Manon*
Queena Mario (Manon);
Tito Schipa (des Grieux),
Giuseppe De Luca (Lescaut)
Gaetano Merola
Sept. 30

1930

Massenet, *Manon*
Queena Mario (Manon);
Beniamino Gigli (des Grieux),
Millo Picco (Lescaut)
Gaetano Merola
Sept. 11

Strauss, *Salome*
Maria Jeritza (Salome),
Dorothee Manski (Herodias);
Sydney Rayner (Herod), John
Charles Thomas (Jokanaan)
Gaetano Merola
Sept. 12, 27m

Verdi, *La Traviata*
Claire Clairbert** (Violetta);
Beniamino Gigli (Alfredo),
Gaetano Viviani** (Germont)
Gaetano Merola
Sept. 13

Puccini,
La Fanciulla del West
Maria Jeritza (Minnie);
Frederick Jagel (Johnson),
Gaetano Viviani (Rance)
Gaetano Merola
Sept. 15

Puccini, *La Bohème*
Queena Mario (Mimì),
Audrey Farncroft (Musetta);
Beniamino Gigli (Rodolfo),
Gaetano Viviani (Marcello),
Ezio Pinza (Colline)
Antonio Dell'Orefice
Sept. 17

Ravel,
L'Enfant et les Sortilèges
Queena Mario (Boy), Audrey
Farncroft (Fire, Princess,
Lark), Eva Gruninger
(Mother, Butterfly); Louis
D'Angelo (Armchair, Tree)
Gaetano Merola
and
Humperdinck,
Hänsel und Gretel
Elinor Marlo (Hänsel),
Queena Mario (Gretel),
Dorothee Manski (Witch),
Eva Gruninger (Gertrude);
Eugenio Sandrini (Peter)
Karl Riedel
Sept. 19

Mascagni,
Cavalleria Rusticana
Maria Jeritza (Santuzza);
Frederick Jagel (Turiddu),
Millo Picco (Alfio)
Antonio Dell'Orefice
and
Leoncavallo, *Pagliacci*
Maria Jeritza (Nedda);
Sydney Rayner (Canio), John
Charles Thomas (Tonio),

Millo Picco (Silvio)
Antonio Dell'Orefice
Sept. 20

Thomas, *Mignon*
Queena Mario (Mignon),
Claire Clairbert (Philine);
Beniamino Gigli
(Wilhelm Meister),
Ezio Pinza (Lothario)
Wilfred Pelletier
Sept. 22

Wagner, *Tannhäuser*
Maria Jeritza (Elisabeth),
Dorothee Manski (Venus);
Sydney Rayner (Tannhäuser),
John Charles Thomas
(Wolfram),
Ezio Pinza (Hermann)
Karl Riedel
Sept. 23

Gounod, *Faust*
Hope Hampton (Marguerite),
Suzanne Torres (Siebel);
Frederick Jagel (Faust), John
Charles Thomas (Valentin),
Ezio Pinza (Méphistophélès)
Wilfred Pelletier
Sept. 25

Donizetti,
Lucia di Lammermoor
Claire Clairbert (Lucia);
Beniamino Gigli (Edgardo),
Gaetano Viviani (Enrico),
Louis D'Angelo (Raimondo)
Gaetano Merola
Sept. 27

1931

Rabaud, *Mârouf*
Yvonne Gall (Princess),
Eva Gruninger (Fattoumah);
Mario Chamlee (Mârouf),
Louis D'Angelo (Sultan)
Gaetano Merola
Sept. 10

Verdi, *Aida*
Elisabeth Rethbert (Aida),
Faina Petrova (Amneris);
Giovanni Martinelli
(Radames), Giuseppe
Danise (Amonasro)
Gaetano Merola
Sept. 12

Wagner, *Lohengrin*
Maria Müller (Elsa),
Faina Petrova (Ortrud);
Gotthelf Pistor**
(Lohengrin), Friedrich
Schorr (Telramund),
Louis D'Angelo (Heinrich)
Hans Blechschmidt
Sept. 14

Giordano, *Andrea Chénier*
Elisabeth Rethberg
(Maddalena); Giovanni
Martinelli (Chénier),
Giuseppe Danise (Gérard)
Gaetano Merola
Sept. 16

Puccini, *Madama Butterfly*
Maria Müller (Cio-Cio-San),
Faina Petrova (Suzuki);
Mario Chamlee (Pinkerton),
Andrés de Segurola
(Sharpless)
Wilfred Pelletier
Sept. 18

Verdi,
Un Ballo in Maschera
Elisabeth Rethberg (Amelia),
Audrey Farncroft (Oscar),
Luisa Silva (Ulrica); Giovanni
Martinelli (Riccardo),
Giuseppe Danise (Renato)
Pietro Cimini
Sept. 19

Puccini, *Tosca*
Yvonne Gall (Tosca); Mario
Chamlee (Cavaradossi),
Giuseppe Danise (Scarpia)
Pietro Cimini
Sept. 21

Wagner, *Tannhäuser*
Elisabeth Rethberg
(Elisabeth), Maxine
Castleton (Venus);
Gotthelf Pistor (Tannhäuser),
Friedrich Schorr (Wolfram),
Ezio Pinza (Hermann)
Hans Blechschmidt
Sept. 23

Puccini, *La Bohème*
Maria Müller (Mimì), Audrey
Farncroft (Musetta); Mario
Chamlee (Rodolfo), Andrés
de Segurola (Marcello),
Ezio Pinza (Colline)
Antonio Dell'Orefice
Sept. 25

Verdi, *Il Trovatore*
Elisabeth Rethberg
(Leonora), Luisa
Silva (Azucena);
Giovanni Martinelli
(Manrico), Giuseppe
Danise (Count Di Luna)
Gaetano Merola
Sept. 26

Wagner, *Die Meistersinger*
Maria Müller (Eva),
Eva Gruninger (Magdalene);
Gotthelf Pistor (Walther),
Friedrich Schorr (Hans
Sachs), Arnold Gabor
(Beckmesser),
Ezio Pinza (Pogner),
Marek Windheim (David)
Hans Blechschmidt
Sept. 28

Bizet, *Carmen*
Faina Petrova (Carmen),
Audrey Farncroft (Micaëla);
Giovanni Martinelli (Don
José), Ezio Pinza (Escamillo)
Wilfred Pelletier
Sept. 29

1932

Puccini, *Tosca*
Claudia Muzio (Tosca);
Dino Borgioli (Cavaradossi),
Alfredo Gandolfi (Scarpia)
Gaetano Merola
Oct. 15

Donizetti,
Lucia di Lammermoor
Lily Pons (Lucia);
Francesco Merli/
Dino Borgioli (Edgardo),
Alfredo Gandolfi (Enrico),
Louis D'Angelo (Raimondo)
Gaetano Merola
Oct. 17, 23m

Wagner, *Die Meistersinger*
Maria Müller (Eva),
Evelyn MacNevin
(Magdalena); Mario
Chamlee (Walther),
Friedrich Schorr (Hans
Sachs), Arnold Gabor
(Beckmesser),
Ezio Pinza (Pogner),
Marek Windheim (David)
Hans Blechschmidt
Oct. 18, 30m

Verdi, *Rigoletto*
Lily Pons (Gilda),
Eva Gruninger (Maddalena);
Richard Bonelli (Rigoletto),
Dino Borgioli (Duke),
Ezio Pinza (Sparafucile)
Gaetano Merola
Oct. 20

Humperdinck,
Hänsel und Gretel
Marie Lothrop (Hänsel),
Queena Mario (Gretel),
Kathryn Meisle (Witch),
Evelyn MacNevin (Gertrude);
Arnold Gabor (Peter)
Hans Blechschmidt
and
Ravel,
La Valse and *Bolero*
Estelle Reed (Dancer, *Bolero*)
Gaetano Merola
Oct. 22m

Mascagni,
Cavalleria Rusticana
Claudia Muzio (Santuzza);
Mario Chamlee (Turiddu),
Alfredo Gandolfi (Alfio)
Gaetano Merola
and
Leoncavallo, *Pagliacci*
Claudia Muzio (Nedda);
Tandy MacKenzie (Canio),
Richard Bonelli (Tonio),
Marsden Argall (Silvio)
Pietro Cimini
Oct. 22

Wagner, *Lohengrin*
Maria Müller (Elsa),
Kathryn Meisle (Ortrud);
Mario Chamlee (Lohengrin),
Friedrich Schorr
(Telramund),

Louis D'Angelo (Heinrich)
Hans Blechschmidt
Oct. 25

Gounod, *Faust*
Queena Mario (Marguerite),
Katerina Malova (Siebel);
Dino Borgioli (Faust),
Richard Bonelli (Valentin),
Ezio Pinza (Méphistophélès)
Hans Blechschmidt
Oct. 27

Verdi, *Il Trovatore*
Claudia Muzio (Leonora),
Kathryn Meisle (Azucena);
Tandy MacKenzie (Manrico),
Richard Bonelli (Count
Di Luna)
Pietro Cimini
Oct. 29

Verdi, *La Traviata*
Claudia Muzio (Violetta);
Dino Borgioli (Alfredo),
Richard Bonelli (Germont)
Gaetano Merola
Nov. 1

1933

Saint-Saëns,
Samson et Dalila
Cyrena Van Gordon (Dalila);
Giovanni Martinelli (Samson),
Ezio Pinza (Priest)
Gaetano Merola
Nov. 3, 12m

Rimsky-Korsakov,
The Golden Cockerel
(Dance Pantomime with
Vocal Accompaniment)
Emily Hardy (Queen of
Shemakha), Querita Eybel
(Voice of the Cockerel);
Nathan Stewart (King
Dodon), Raymond Marlowe
(Astrologer), Amerigo
Frediani (Prince)
  Principal dancers:
Maclovia Ruiz and Adolph
Bolm
Wilfred Pelletier
Nov. 6, 26m

Verdi, *Aida*
Claudia Muzio (Aida),
Kathryn Meisle (Amneris);
Giovanni Martinelli
(Radames), Richard
Bonelli (Amonasro)
Gaetano Merola
Nov. 8

Wagner,
Tristan und Isolde
Gertrude Kappel (Isolde),
Kathryn Meisle (Brangäne);
Paul Althouse (Tristan),
Richard Bonelli (Kurwenal),
Ezio Pinza (King Marke)
Alfred Hertz
Nov. 10, 19m

Massenet, *Manon*
Lucrezia Bori (Manon); Dino
Borgioli (des Grieux), Alfredo

Gandolfi (Lescaut)
Wilfred Pelletier
Nov. 14, Dec. 2

Wolf-Ferrari,
The Secret of Suzanne
Nina Morgana (Suzanne);
Alfredo Gandolfi (Count Gil)
Antonio Dell'Orefice
and
Gruenberg,
The Emperor Jones
Lawrence Tibbett (Brutus
Jones), Raymond Marlowe
(Henry Smithers)
Wilfred Pelletier
Nov. 17, 30m

Mascagni,
Cavalleria Rusticana
Claudia Muzio (Santuzza);
Dino Borgioli (Turiddu),
Alfredo Gandolfi (Alfio)
Antonio Dell'Orefice
and
Leoncavallo, *Pagliacci*
Lucrezia Bori (Nedda);
Giovanni Martinelli (Canio),
Lawrence Tibbett (Tonio),
Alfredo Gandolfi (Silvio)
Gaetano Merola
Nov. 21

Verdi, *La Traviata*
Claudia Muzio (Violetta);
Dino Borgioli (Alfredo),
Lawrence Tibbett (Germont)
Gaetano Merola
Nov. 24

Puccini, *La Bohème*
Lucrezia Bori (Mimi),
Emily Hardy (Musetta);
Dino Borgioli (Rodolfo),
Richard Bonelli (Marcello),
Ezio Pinza (Colline)
Gaetano Merola
Nov. 28

Verdi,
La Forza del Destino
Claudia Muzio (Leonora),
Myrtle Leonard (Preziosilla);
Giovanni Martinelli
(Don Alvaro), Richard
Bonelli (Don Carlo), Ezio
Pinza (Padre Guardiano)
Gaetano Merola
Dec. 1

1934

Smetana,
Die Verkaufte Braut
(The Bartered Bride)
Elisabeth Rethberg (Marie);
Mario Chamlee (Jenik),
Marek Windheim (Vasek),
Louis D'Angelo (Kecal)
Alfred Hertz
Nov. 14

Puccini, *Tosca*
Lotte Lehmann (Tosca);
Dino Borgioli (Cavaradossi),
Alfredo Gandolfi (Scarpia)
Gaetano Merola
Nov. 16

Bizet, *Carmen*
Ninon Vallin (Carmen),
Lillian Clark (Micaëla);
Mario Chamlee (Don José),
Ezio Pinza (Escamillo)
Gaetano Merola
Nov. 17

Massenet, *Manon*
Lucrezia Bori (Manon);
Richard Crooks (des Grieux),
Alfredo Gandolfi (Lescaut)
Pietro Cimini
Nov. 19, Dec. 1

Puccini, *Madama Butterfly*
Lotte Lehmann/Elisabeth
Rethberg (Cio-Cio-San),
Elinor Marlo (Suzuki);
Dino Borgioli/
Mario Chamlee (Pinkerton),
Alfredo Gandolfi (Sharpless)
Pietro Cimini
Nov. 22, Dec. 2m

Wagner, *Tannhäuser*
Elisabeth Rethberg
(Elisabeth), Querita
Eybel (Venus); Lauritz
Melchior (Tannhäuser),
Richard Bonelli/Nelson
Eddy (Wolfram),
Ezio Pinza (Hermann)
Alfred Hertz
Nov. 26, Dec. 8

Verdi, *La Traviata*
Lucrezia Bori (Violetta);
Richard Crooks (Alfredo),
Richard Bonelli (Germont)
Gaetano Merola
Nov. 28

Gounod, *Faust*
Ninon Vallin (Marguerite),
Lillian Clark (Siebel);
Richard Crooks (Faust),
Richard Bonelli (Valentin),
Ezio Pinza (Méphistophélès)
Gaetano Merola
Nov. 30

Puccini, *La Rondine*
Lucrezia Bori (Magda),
Lillian Clark (Lisette);
Dino Borgioli (Ruggero),
Marek Windheim (Prunier)
Gaetano Merola
Dec. 3

Delibes, *Lakmé*
Emily Hardy (Lakmé),
Eva Gruninger (Mallika);
Mario Chamlee (Gerald),
Ezio Pinza (Nilakantha),
Alfredo Gandolfi (Frederic)
Gaetano Merola
Dec. 4

Verdi, *Otello*
Elisabeth Rethberg
(Desdemona);
Lauritz Melchior (Otello),
Richard Bonelli (Iago)
Gaetano Merola
Dec. 5

Thomas, *Mignon*
Lucrezia Bori (Mignon),
Emily Hardy (Philine); Dino
Borgioli (Wilhelm Meister),
Ezio Pinza (Lothario),
Pietro Cimini
Dec. 7

1935

Wagner, *Das Rheingold*
Querita Eybel (Fricka),
Kathryn Meisle (Erda);
Friedrich Schorr (Wotan),
Hans Clemens (Loge), Gustav
Schützendorf (Alberich)
Artur Bodanzky
Nov. 1

Wagner, *Die Walküre*
Kirsten Flagstad
(Brünnhilde), Elisabeth
Rethberg (Sieglinde),
Kathryn Meisle (Fricka);
Lauritz Melchior (Siegmund),
Friedrich Schorr (Wotan),
Chase Baromeo/Emanuel
List (Hunding)
Artur Bodanzky
Nov. 4, 13

Wagner, *Siegfried*
Kirsten Flagstad
(Brünnhilde), Kathryn
Meisle (Erda); Lauritz
Melchior (Siegfried), Gustav
Schützendorf (Alberich),
Marek Windheim (Mime),
Friedrich Schorr (Wanderer)
Artur Bodanzky
Nov. 6

Wagner, *Götterdämmerung*
Kirsten Flagstad
(Brünnhilde), Dorothee
Manski (Gutrune); Lauritz
Melchior (Siegfried),
Friedrich Schorr (Gunther),
Emanuel List (Hagen)
Artur Bodanzky
Nov. 9

Verdi, *Aida*
Elisabeth Rethberg (Aida),
Kathryn Meisle/Coe
Glade (Amneris); Giovanni
Martinelli (Radames),
Nelson Eddy/
Richard Bonelli (Amonasro)
Gaetano Merola
Nov. 11, 23

Flotow, *Martha* (in Italian)
Helen Jepson (Lady Harriet),
Coe Glade/
Eva Gruninger (Nancy);
Tito Schipa (Lionel),
Henri Shefoff (Plunkett)
Richard Lert
Nov. 16, Dec. 1m

Halévy, *La Juive*
Elisabeth Rethberg (Rachel),
Emily Hardy (Eudoxia);
Giovanni Martinelli (Eleazar),
Ezio Pinza (Cardinal)
Richard Lert
Nov. 18

Massenet, *Werther*
Coe Glade (Charlotte),
Anna Young (Sophie);
Tito Schipa (Werther),
Alfredo Gandolfi (Albert)
Gaetano Merola
Nov. 22

Rossini,
Il Barbiere di Siviglia
Josephine Tumminia (Rosina);
Richard Bonelli (Figaro),
Tito Schipa (Almaviva),
Ezio Pinza (Basilio),
Louis D'Angelo (Bartolo)
Gaetano Merola
Nov. 25

Puccini, *La Bohème*
Helen Jepson (Mimi),
Edna Smith (Musetta);
Giovanni Martinelli (Rodolfo),
Richard Bonelli (Marcello),
Ezio Pinza (Colline)
Richard Lert
Nov. 27

Verdi, *Rigoletto*
Emily Hardy (Gilda),
Eva Gruninger (Maddalena);
Richard Bonelli (Rigoletto),
Tito Schipa (Duke),
Ezio Pinza (Sparafucile)
Gaetano Merola
Nov. 29

Puccini, *Suor Angelica*
Helen Gahagan** (Angelica),
Margaret O'Dea (Princess)
Gaetano Merola
and
Rimsky-Korsakov,
The Golden Cockerel
(Dance Pantomime with
Vocal Accompaniment)
Emily Hardy (Queen
of Shemakha), Querita
Eybel (Voice of the
Cockerel); Douglas Beattie
(King Dodon), Raymond
Marlowe (Astrologer),
C. Martin Friberg (Prince)
Gaetano Merola
Dec. 2

1936

Halévy, *La Juive*
Elisabeth Rethberg (Rachel),
Charlotte Boerner (Eudoxia);
Giovanni Martinelli (Eleazar),
Ezio Pinza (Cardinal)
Gaetano Merola
Oct. 30

Rossini,
Il Barbiere di Siviglia
Josephine Tumminia (Rosina);
Carlo Morelli (Figaro),
Charles Kullman (Almaviva),
Ezio Pinza (Basilio),
Louis D'Angelo (Bartolo)
Gaetano Merola
Oct. 31

Wagner, *Tristan und Isolde*
Kirsten Flagstad (Isolde),
Kathryn Meisle/

Doris Doe (Brangäne);
Lauritz Melchior (Tristan),
Friedrich Schorr (Kurwenal),
Emanuel List (King Marke)
Fritz Reiner
Nov. 2, 17

Bizet, *Carmen*
Bruna Castagna (Carmen),
Josephine Tumminia
(Micaëla); Charles
Kullman (Don José), Ezio
Pinza (Escamillo)
Gennaro Papi
Nov. 4, 15m

Verdi, *Rigoletto*
Josephine Tumminia (Gilda),
Eva Gruninger (Maddalena);
Lawrence Tibbett (Rigoletto),
Charles Kullman (Duke),
Ezio Pinza (Sparafucile)
Gennaro Papi
Nov. 6

Wagner, *Götterdämmerung*
Kirsten Flagstad
(Brünnhilde), Dorothee
Manski (Gutrune); Lauritz
Melchior (Siegfried),
Friedrich Schorr (Gunther),
Emanuel List (Hagen)
Fritz Reiner
Nov. 7

Mozart, *Le Nozze di Figaro*
Charlotte Boerner (Susanna),
Elisabeth Rethberg
(Countess), Gina
Vanna (Cherubino);
Ezio Pinza (Figaro),
Perry Askam (Count)
Richard Lert
Nov. 9

Leoncavallo, *Pagliacci*
Gina Vanna (Nedda);
Giovanni Martinelli (Canio),
Lawrence Tibbett (Tonio),
John Howell (Silvio)
Gennaro Papi
and
Puccini, *Gianni Schicchi*
Gina Vanna (Lauretta);
Lawrence Tibbett (Schicchi),
Charles Kullman (Rinuccio)
Gennaro Papi
Nov. 11

Wagner, *Die Walküre*
Kirsten Flagstad
(Brünnhilde), Lotte
Lehmann (Sieglinde),
Kathryn Meisle (Fricka);
Lauritz Melchior (Siegmund),
Friedrich Schorr (Wotan),
Emanuel List (Hunding)
Fritz Reiner
Nov. 13, 22m

Verdi, *Il Trovatore*
Elisabeth Rethberg
(Leonora), Bruna Castagna
(Azucena); Giovanni
Martinelli (Manrico), Carlo
Morelli (Count Di Luna)
Gennaro Papi
Nov. 14m

Verdi,
La Forza del Destino
Elisabeth Rethberg
(Leonora), Doris
Doe (Preziosilla);
Giovanni Martinelli
(Don Alvaro), Carlo
Morelli (Don Carlo), Ezio
Pinza (Padre Guardiano)
Gennaro Papi
Nov. 16

Puccini, *Tosca*
Lotte Lehmann (Tosca);
Charles Kullman
(Cavaradossi), Lawrence
Tibbett (Scarpia)
Gennaro Papi
Nov. 18

Verdi, *Otello*
Elisabeth Rethberg
(Desdemona);
Giovanni Martinelli (Otello),
Lawrence Tibbett (Iago)
Gaetano Merola
Nov. 20

Wagner, *Das Rheingold*
Dorothee Manski (Fricka),
Margaret O'Dea (Erda);
Friedrich Schorr (Wotan),
Hans Clemens (Loge),
Arnold Gabor (Alberich)
Karl Riedel
Nov. 21

Massenet, *Werther*
Coe Glade (Charlotte),
Anna Young (Sophie);
Tito Schipa (Werther),
Alfredo Gandolfi (Albert)
Gaetano Merola
Nov. 22

1937

Verdi, *Aida*
Gina Cigna (Aida), Bruna
Castagna (Amneris); Giovanni
Martinelli (Radames),
Richard Bonelli (Amonasro)
Gaetano Merola
Oct. 15, 26
Nov. 18 (Los Angeles)

Puccini, *La Bohème*
Vina Bovy (Mimi),
Charlotte Boerner (Musetta);
Charles Kullman (Rodolfo),
Richard Bonelli (Marcello),
Ezio Pinza (Colline)
Gennaro Papi
Oct. 18

Verdi,
Un Ballo in Maschera
Gina Cigna (Amelia), Bruna
Castagna (Ulrica), Charlotte
Boerner (Oscar); Giovanni
Martinelli (Riccardo),
Richard Bonelli (Renato)
Gennaro Papi
Oct. 20

Gounod, *Faust*
Charlotte Boerner
(Marguerite),

Helen Beatty (Siebel);
Giovanni Martinelli (Faust),
Perry Askam (Valentin),
Ezio Pinza (Méphistophélès)
Pietro Cimini
Oct. 23

Wagner, *Tristan und Isolde*
Kirsten Flagstad (Isolde),
Kathryn Meisle/
Doris Doe (Brangäne);
Lauritz Melchior (Tristan),
Julius Huehn (Kurwenal),
Ludwig Hofmann/
(10/31, 11/15) Emanuel
List (King Marke)
Fritz Reiner
Oct. 25, 31m, Nov. 1
Nov. 15 (Los Angeles)

Puccini, *Madama Butterfly*
Rosa Tentoni (Cio-Cio-San),
Dorothy Cornish (Suzuki);
Charles Kullman (Pinkerton),
Julius Huehn (Sharpless)
Gennaro Papi
Oct. 27

Delibes, *Lakmé*
Lily Pons (Lakmé),
Helen Beatty (Mallika);
René Maison (Gerald),
Ezio Pinza (Nilakantha),
George Cehanovsky
(Frederic)
Pietro Cimini
Oct. 29, Nov. 3
Nov. 16 (Los Angeles)

Verdi, *La Traviata*
Gina Cigna (Violetta);
Charles Kullman (Alfredo),
Richard Bonelli (Germont)
Gaetano Merola
Oct. 30

Gounod, *Roméo et Juliette*
Vina Bovy (Juliette); René
Maison (Roméo), Perry
Askam (Mercutio), Emanuel
List (Laurence)
Gaetano Merola
Nov. 1

Wagner, *Lohengrin*
Kirsten Flagstad (Elsa),
Kathryn Meisle (Ortrud);
Lauritz Melchior (Lohengrin),
Julius Huehn (Telramund),
Ludwig Hofmann (Heinrich)
Fritz Reiner
Nov. 5, 11
Nov. 19 (Los Angeles)

Verdi, *Rigoletto*
Josephine Tumminia (Gilda),
Dorothy Cornish
(Maddalena); Richard
Bonelli (Rigoletto),
Charles Kullman (Duke),
Norman Cordon (Sparafucile)
Gennaro Papi
Nov. 6

Beethoven, *Fidelio*
Kirsten Flagstad (Leonore),
Charlotte Boerner
(Marzelline); René

Maison (Florestan),
Ludwig Hofmann (Pizarro),
Emanuel List (Rocco)
Fritz Reiner
Nov. 8

Massenet, *Manon*
Vina Bovy (Manon);
René Maison (des Grieux),
Richard Bonelli (Lescaut)
Pietro Cimini
Nov. 10

Bellini, *Norma*
Gina Cigna (Norma),
Bruna Castagna
(Adalgisa); Giovanni
Martinelli (Pollione),
Ezio Pinza (Oroveso)
Gaetano Merola
Nov. 13

Puccini, *Tosca*
Maria Jeritza (Tosca);
Frank Forest (Cavaradossi),
Richard Bonelli (Scarpia)
Gaetano Merola
Nov. 20 (Los Angeles)

1938

Giordano, *Andrea Chénier*
Elisabeth Rethberg
(Maddalena); Beniamino
Gigli (Chénier),
Richard Bonelli/(10/15)
Carlo Tagliabue** (Gérard)
Gaetano Merola
Oct. 7, 15
Nov. 5 (Los Angeles)

Mozart, *Don Giovanni*
Elisabeth Rethberg
(Donna Anna), Irene Jessner
(Donna Elvira), Mafalda
Favero** (Zerlina);
Ezio Pinza (Giovanni), Dino
Borgioli (Ottavio), Salvatore
Baccaloni (Leporello)
Fritz Reiner
Oct. 10, 20

Flotow, *Martha* (in Italian)
Mafalda Favero (Lady
Harriet), Doris Doe (Nancy);
Beniamino Gigli (Lionel),
Louis D'Angelo (Plunkett)
Gennaro Papi
Oct. 12

Wagner, *Die Meistersinger*
Irene Jessner/(11/7)
Elisabeth Rethberg
(Eva), Kerstin Thorborg
(Magdalene); Charles
Kullman (Walther), Friedrich
Schorr (Hans Sachs),
Arnold Gabor (Beckmesser),
Carlton Gauld (Pogner),
Karl Laufkötter (David)
Fritz Reiner
Oct. 14, 26
Nov. 7 (Los Angeles)

Mascagni,
Cavalleria Rusticana
Ebe Stignani** (Santuzza);
Alessandro Ziliani**/

Galliano Masini (Turiddu),
Carlo Tagliabue (Alfio)
Gaetano Merola
and
Donizetti, *Don Pasquale*
Mafalda Favero (Norina);
Salvatore Baccaloni
(Pasquale),
Dino Borgioli (Ernesto),
Richard Bonelli (Malatesta)
Gennaro Papi
Oct. 17, 22

Debussy,
Pelléas et Mélisande
Janine Micheau**
(Mélisande), Doris
Doe (Geneviève); Georges
Cathelat** (Pelléas),
Carlton Gauld (Golaud),
Louis D'Angelo (Arkel)
Erich Leinsdorf
Oct. 19
Nov. 8 (Los Angeles)

Donizetti,
Lucia di Lammermoor
Lily Pons (Lucia);
Galliano Masini (Edgardo),
Carlo Tagliabue (Enrico),
Norman Cordon (Raimondo)
Gennaro Papi
Oct. 21, 29
Oct. 27 (Sacramento)

Rossini,
Il Barbiere di Siviglia
Janine Micheau (Rosina);
Carlo Tagliabue (Figaro),
Dino Borgioli (Almaviva),
Norman Cordon (Basilio),
Salvatore Baccaloni (Bartolo)
Gaetano Merola
Oct. 23m

Strauss, *Elektra*
Rose Pauly (Elektra),
Irene Jessner (Chrysothemis),
Kerstin Thorborg
(Klytemnestra);
Karl Laufkötter (Aegisth),
Julius Huehn (Orest)
Fritz Reiner
Oct. 24, 30m
Nov. 10 (Los Angeles)

Verdi,
La Forza del Destino
Elisabeth Rethberg
(Leonora), Doris
Doe (Preziosilla);
Beniamino Gigli (Don
Alvaro), Richard Bonelli/
Carlo Tagliabue (Don Carlo),
Ezio Pinza (Padre
Guardiano)
Gennaro Papi
Oct. 28, Nov. 1

Puccini, *La Bohème*
Mafalda Favero (Mimi),
Anne Jamison (Musetta);
Galliano Masini/
Beniamino Gigli (Rodolfo),
Carlo Tagliabue/Richard
Bonelli (Marcello), Norman
Cordon/Ezio Pinza (Colline)

Gennaro Papi
Oct. 31
Nov. 12 (Los Angeles)

Rimsky-Korsakov,
Le Coq d'Or (in French)
Lily Pons (Queen of
Shemakha), Thelma Votipka
(Voice of the Cockerel);
Ezio Pinza (King Dodon),
Nicholas Massue (Astrologer)
Gennaro Papi
Nov. 3
Nov. 11 (Los Angeles)

Mascagni,
Cavalleria Rusticana
Ebe Stignani (Santuzza),
Alessandro Ziliani (Turiddu),
Carlo Tagliabue (Alfio)
Gaetano Merola
and
Puccini, *La Bohème*
Mafalda Favero (Mimi),
Anne Jamison (Musetta);
Beniamino Gigli (Rodolfo),
Richard Bonelli (Marcello),
Ezio Pinza (Colline)
Gennaro Papi
Nov. 12 (Los Angeles)

1939

Massenet, *Manon*
Bidú Sayão (Manon);
Tito Schipa (des Grieux),
Richard Bonelli (Lescaut)
Gaetano Merola
Oct. 13
Nov. 11 (Los Angeles)

Wagner, *Die Walküre*
(10/17) Marjorie
Lawrence/Kirsten Flagstad
(Brünnhilde), (10/17) Kirsten
Flagstad/Marjorie Lawrence
(Sieglinde), (10/17, 11/7)
Kathryn Meisle/Herta
Glaz (Fricka); Lauritz
Melchior (Siegmund), (10/17,
11/7) Julius Huehn/
Fred Destal (Wotan),
Norman Cordon (Hunding)
Erich Leinsdorf/(10/24)
Edwin McArthur
Oct. 17, 24
Oct. 28 (Sacramento)
Nov. 7 (Los Angeles)

Puccini, *Madama Butterfly*
Jarmila Novotná** (Cio-Cio-
San), Herta Glaz (Suzuki);
Michael Bartlett (Pinkerton),
Julius Huehn/George
Cehanovsky (Sharpless)
Gennaro Papi
Oct. 18, Nov. 3m (student
performance)

Wagner, *Tristan und Isolde*
Kirsten Flagstad (Isolde),
(10/20) Kathryn
Meisle/Herta Glaz
(Brangäne); Lauritz
Melchior (Tristan),
Julius Huehn/(11/10)
Fred Destal (Kurwenal),

Alexander Kipnis (King
Marke)
Edwin McArthur
Oct. 20, Nov. 2
Nov. 10 (Los Angeles)

Leoncavallo, *Pagliacci*
Charlotte Boerner (Nedda);
George Stinson (Canio),
Richard Bonelli (Tonio),
George Cehanovsky (Silvio)
Gaetano Merola
and
Mascagni,
Cavalleria Rusticana
Dusolina Giannini (Santuzza);
Frederick Jagel (Turiddu),
George Cehanovsky (Alfio)
Gennaro Papi
Oct. 21

Verdi, *Rigoletto*
Lily Pons (Gilda), (10/23)
Herta Glaz/Sandra
Gahle (Maddalena);
Lawrence Tibbett (Rigoletto),
Frederick Jagel (Duke),
Norman Cordon (Sparafucile)
Gennaro Papi
Oct. 23, 29m
Nov. 6 (Los Angeles)

Donizetti,
Lucia di Lammermoor
Lily Pons (Lucia);
Tito Schipa (Edgardo),
Stefan Ballarini (Enrico),
Norman Cordon (Raimondo)
Gennaro Papi
Oct. 25

Verdi, *Otello*
Elisabeth Rethberg
(Desdemona); Giovanni
Martinelli (Otello),
Lawrence Tibbett (Iago)
Gaetano Merola
Oct. 27
Nov. 9 (Los Angeles)

Verdi, *La Traviata*
Jarmila Novotná (Violetta);
Nino Martini (Alfredo),
Lawrence Tibbett (Germont)
Gaetano Merola
Oct. 30

Leoncavallo, *Pagliacci*
Charlotte Boerner (Nedda);
George Stinson (Canio),
Richard Bonelli (Tonio),
George Cehanovsky (Silvio)
Gaetano Merola
and
Delibes, *Coppélia* (Ballet)
Janet Reed
(Swanilda/Coppélia),
Willam Christensen (Frantz)
Willem Van Den Burg
Oct. 31

Rossini,
Il Barbiere di Siviglia
Lily Pons (Rosina);
Richard Bonelli (Figaro),
Nino Martini (Almaviva),
Norman Cordon (Basilio),

Louis D'Angelo (Bartolo)
Gennaro Papi
Nov. 1
Nov. 8 (Pasadena)

Beethoven, *Fidelio*
Kirsten Flagstad (Leonore),
Charlotte Boerner
(Marzelline); Lauritz
Melchior (Florestan),
Fred Destal (Pizarro),
Alexander Kipnis (Rocco)
Erich Leinsdorf
Nov. 3

Verdi, *Il Trovatore*
Elisabeth Rethberg
(Leonora), Kathryn
Meisle (Azucena); Giovanni
Martinelli (Manrico), Richard
Bonelli (Count Di Luna)
Gennaro Papi
Nov. 4

1940

Mozart, *Le Nozze di Figaro*
Bidú Sayão (Susanna),
Elisabeth Rethberg
(Countess), Risë
Stevens (Cherubino);
Ezio Pinza (Figaro),
John Brownlee (Count)
Erich Leinsdorf
Oct. 12
Nov. 8 (Los Angeles)

Delibes, *Lakmé*
Lily Pons (Lakmé),
Irra Petina (Mallika); Raoul
Jobin (Gerald), Alexander
Kipnis (Nilakantha), George
Cehanovsky (Frederic)
Gaetano Merola
Oct. 14, 20m

Strauss, *Der Rosenkavalier*
Risë Stevens (Octavian),
Lotte Lehmann
(Marschallin), Margit Bokor
(Sophie); Alexander Kipnis
(Baron Ochs), Francisco
Naya (Italian Singer),
Walter Olitzki (Faninal)
Erich Leinsdorf
Oct. 16, 27m
Nov. 9 (Los Angeles)

Puccini, *La Bohème*
Bidú Sayão (Mimi),
Margit Bokor (Musetta);
Jussi Bjoerling (Rodolfo),
John Brownlee (Marcello),
Ezio Pinza (Colline)
Gennaro Papi
Oct. 18, 29

Mozart, *Don Giovanni*
Elisabeth Rethberg (Donna
Anna), Elsa Zebranska
(Donna Elvira), Margit
Bokor (Zerlina); Ezio
Pinza (Giovanni), Alessio
De Paolis (Ottavio),
Alexander Kipnis (Leporello)
Erich Leinsdorf
Oct. 21
Nov. 4 (Los Angeles)

Verdi,
Un Ballo in Maschera
Elisabeth Rethberg (Amelia),
Suzanne Sten (Ulrica),
Margit Bokor (Oscar);
Jussi Bjoerling (Riccardo),
Richard Bonelli (Renato)
Gennaro Papi
Oct. 23
Nov. 4 (Los Angeles)

Bizet, *Carmen*
Marjorie Lawrence (Carmen),
Verna Osborne (Micaëla);
Raoul Jobin (Don José),
Ezio Pinza (Escamillo)
Gaetano Merola
Oct. 25, Nov. 2

Verdi, *Rigoletto*
Lily Pons (Gilda),
Alice Avakian (Maddalena);
Robert Weede (Rigoletto),
Francisco Naya (Duke),
Lorenzo Alvary (Sparafucile)
Gennaro Papi
Oct. 28

Verdi, *Aida*
Elisabeth Rethberg (Aida),
Suzanne Sten (Amneris);
Frederick Jagel (Radames),
Robert Weede (Amonasro)
Gennaro Papi
Oct. 30

Massenet, *Manon*
Bidú Sayão (Manon),
Tito Schipa (des Grieux),
John Brownlee (Lescaut)
Gaetano Merola
Nov. 1
Nov. 5 (Pasadena)

Donizetti,
Lucia di Lammermoor
Lily Pons (Lucia);
Tito Schipa (Edgardo),
Richard Bonelli (Enrico),
Lorenzo Alvary (Raimondo)
Gennaro Papi
Nov. 7 (Los Angeles)

1941

Massenet, *Manon*
Grace Moore (Manon);
Raoul Jobin (des Grieux),
John Brownlee (Lescaut)
Gaetano Merola
Oct. 2 (Portland)
Oct. 6 (Seattle)

Wagner, *Tannhäuser*
Stella Roman (Elisabeth),
Karin Branzell (Venus);
Lauritz Melchior
(Tannhäuser), Julius
Huehn (Wolfram), (10/3, 8)
Lorenzo Alvary/Alexander
Kipnis (Hermann)
Erich Leinsdorf
Oct. 3 (Portland)
Oct. 8 (Seattle)
Oct. 24, 30
Nov. 9m (Los Angeles)

Verdi, *Rigoletto*
Bidú Sayão/(10/19)
Lily Pons (Gilda),
Irra Petina (Maddalena);
Lawrence Tibbett (Rigoletto),
Jan Peerce (Duke),
Lorenzo Alvary (Sparafucile)
Gennaro Papi
Oct. 4 (Portland)
Oct. 7 (Seattle)
Oct. 11 (Sacramento)
Oct. 19m
Nov. 5 (Pasadena)

Donizetti, *Don Pasquale*
Bidú Sayão (Norina);
Salvatore Baccaloni
(Pasquale), Franco
Perulli (Ernesto), John
Brownlee (Malatesta)
Gennaro Papi
Oct. 13

Strauss, *Der Rosenkavalier*
Risë Stevens (Octavian),
Lotte Lehmann
(Marschallin), Margit
Bokor (Sophie); Alexander
Kipnis (Baron Ochs),
Leslie George/Anthony
Marlowe (Italian Tenor),
Walter Olitzki (Faninal)
Erich Leinsdorf
Oct. 14
Nov. 6 (Los Angeles)

Donizetti,
La Fille du Régiment
Lily Pons (Marie),
Irra Petina (Marquise);
Raoul Jobin (Tonio),
Salvatore Baccaloni (Sulpice)
Gennaro Papi
Oct. 16, 28
Nov. 4 (Los Angeles)

Puccini, *Tosca*
Stella Roman (Tosca);
Charles Kullman
(Cavaradossi), John
Brownlee (Scarpia)
Gaetano Merola
Oct. 18

Puccini, *Madama Butterfly*
Licia Albanese (Cio-Cio-San),
Irra Petina (Suzuki);
Frederick Jagel (Pinkerton),
John Brownlee (Sharpless)
Gennaro Papi
Oct. 20, 23
Oct. 25 (Sacramento)

Rossini,
Il Barbiere di Siviglia
Bidú Sayão (Rosina);
Lawrence Tibbett (Figaro),
Franco Perulli (Almaviva),
Ezio Pinza (Basilio),
Salvatore Baccaloni (Bartolo)
Gaetano Merola
Oct. 22
Nov. 8 (Los Angeles)

Bizet, *Carmen*
Gladys Swarthout (Carmen),
Licia Albanese (Micaëla);

Raoul Jobin (Don José),
Ribert Weede (Escamillo)
Erich Leinsdorf
Oct. 27

Montemezzi,
L'Amore dei Tre Re
Grace Moore (Fiora),
Charles Kullman (Avito),
Robert Weede (Manfredo),
Ezio Pinza (Archibaldo)
Italo Montemezzi
Oct. 29
Nov. 7 (Los Angeles)

Verdi, *Simon Boccanegra*
Stella Roman (Amelia);
Lawrence Tibbett (Simon),
Frederick Jagel (Gabriele),
Ezio Pinza (Fiesco)
Erich Leinsdorf
Nov. 1
Nov. 3 (Los Angeles)

1942

Verdi, *Aida*
Stella Roman (Aida),
Bruna Castagna (Amneris);
Frederick Jagel (Radames),
Robert Weede (Amonasro)
Gaetano Merola
Oct. 9, 25m
Nov. 7 (Los Angeles)

Verdi, *La Traviata*
Bidú Sayão (Violetta);
Jan Peerce (Alfredo),
Richard Bonelli (Germont)
Fausto Cleva
Oct. 10 (Sacramento)
Oct. 14
Nov. 2 (Los Angeles)

Donizetti,
La Fille du Régiment
Lily Pons (Marie),
Irra Petina (Marquise);
Raoul Jobin (Tonio),
Salvatore Baccaloni (Sulpice)
Pietro Cimara
Oct. 12, 22

Smetana,
The Bartered Bride
Josephine Antoine (Marie);
Charles Kullman (Jenik),
Marek Windheim (Vashek),
Douglas Beattie (Kezal)
Walter Herbert
Oct. 16

Donizetti,
Lucia di Lammermoor
Lily Pons (Lucia); Jan Peerce
(Edgardo), Richard Bonelli
(Enrico), Lorenzo Alvary
(Raimondo)
Pietro Cimara
Oct. 18m

Bizet, *Carmen*
Irra Petina (Carmen),
Licia Albanese (Micaëla);
Raoul Jobin (Don José),
John Brownlee/(10/24)
Ezio Pinza (Escamillo)

Gaetano Merola/(10/24)
Fausto Cleva
Oct. 19
Oct. 24 (Sacramento)
Nov. 4 (Los Angeles)

Gounod, *Faust*
Licia Albanese (Marguerite),
Verna Osborne (Siebel);
Charles Kullman (Faust),
John Brownlee (Valentin),
Ezio Pinza (Méphistophélès)
Fausto Cleva
Oct. 21, 31

Montemezzi,
L'Amore dei Tre Re
Jean Tennyson (Fiora);
Charles Kullman (Avito),
Robert Weede (Manfredo),
Ezio Pinza (Archibaldo)
Italo Montemezzi
Oct. 23

Strauss, Johann Jr.,
The Bat (Die Fledermaus)
Margit Bokor (Rosalinda),
Josephine Antoine (Adele),
Irra Petina (Orlofsky); Marek
Windheim (Eisenstein),
Robert Marshall (Alfred),
John Brownlee (Falke)
Walter Herbert
Oct. 26
Nov. 6 (Los Angeles)

Rossini,
Il Barbiere di Siviglia
Bidú Sayão (Rosina);
John Brownlee (Figaro),
Charles Kullman (Almaviva),
Ezio Pinza (Basilio),
Salvatore Baccaloni (Bartolo)
Fausto Cleva
Oct. 27

Verdi,
Un Ballo in Maschera
Stella Roman (Amelia),
Bruna Castagna (Ulrica),
Margit Bokor (Oscar);
Frederick Jagel (Riccardo),
Richard Bonelli (Renato)
Fausto Cleva
Oct. 28

Rimsky-Korsakov,
The Golden Cockerel
Josephine Antoine (Queen of
Shemakha), Thelma Votipka
(Voice of the Cockerel);
Salvatore Baccaloni
(King Dodon), Alessio
De Paolis (Astrologer),
Paul Walti (Prince)
Gaetano Merola
Oct. 30

1943

Saint-Saëns,
Samson et Dalila
Kerstin Thorborg (Dalila);
Raoul Jobin (Samson),
Leonard Warren (Priest)
Gaetano Merola
Oct. 7, 26

Verdi, *La Traviata*
Licia Albanese (Violetta);
Charles Kullman (Alfredo),
Francesco Valentino
(Germont)
Fausto Cleva
Oct. 10m

Verdi,
La Forza del Destino
Zinka Milanov/(11/6)
Dusolina Giannini (Leonora),
Irra Petina/(11/6)
Christine Johnson
(Preziosilla); Frederick
Jagel/(10/17) Kurt Baum
(Don Alvaro), Leonard
Warren (Don Carlo), Ezio
Pinza (Padre Guardiano)
Gaetano Merola
Oct. 11, 17m
Nov. 6 (Los Angeles)

Mascagni,
Cavalleria Rusticana
Dusolina Giannini (Santuzza),
Charles Kullman/
Kurt Baum (Turiddu),
George Cehanovsky (Alfio)
Kurt Herbert Adler
and
Leoncavallo, *Pagliacci*
Licia Albanese (Nedda);
Raoul Jobin (Canio),
John Charles Thomas/
Robert Weede (Tonio),
Francesco Valentino (Silvio)
Pietro Cimara
Oct. 13, 30

Puccini, *The Girl of
the Golden West*
Florence Kirk (Minnie);
Frederick Jagel (Johnson),
Robert Weede (Rance)
Fausto Cleva
Oct. 9 (Sacramento)
Oct. 15, 24m
Nov. 3 (Los Angeles)

Donizetti,
Lucia di Lammermoor
Lily Pons (Lucia);
Jan Peerce (Edgardo),
Leonard Warren/
Ivan Petroff (Enrico),
Lorenzo Alvary (Raimondo)
Pietro Cimara
Oct. 18
Nov. 1 (Los Angeles)

Puccini, *La Bohème*
Licia Albanese (Mimi);
Charles Kullman/(11/7)
Frederick Jagel (Rodolfo),
Francesco Valentino
(Marcello), Ezio
Pinza/(10/24) Roberto
Silva (Colline)
Gaetano Merola
Oct. 20, 24m
Oct. 23 (Sacramento)
Nov. 7 (Los Angeles)

Verdi, *Il Trovatore*
Zinka Milanov (Leonora),
Kerstin Thorborg (Azucena);

Kurt Baum (Manrico), Robert
Weede (Count Di Luna)
Fausto Cleva
Oct. 22
Nov. 4 (Pasadena)

Bizet, *Carmen*
Irra Petina (Carmen),
Irma Gonzales (Micaëla);
Raoul Jobin (Don José),
Ezio Pinza (Escamillo)
Thomas Beecham
Oct. 24

Verdi, *Rigoletto*
Lily Pons (Gilda), Christine
Johnson (Maddalena);
(10/25) Ivan Petroff/John
Charles Thomas (Rigoletto),
Jan Peerce (Duke),
Lorenzo Alvary/(11/1)
Roberto Silva (Sparafucile)
Pietro Cimara
Oct. 25, 28
Nov. 1 (Los Angeles)

Mozart, *Don Giovanni*
Zinka Milanov (Donna
Anna), Florence Kirk
(Donna Elvira),
Licia Albanese (Zerlina);
Ezio Pinza (Giovanni),
Charles Kullman (Ottavio),
Salvatore Baccaloni
(Leporello)
Thomas Beecham
Oct. 27

Donizetti, *Don Pasquale*
Licia Albanese (Norina);
Salvatore Baccaloni
(Pasquale), John
Garris (Ernesto),
Ivan Petroff (Malatesta)
Pietro Cimara
Oct. 29

1944

Verdi, *Aida*
Stella Roman (Aida),
Margaret Harshaw
(Amneris); Frederick
Jagel (Radames), Leonard
Warren (Amonasro)
Gaetano Merola
Sept. 29, 15m

Verdi,
La Forza del Destino
Stella Roman (Leonora),
Herta Glaz (Preziosilla);
Frederick Jagel (Don Alvaro),
Leonard Warren (Don Carlo),
Ezio Pinza (Padre
Guardiano)
Gaetano Merola
Oct. 1m
Oct. 7 (Sacramento)
Nov. 2 (Los Angeles)

Flotow, *Martha* (in Italian)
Licia Albanese (Lady
Harriet), Herta Glaz (Nancy);
Bruno Landi (Lionel),
Lorenzo Alvary (Plunkett)
Gaetano Merola/Karl Riedel
Oct. 3, 8m

Puccini, *La Bohème*
Licia Albanese (Mimi),
Virginia MacWatters
(Musetta); Charles
Kullman (Rodolfo),
Francesco Valentino
(Marcello),
Ezio Pinza (Colline)
Gaetano Merola
Oct. 5
Oct. 31 (Pasadena)

Delibes, *Lakmé*
Lily Pons (Lakmé), Herta
Glaz (Mallika); Raoul
Jobin (Gerald), Roberto
Silva (Nilakantha), George
Cehanovsky (Frederic)
Pietro Cimara
Oct. 6
Oct. 14 (Sacramento)
Oct. 30 (Los Angeles)

Massenet, *Manon*
Licia Albanese (Manon);
Charles Kullman (des
Grieux), Francesco
Valentino (Lescaut)
Pietro Cimara
Oct. 10, 22m

Donizetti,
Lucia di Lammermoor
Lily Pons (Lucia);
Jan Peerce (Edgardo),
Ivan Petroff (Enrico),
Lorenzo Alvary (Raimondo)
Pietro Cimara
Oct. 11
Oct. 23 (San Jose)
Nov. 3 (Los Angeles)

Wolf-Ferrari,
The Secret of Suzanne
(Il Segreto di Susanna)
Virginia MacWatters
(Suzanne);
Hugh Thompson (Count Gil)
Kurt Herbert Adler
and
Strauss, *Salome*
Lili Djanel (Salome),
Margaret Harshaw
(Herodias); Frederick
Jagel (Herod),
John Shafer (Jokanaan)
Georges Sebastian
Oct. 13, 19

Verdi, *Falstaff*
Vivian Della Chiesa (Alice),
Licia Albanese (Nannetta),
Margaret Harshaw (Quickly),
Herta Glaz (Meg);
Salvatore Baccaloni
(Falstaff), Bruno
Landi (Fenton),
Ivan Petroff (Ford)
William Steinberg
Oct. 16, 26
Nov. 4 (Los Angeles)

Verdi, *Rigoletto*
Lily Pons (Gilda),
Herta Glaz (Maddalena);
Leonard Warren (Rigoletto),
Jan Peerce (Duke),

Roberto Silva (Sparafucile)
Pietro Cimara
  Oct. 17

Gounod, *Faust*
Vivian Della Chiesa (Marguerite), Herta Glaz (Siebel); Raoul Jobin (Faust), Leonard Warren (Valentin), Ezio Pinza (Méphistophélès) William Steinberg
  Oct. 18
  Oct. 21 (Sacramento)

Verdi, *Un Ballo in Maschera*
Stella Roman (Amelia), Margaret Harshaw (Ulrica), Virginia MacWatters (Oscar); Jan Peerce (Riccardo), Leonard Warren (Renato) William Steinberg
  Oct. 20

Offenbach, *Les Contes d'Hoffmann*
Virginia MacWatters (Olympia), Licia Albanese (Antonia), Lily Djanel (Giulietta), Herta Glaz (Nicklausse); Raoul Jobin (Hoffmann), Ezio Pinza (Coppélius, Dr. Miracle), Francesco Valentino (Dapertutto) Gaetano Merola
  Oct. 24, 28
  Nov. 5m (Los Angeles)

Bizet, *Carmen*
Risë Stevens (Carmen), Virginia MacWatters (Micaëla); Charles Kullman (Don José), Francesco Valentino (Escamillo) Georges Sebastian
  Oct. 27
  Nov. 1 (Los Angeles)

1945

Bizet, *Carmen*
Risë Stevens (Carmen), Eleanor Steber/(11/10) Nadine Conner (Micaëla); Raoul Jobin (Don José), Mack Harrell (Escamillo) Gaetano Merola
  Sept. 25, Oct. 11
  Nov. 10 (Los Angeles)

Puccini, *La Bohème*
Licia Albanese/(10/24) Vivian Della Chiesa/(11/9) Dorothy Kirsten (Mimì), Nadine Conner (Musetta); Charles Kullman/(11/9) Jussi Bjoerling (Rodolfo), (9/28)Mack Harrell/ Francesco Valentino (Marcello), Ezio Pinza/(11/9) Lorenzo Alvary (Colline) Gaetano Merola
  Sept. 28, Oct. 24
  Oct. 8 (San Jose)
  Nov. 9 (Los Angeles)

Verdi, *La Traviata*
Licia Albanese/(11/11) Nadine Conner (Violetta); Charles Kullman (Alfredo), Francesco Valentino (Germont) Gaetano Merola/(10/17) Pietro Cimara
  Sept. 30m, Oct. 17
  Nov. 11m (Los Angeles)

Strauss, *Der Rosenkavalier*
Risë Stevens (Octavian), Lotte Lehmann (Marschallin), Eleanor Steber/(10/18) Nadine Conner (Sophie); Lorenzo Alvary (Baron Ochs), Bruno Landi (Italian Singer), Walter Olitzki (Faninal) Georges Sebastian
  Oct. 2, 18
  Oct. 6 (Sacramento)

Offenbach, *Les Contes d'Hoffmann*
Evelynn Corvello (Olympia), Licia Albanese (Antonia), Lily Djanel (Giulietta), Herta Glaz (Nicklausse); Raoul Jobin (Hoffmann), Ezio Pinza (Coppélius, Dr. Miracle), Francesco Valentino/Mack Harrell (Dapertutto) Gaetano Merola
  Oct. 4
  Oct. 30 (Pasadena)

Wagner, *Tristan und Isolde*
Helen Traubel (Isolde), (10/5) Herta Glaz/Margaret Harshaw (Brangäne); Lauritz Melchior (Tristan), Herbert Janssen (Kurwenal), Lorenzo Alvary (King Marke) William Steinberg
  Oct. 5, 14m
  Oct. 29 (Los Angeles)

Mascagni, *Cavalleria Rusticana*
Vivian Della Chiesa (Santuzza); Charles Kullman (Turiddu), Ivan Petroff (Alfio) Kurt Herbert Adler
  and
Leoncavallo, *Pagliacci*
Licia Albanese/ Nadine Conner (Nedda); Raoul Jobin (Canio), Francesco Valentino (Tonio), Mack Harrell (Silvio) Kurt Herbert Adler
  Oct. 7m
  Nov. 6 (Pasadena)

Wagner, *Die Walküre*
Helen Traubel (Brünnhilde), Lily Djanel (Sieglinde), Margaret Harshaw (Fricka); Lauritz Melchior (Siegmund), Herbert Janssen (Wotan),

Lorenzo Alvary (Hunding) William Steinberg
  Oct. 9
  Nov. 3 (Los Angeles)

Mussorgsky, *Boris Godunov* (in Italian)
Vivian Della Chiesa (Marina); Ezio Pinza (Boris), Frederick Jagel (Dimitri), Lorenzo Alvary (Pimen), Alessio de Paolis (Shuisky) Georges Sebastian
  Oct. 12, 22
  Nov. 5 (Los Angeles)

Mozart, *Don Giovanni*
Stella Roman (Donna Anna), Vivian Della Chiesa/Eleanor Steber (Donna Elvira), Licia Albanese/Nadine Conner (Zerlina); Ezio Pinza (Giovanni), Bruno Landi (Ottavio), Salvatore Baccaloni (Leporello) William Steinberg
  Oct. 16, 25

Donizetti, *Lucia di Lammermoor*
Lily Pons (Lucia); Jan Peerce (Edgardo), Ivan Petroff (Enrico), Lorenzo Alvary (Raimondo) Pietro Cimara
  Oct. 13 (Sacramento)
  Oct. 19
  Nov. 4m (Los Angeles)

Rossini, *Il Barbiere di Siviglia*
Hilde Reggiani (Rosina), Francesco Valentino (Figaro), Bruno Landi (Almaviva), Ezio Pinza (Basilio), Salvatore Baccaloni (Bartolo) Pietro Cimara
  Oct. 21m
  Oct. 31 (Los Angeles)

Ravel, *L'Heure Espagnole*
Licia Albanese (Concepcion); John Garris (Gonzalve), Mack Harrell (Ramiro), Salvatore Baccaloni (Inigo Gomez) Gaetano Merola
  and
Strauss, *Salome*
Lily Djanel (Salome), Margaret Harshaw (Herodias); Frederick Jagel (Herod), Herbert Janssen (Jokanaan) Georges Sebastian
  Oct. 23
  Nov. 1 (Los Angeles)

Verdi, *Rigoletto*
Lily Pons (Gilda), Herta Glaz (Maddalena); Ivan Petroff (Rigoletto), Jan Peerce (Duke), Lorenzo Alvary (Sparafucile) Pietro Cimara
  Oct. 26
  Nov. 7 (Los Angeles)

Verdi, *Aida*
Stella Roman (Aida), Margaret Harshaw (Amneris); Frederick Jagel (Radames), Ivan Petroff (Amonasro) Gaetano Merola/(10/27) Karl Kritz
  Oct. 20 (Sacramento)
  Oct. 27
  Nov. 2 (Los Angeles)

1946

Wagner, *Lohengrin*
Astrid Varnay (Elsa), Margaret Harshaw (Ortrud); Set Svanholm (Lohengrin), George Czaplicki (Telramund), Nicola Moscona (Heinrich) William Steinberg
  Sept. 9 (Portland)
  Sept. 14 (Seattle)
  Sept. 17, Oct. 2
  Sept. 28 (Sacramento)
  Oct. 23 (Los Angeles)

Bizet, *Carmen*
Lily Djanel (Carmen), Nadine Conner (Micaëla); Raoul Jobin (Don José), George Czaplicki/(9/12) Mack Harrell (Escamillo) Paul Breisach
  Sept. 7 (Portland)
  Sept. 12 (Seattle)
  Sept. 19

Lily Djanel (Carmen), Florence George/(11/2) Nadine Conner (Micaëla); Raoul Jobin/(11/2) Charles Kullman (Don José), Mack Harrell/(11/2) George Czaplicki (Escamillo) Paul Breisach
  Sept. 29m
  Nov. 2 (Los Angeles)

Verdi, *La Traviata*
Licia Albanese (Violetta); Charles Kullman/ Jan Peerce (Alfredo), Francesco Valentino (Germont) Pietro Cimara/ Gaetano Merola
  Sept. 8m (Portland)
  Sept. 13 (Seattle)

Licia Albanese/(10/31) Bidú Sayão (Violetta); Jan Peerce (Alfredo), Francesco Valentino/(9/30) Mack Harrell (Germont) Gaetano Merola/(10/31) Paul Breisach
  Sept. 20, 30
  Oct. 31 (Pasadena)

Donizetti, *Don Pasquale*
Licia Albanese (Norina); Salvatore Baccaloni (Pasquale), John Garris (Ernesto),

John Brownlee (Malatesta) Karl Kritz
  Sept. 22m

Gounod, *Roméo et Juliette*
Bidú Sayão (Juliette); Raoul Jobin/(11/3) Jussi Bjoerling (Roméo), John Brownlee/(10/12) George Cehanovsky (Mercutio), Nicola Moscona/(11/3) Lorenzo Alvary (Laurence) Paul Breisach
  Sept. 24
  Oct. 12 (Sacramento)
  Nov. 3 (Los Angeles)

Puccini, *La Bohème*
Dorothy Kirsten (Mimì), Maria Sa Earp ** (Musetta); Charles Kullman (Rodolfo), Francesco Valentino (Marcello), Ezio Pinza (Colline) Gaetano Merola/ Pietro Cimara
  Sept. 10 (Portland)
  Sept. 15m (Seattle)

Bidú Sayão/(10/14) Stella Roman (Mimì), Maria Sa Earp (Musetta); (9/26) Charles Kullman/Jussi Bjoerling (Rodolfo), (9/26) Francesco Valentino/ Mack Harrell (Marcello), (9/26) Ezio Pinza/ Nicola Moscona (Colline) Gaetano Merola/(10/14) Pietro Cimara
  Sept. 26
  Oct. 14
  Oct. 29 (Los Angeles)

Mussorgsky, *Boris Godunov* (in Italian)
Herta Glaz (Marina); Ezio Pinza (Boris), Mario Berini (Dimitri), Lorenzo Alvary (Pimen), Alessio De Paolis (Shuisky) Georges Sebastian
  Sept. 27, Oct. 7
  Oct. 5 (Sacramento)
  Oct. 21 (Los Angeles)

Delibes, *Lakmé*
Lily Pons (Lakmé, Herta Glaz (Mallika); Raoul Jobin (Gerald), Nicola Moscona (Nilakantha), George Cehanovsky (Frederic) Pietro Cimara
  Oct. 1, 6m
  Oct. 22 (Los Angeles)

Verdi, *La Forza del Destino*
Stella Roman (Leonora), Herta Glaz (Preziosilla); Kurt Baum (Don Alvaro), Francesco Valentino (Don Carlo), Ezio Pinza (Padre Guardiano) Gaetano Merola/Karl Kritz
  Oct. 3
  Oct. 28 (Los Angeles)

Strauss, *Der Rosenkavalier*
Jarmila Novotná (Octavian), Lotte Lehmann (Marschallin), Nadine Conner (Sophie); Lorenzo Alvary (Ochs), Kurt Baum/Kayton Nesbitt (Italian Singer), Walter Olitzki (Faninal) Georges Sebastian
  Oct. 8, 13m
  Nov. 1 (Los Angeles)

Donizetti, *Lucia di Lammermoor*
Lily Pons (Lucia); Jan Peerce (Edgardo), Ivan Petroff (Enrico), Lorenzo Alvary (Raimondo) Pietro Cimara
  Oct. 10

Beethoven, *Fidelio*
Regina Resnik (Leonore), Nadine Conner (Marzelline); Mario Berini (Florestan), Kenneth Schon (Pizarro), Lorenzo Alvary (Rocco) Paul Breisach
  Oct. 11, 17

Puccini, *Madama Butterfly*
Licia Albanese (Cio-Cio-San), Herta Glaz (Suzuki); Charles Kullman (Pinkerton), John Brownlee (Sharpless) Gaetano Merola
  Oct. 15, 20m
  Oct. 24 (Pasadena)
  Oct. 30 (Los Angeles)

Verdi, *Il Trovatore*
Stella Roman (Leonora), Margaret Harshaw (Azucena); Jussi Bjoerling (Manrico), Francesco Valentino (Count Di Luna) Kurt Herbert Adler
  Oct. 16
  Oct. 26 (Los Angeles)

Mozart, *Le Nozze di Figaro*
Bidú Sayão (Susanna), Stella Roman (Countess), Jarmila Novotná (Cherubino); Ezio Pinza (Figaro), John Brownlee (Count) William Steinberg
  Oct. 18
  Oct. 25 (Los Angeles)

Verdi, *Rigoletto*
Lily Pons (Gilda), Eleanor Knapp (Maddalena); Lawrence Tibbett (Rigoletto), Jan Peerce (Duke), Lorenzo Alvary (Sparafucile) Pietro Cimara
  Oct. 19
  Oct. 27m (Los Angeles)

1947

Verdi, *Aida*
Stella Roman (Aida), Blanche Thebom/(10/25) Margaret Harshaw (Amneris); Kurt Baum (Radames), Robert Weede/(9/25) Leonard

Warren (Amonasro) Paul Breisach
  Sept. 8 (Seattle
  Sept. 11 (Portland)
  Sept. 25
  Oct. 25 (Los Angeles)

Puccini, *Madama Butterfly*
Licia Albanese (Cio-Cio-San), Herta Glaz (Suzuki), Jan Peerce (Pinkerton), Giuseppe Valdengo/Francesco Valentino (Sharpless) Pietro Cimara
  Sept. 9 (Seattle)
  Sept. 22

Licia Albanese (Cio-Cio-San), Herta Glaz (Suzuki), Charles Kullman (Pinkerton), Francesco Valentino/Giuseppe Valdengo (Sharpless) Pietro Cimara
  Oct. 18
  Oct. 27 (Los Angeles)

Gounod, *Faust*
Florence Quartararo/ Nadine Conner (Marguerite), Herta Glaz (Siebel); Raoul Jobin (Faust), Giuseppe Valdengo (Valentin), Ezio Pinza (Méphistophélès) Gaetano Merola
  Sept. 10 (Seattle)
  Sept. 13 (Portland)

Claudia Pinza (Marguerite), Herta Glaz (Siebel); Raoul Jobin (Faust), Giuseppe Valdengo/ Robert Weede (Valentin), Ezio Pinza (Méphistophélès) Wilfred Pelletier
  Sept 21m, Oct. 6

Claudia Pinza (Marguerite), Herta Glaz (Siebel); Raoul Jobin (Faust), Martial Singher (Valentin), Ezio Pinza (Méphistophélès) Wilfred Pelletier
  Oct. 30 (Pasadena)

Verdi, *La Traviata*
Licia Albanese (Violetta); Jan Peerce/Charles Kullman (Alfredo), Leonard Warren (Germont) Gaetano Merola/ Kurt Herbert Adler
  Sept. 16, Oct. 4m

Gounod, *Roméo et Juliette*
Bidú Sayão (Juliette); Raoul Jobin (Roméo), Martial Singher (Mercutio), Nicola Moscona (Laurence) Wilfred Pelletier
  Sept. 18, 24

Mozart, *Don Giovanni*
Stella Roman (Anna), Florence Quartararo/ Regina Resnik (Elvira), Licia Albanese/Nadine Conner (Zerlina); Ezio Pinza (Giovanni),

Charles Kullman (Ottavio), Salvatore Baccaloni (Leporello) Paul Breisach
Sept. 19, Oct. 8

Stella Roman/ Regina Resnik (Anna), Florence Quartararo/ Claudia Pinza (Elvira), Nadine Conner (Zerlina); Ezio Pinza (Giovanni), Charles Kullman (Ottavio), Salvatore Baccaloni (Leporello) Paul Breisach
Sept. 27 (Sacramento)
Nov. 1 (Los Angeles)

Wagner, *Götterdämmerung*
Helen Traubel (Brünnhilde), Regina Resnik (Gutrune); Set Svanholm (Siegfried), Lorenzo Alvary (Hagen) William Steinberg
Sept. 26, Oct. 9
Oct. 23 (Los Angeles)

Puccini, *La Bohème*
Bidú Sayão (Mimì), Lois Hartzell (Musetta); Jan Peerce (Rodolfo), Francesco Valentino/ (10/29) Giuseppe Valdengo (Marcello), Nicola Moscona/(10/15) Virgilio Lazzari (Colline) Gaetano Merola
Sept. 28m
Oct. 15
Oct. 29 (Los Angeles)

Ponchielli, *La Gioconda*
Stella Roman/(10/16) Regina Resnik (Gioconda), Blanche Thebom (Laura), Margaret Harshaw (La Cieca); Kurt Baum (Enzo), Leonard Warren (Barnaba), Nicola Moscona (Alvise) Dick Marzollo
Sept. 30
Oct. 16
Oct. 20 (Los Angeles)

Wagner, *Tristan und Isolde*
Helen Traubel (Isolde), Blanche Thebom/ Margaret Harshaw/ Herta Glaz (Brangäne); Set Svanholm (Tristan), George Czaplicki (Kurwenal), Lorenzo Alvary (King Marke) William Steinberg
Oct. 2, 13
Nov. 2m (Los Angeles)

Charpentier, *Louise*
Dorothy Kirsten (Louise), Claramae Turner (Mother); Raoul Jobin (Julien), Ezio Pinza (Father) Paul Breisach
Oct. 3, 19m
Oct. 11 (Sacramento)
Oct. 28 (Los Angeles)

Mozart, *Le Nozze di Figaro*
Bidú Sayão (Susanna), Florence Quartararo (Countess), Blanche Thebom/ Herta Glaz (Cherubino); Ezio Pinza (Figaro), Martial Singher (Count) William Steinberg
Oct. 5m
Oct. 22 (Los Angeles)

Verdi, *Otello*
Licia Albanese (Desdemona); Set Svanholm (Otello), Lawrence Tibbett (Iago) William Steinberg
Oct. 7
Oct. 31 (Los Angeles)

Debussy, *Pelléas et Mélisande*
Bidú Sayão (Mélisande), Margaret Harshaw (Geneviève); Martial Singher (Pelléas), Lawrence Tibbett (Golaud), Lorenzo Alvary (Arkel) Wilfred Pelletier
Oct. 10

Verdi, *Rigoletto*
Nadine Conner (Gilda), Claramae Turner (Maddalena); Lawrence Tibbett (Rigoletto), Jan Peerce (Duke), Virgilio Lazzari (Sparafucile) Pietro Cimara
Sept. 20 (San Jose)

Lily Pons (Gilda), Herta Glaz/Claramae Turner (Maddalena); Lawrence Tibbett (Rigoletto), Jan Peerce (Duke), Virgilio Lazzari (Sparafucile) Pietro Cimara
Oct. 12m
Oct. 26m (Los Angeles)

Montemezzi, *L'Amore dei Tre Re*
Dorothy Kirsten (Fiora), Charles Kullman (Avito), Robert Weede (Manfredo), Ezio Pinza (Archibaldo) Italo Montemezzi
Oct. 14
Oct. 24 (Los Angeles)

Donizetti, *Lucia di Lammermoor*
Josephine Tumminia/ Lily Pons (Lucia); Jan Peerce (Edgardo), Francesco Valentino (Enrico), Virgilio Lazzari/Lorenzo Alvary (Raimondo) Pietro Cimara
Oct. 17
Oct. 21 (Los Angeles)

Verdi, *Falstaff*
Regina Resnik (Alice), Licia Albanese/(10/7) Dorothy Warenskjold (Nannetta), Ebe Stignani/ (10/7) Cloe Elmo (Quickly), Herta Glaz (Meg); Salvatore Baccaloni (Falstaff), Max Lichtegg** (Fenton), Robert Weede (Ford) William Steinberg
Sept. 14, Oct. 7
Oct. 19 (Los Angeles)

Verdi, *La Traviata*
(9/16) Licia Albanese/ Dorothy Kirsten (Violetta); Jan Peerce/(10/15) Ferruccio Tagliavini (Alfredo), Giuseppe Valdengo/(10/15) Robert Weede (Germont) Pietro Cimara
Sept. 16, Oct. 15
Oct. 22 (Los Angeles)

Massenet, *Manon*
Bidú Sayão (Manon); Raoul Jobin (des Grieux), Francesco Valentino (Lescaut) Paul Breisach
Sept. 17, Oct. 4
Oct. 30 (Los Angeles)

Mozart, *Don Giovanni*
Regina Resnik (Anna), Claudia Pinza (Elvira), Bidú Sayão/(10/28) Nadine Conner (Zerlina); Ezio Pinza (Giovanni), Max Lichtegg (Ottavio), Salvatore Baccaloni/(9/29) Italo Tajo (Leporello) Paul Breisach
Sept. 19m, 29
Oct. 28 (Los Angeles)

Wagner, *Die Meistersinger*
Astrid Varnay (Eva), Herta Glaz (Magdalene); (9/21) Charles Kullman/ Set Svanholm (Walther), Herbert Janssen (Sachs), Walter Olitzki (Beckmesser), Nicola Moscona (Pogner), John Garris (David) William Steinberg
Sept. 21, Oct. 10m
Oct. 24m (Los Angeles)

Rossini, *Il Barbiere di Siviglia*
Nadine Conner (Rosina); Giuseppe Valdengo/ Tito Gobbi** (Figaro), John Garris (Almaviva), Italo Tajo (Basilio), Salvatore Baccaloni (Bartolo) Paul Breisach
Sept. 22, Oct. 2m

Puccini, *La Bohème*
Bidú Sayão/ Licia Albanese (Mimì), Lois Hartzell (Musetta);

Jan Peerce/Jussi Bjoerling (Rodolfo), Francesco Valentino/ Tito Gobbi (Marcello), Italo Tajo (Colline) Gaetano Merola
Sept. 23, Oct. 12

Bidú Sayão/ Licia Albanese (Mimì), Lois Hartzell (Musetta); Jan Peerce/Jussi Bjoerling (Rodolfo), Tito Gobbi/Giuseppe Valdengo (Marcello), Italo Tajo (Colline) Gaetano Merola
Oct. 18 (Bakersfield)
Oct. 31m (Los Angeles)

Verdi, *La Forza del Destino*
Sara Menkes (Leonora), Claramae Turner/(10/21) Ebe Stignani (Preziosilla); Kurt Baum (Don Alvaro), (9/24) Leonard Warren/Robert Weede (Don Carlo), Ezio Pinza (Padre Guardiano) (9/24) Gaetano Merola/ Dick Marzollo
Sept. 24, Oct. 6
Oct. 21 (Los Angeles)

Verdi, *Rigoletto*
Nadine Conner (Gilda), Herta Glaz (Maddalena); Leonard Warren (Rigoletto), Jan Peerce (Duke), Lorenzo Alvary (Sparafucile) Kurt Herbert Adler
Sept. 26m

Mascagni, *Cavalleria Rusticana*
Ebe Stignani (Santuzza); Mario Binci (Turiddu), Francesco Valentino (Alfio) Dick Marzollo
and

Leoncavallo, *Pagliacci*
Licia Albanese (Nedda); Raoul Jobin/Kurt Baum (Canio), Robert Weede (Tonio), George Cehanovsky (Silvio) Pietro Cimara
Sept. 25 (Sacramento)
Sept. 28

Verdi, *Il Trovatore*
Sara Menkes (Leonora), Cloe Elmo (Azucena); Kurt Baum/Jussi Bjoerling (Manrico), Leonard Warren (Count Di Luna) Dick Marzollo
Sept. 30
Oct. 9 (Sacramento)

Mussorgsky, *Boris Godunov* (in Italian)
Winifred Heidt (Marina); Ezio Pinza (Boris), Charles Kullman (Dimitri), Lorenzo Alvary (Pimen), Alessio De Paolis (Shuisky),

(10/1) Francesco Valentino/ Daniel Duno (Rangoni) Erich Leinsdorf
Oct. 1, 13
Oct. 25 (Los Angeles)

Ponchielli, *La Gioconda*
Astrid Varnay (Gioconda), Ebe Stignani (Laura), Claramae Turner (La Cieca); Kurt Baum (Enzo), Francesco Valentino (Barnaba), Nicola Moscona (Alvise) Dick Marzollo
Oct. 3m
Oct. 26 (Los Angeles)

Bizet, *Carmen*
Winifred Heidt (Carmen), Nadine Conner/Dorothy Warenskjold (Micaëla); Charles Kullman/Raoul Jobin (Don José), Giuseppe Valdengo (Escamillo) Erich Leinsdorf
Oct. 5, 17m

Winifred Heidt (Carmen), Claudia Pinza (Micaëla); Raoul Jobin (Don José), Giuseppe Valdengo (Escamillo) Erich Leinsdorf
Oct. 23 (Los Angeles)

Puccini, *Madama Butterfly*
Licia Albanese/Dorothy Kirsten (Cio-Cio-San), Herta Glaz (Suzuki); Charles Kullman/Jan Peerce (Pinkerton), Alessio De Paolis/Giuseppe Valdengo (Sharpless) Pietro Cimara
Oct. 2 (San Jose)
Oct. 8

Donizetti, *L'Elisir d'Amore*
Bidú Sayão (Adina); Ferruccio Tagliavini (Nemorino), Tito Gobbi (Belcore), Salvatore Baccaloni/ Italo Tajo (Dulcamara) Paul Breisach
Oct. 11
Oct. 20 (Los Angeles)

Wagner, *Siegfried*
Astrid Varnay (Brünnhilde), Eula Beal (Erda); Set Svanholm (Siegfried), Walter Olitzki (Alberich), John Garris (Mime), Herbert Janssen (Wanderer) Erich Leinsdorf
Oct. 14
Oct. 27 (Los Angeles)

Verdi, *Otello*
Licia Albanese (Desdemona); Set Svanholm (Otello), Leonard Warren (Iago) William Steinberg
Oct. 16
Oct. 29 (Los Angeles)

Puccini, *Tosca*
Elisabetta Barbato** (Tosca); (9/20) Jussi Bjoerling/Ferruccio Tagliavini (Cavaradossi), Lawrence Tibbett (Scarpia) Fausto Cleva
Sept. 20, 29, Oct. 8

Elisabetta Barbato; Jan Peerce (Cavaradossi), Lawrence Tibbett (Scarpia) Fausto Cleva
Oct. 29 (Los Angeles)

Gounod, *Faust*
(9/22) Licia Albanese/ Florence Quartararo (Marguerite), Herta Glaz (Siebel); Raoul Jobin/(10/2) Jussi Bjoerling (Faust), Enzo Mascherini/(10/24) Robert Weede (Valentin), Italo Tajo/ (10/2) Nicola Moscona (Méphistophélès) Gaetano Merola/(10/2) Kurt Herbert Adler
Sept. 22, Oct. 2m
Oct. 24 (Bakersfield)

Bizet, *Carmen*
Winifred Heidt (Carmen), Uta Graf/Dorothy Warenskjold (Micaëla); Ramon Vinay (Don José), Francesco Valentino (Escamillo) Paul Breisach
Sept. 24
Nov. 4 (Los Angeles)

Puccini, *La Bohème*
Licia Albanese (Mimì), Lois Hartzell (Musetta); (9/25) Jussi Bjoerling/Ferruccio Tagliavini (Rodolfo), (9/25) Enzo Mascherini/Francesco Valentino (Marcello), Nicola Moscona (Colline) Karl Kritz
Sept. 25, Oct. 19
Nov. 1 (Los Angeles)

Mozart, *Don Giovanni*
Rose Bampton (Anna), Jarmila Novotná (Elvira), Licia Albanese/(10/31) Uta Graf (Zerlina); Italo Tajo (Giovanni), Jan Peerce (Ottavio), Salvatore Baccaloni (Leporello) Paul Breisach
Sept. 27, Oct. 9m
Oct. 31 (Los Angeles)

Wagner, *Tristan und Isolde*
Kirsten Flagstad (Isolde), Blanche Thebom/(10/6) Herta Glaz (Brangäne); Set Svanholm (Tristan), Herbert Janssen (Kurwenal), Mihaly Szekely (King Marke) William Steinberg
Sept. 30, Oct. 6, 15
Oct. 28 (Los Angeles)

Verdi, *Aida*
Elisabetta Barbato (Aida), Blanche Thebom (Amneris); Set Svanholm (Radames), Robert Weede (Amonasro) William Steinberg
Oct. 4, 13
Nov. 5 (Los Angeles)

Puccini, *Manon Lescaut*
Licia Albanese (Manon); Jussi Bjoerling (des Grieux), (10/7) Enzo Mascherini/ Francesco Valentino (Lescaut) Fausto Cleva
Oct. 7, 16m
Oct. 25 (Los Angeles)

Wagner, *Die Walküre*
Kirsten Flagstad (Brünnhilde), Rose Bampton (Sieglinde), Blanche Thebom (Fricka); Set Svanholm (Siegmund), Richard Sharretts/(10/23) Herbert Janssen (Wotan), Mihaly Szekely (Hunding) William Steinberg
Oct. 11, 23m
Nov. 2 (Los Angeles)

Offenbach, *Les Contes d'Hoffmann*
Uta Graf/Jo Ann O'Connell (Olympia), Licia Albanese/ Dorothy Warenskjold (Antonia), Jarmila Novotná/ Blanche Thebom (Giulietta), Herta Glaz (Nicklausse); Raoul Jobin (Hoffmann), Salvatore Baccaloni (Coppélius), Lawrence Tibbett (Dapertutto, Dr. Miracle) Paul Breisach
Oct. 14, 20

Uta Graf (Olympia), Jarmila Novotná (Antonia), Blanche Thebom (Giulietta), Herta Glaz (Nicklausse); Raoul Jobin (Hoffmann), Salvatore Baccaloni (Coppélius), Lawrence Tibbett (Dapertutto, Dr. Miracle) Paul Breisach
Nov 6m (Los Angeles)

Saint-Saëns, *Samson et Dalila*
Blanche Thebom (Dalila); Raoul Jobin/ Ramon Vinay (Samson), Robert Weede (Priest) Fausto Cleva
Oct. 18
Oct. 30m (Los Angeles)

Donizetti, *Lucia di Lammermoor*
Lily Pons (Lucia); Ferruccio Tagliavini (Edgardo), Francesco Valentino (Enrico), Desiré Ligeti (Raimondo) Gaetano Merola
Oct. 21
Nov. 3 (Los Angeles)

Verdi, *Rigoletto*
Lily Pons (Gilda),
Herta Glaz (Maddalena);
Lawrence Tibbett (Rigoletto),
Jan Peerce (Duke),
Mihaly Szekely (Sparafucile)
Gaetano Merola
    Oct. 26 (Los Angeles)

1950

Verdi, *Aida*
Renata Tebaldi** (Aida),
Elena Nikolaidi (Amneris);
Mario Del Monaco**
(Radames), Robert
Weede (Amonasro)
Fausto Cleva/(11/11)
Gaetano Merola
    Sept. 26, Oct. 1m
    Nov. 11 (Los Angeles)

Donizetti,
Lucia di Lammermoor
Lily Pons (Lucia);
Giuseppe Di Stefano/(10/2)
Eugene Conley (Edgardo),
Enzo Mascherini/(10/2)
Francesco Valentino (Enrico),
Desiré Ligeti (Raimondo)
Paul Breisach
    Sept. 28, Oct. 2
    Nov. 1 (Los Angeles)

Mozart, *Le Nozze di Figaro*
Bidú Sayão (Susanna),
Florence Quartararo
(Countess), (9/29)
Herta Glaz/Dorothy
Warenskjold (Cherubino);
Italo Tajo (Figaro),
John Brownlee (Count)
Jonel Perlea
    Sept. 29, Oct. 4
    Nov. 3 (Los Angeles)

Bidú Sayão (Susanna),
Renata Tebaldi (Countess),
Brenda Lewis (Cherubino);
Italo Tajo (Figaro),
John Brownlee (Count)
Jonel Perlea
    Oct. 30 (Fresno)

Wagner, *Tristan und Isolde*
Kirsten Flagstad (Isolde),
Herta Glaz (Brangäne),
Ramon Vinay (Tristan),
Sigurd Bjoerling**
(Kurwenal), Dezso Ernster/
Desiré Ligeti (King Marke)
Jonel Perlea
    Oct. 3, 12
    Oct. 14 (Sacramento)
    Nov. 2 (Los Angeles)

Giordano, *Andrea Chénier*
Licia Albanese (Maddalena);
Mario Del Monaco (Chénier),
Robert Weede (Gérard)
Fausto Cleva
    Oct. 6, 15m
    Oct. 31 (Los Angeles)

Puccini, *La Bohème*
Bidú Sayão (Mimi), Uta
Graf (Musetta); Giuseppe
Di Stefano (Rodolfo), (10/8)

Enzo Mascherini/Francesco
Valentino (Marcello),
Italo Tajo (Colline)
Karl Kritz
    Oct. 8m, 28
    Nov. 6 (Los Angeles)

Verdi, *Otello*
Renata Tebaldi (Desdemona);
Ramon Vinay (Otello),
Giuseppe Valdengo (Iago)
Fausto Cleva
    Oct. 10, 19
    Nov. 7 (Los Angeles)

Mozart, *The Magic Flute*
Uta Graf/(10/13) Dorothy
Warenskjold (Pamina),
Sari Barabas** (Queen
of the Night); Charles
Kullman/(11/10) James
Schwabacher (Tamino),
John Brownlee (Papageno),
Dezso Ernster (Sarastro)
Paul Breisach
    Oct. 11, 13
    Nov. 10 (Los Angeles)

Rossini,
Il Barbiere di Siviglia
Lily Pons (Rosina);
Enzo Mascherini (Figaro),
Eugene Conley (Almaviva),
Italo Tajo (Basilio),
Salvatore Baccaloni (Bartolo)
Nicola Rescigno
    Oct. 18, 22
    Nov. 3 (Los Angeles)

Puccini, *Suor Angelica*
Licia Albanese (Angelica),
Claramae Turner (Princess)
Kurt Herbert Adler
    and

Strauss, *Salome*
Brenda Lewis (Salome),
Claramae Turner (Herodias);
Frederick Jagel (Herod),
Sigurd Bjoerling/Ralph
Herbert (Jokanaan)
Paul Breisach
    Oct. 20, 26
    Nov. 9 (Los Angeles)

Puccini, *Manon Lescaut*
Dorothy Kirsten/Licia
Albanese (Manon); Mario
Del Monaco (des Grieux),
Giuseppe Valdengo (Lescaut)
Fausto Cleva
    Oct. 24
    Nov. 4 (Los Angeles)

Wagner, *Parsifal*
Kirsten Flagstad (Kundry);
Charles Kullman (Parsifal),
Sigurd Bjoerling (Amfortas),
Dezso Ernster (Gurnemanz),
Ralph Herbert (Klingsor)
Jonel Perlea
    Oct. 27, 29m
    Nov. 5 (Los Angeles)

Verdi, *Rigoletto*
Lily Pons (Gilda), Herta
Glaz (Maddalena); Enzo
Mascherini (Rigoletto),

Giuseppe Di Stefano (Duke),
Desiré Ligeti (Sparafucile)
Richard Karp
    Nov. 12 (Los Angeles)

1951

Verdi, *Otello*
Herva Nelli (Desdemona);
Ramon Vinay (Otello),
Giuseppe Valdengo (Iago)
Fausto Cleva
    Sept. 18, 23m
    Nov. 1 (Los Angeles)

Bizet, *Carmen*
Blanche Thebom (Carmen),
Dorothy Warenskjold/
Uta Graf (Micaëla);
Ramon Vinay (Don José),
Giuseppe Valdengo/
Ralph Herbert (Escamillo)
Paul Breisach/Karl Kritz
    Sept. 20
    Nov. 4 (Los Angeles)

Gounod, *Roméo et Juliette*
Bidú Sayão/(9/27)
Anna Lisa Bjoerling**
(Juliette); Jussi Bjoerling
(Roméo), Ralph Herbert/
(10/29) George Cehanovsky
(Mercutio), Nicola
Moscona/(9/27) Lorenzo
Alvary (Laurence)
Paul Breisach
    Sept. 21, 27
    Oct. 29 (Los Angeles)

Strauss, *Der Rosenkavalier*
Blanche Thebom (Octavian),
Stella Roman (Marschallin),
Uta Graf/(9/30) Dorothy
Warenskjold (Sophie);
Lorenzo Alvary (Ochs),
Eugene Conley/Walter
Fredericks/Ernest Lawrence
(Italian Singer), Ralph
Herbert (Faninal)
Erich Leinsdorf
    Sept. 25, 30m
    Oct. 30 (Los Angeles)

Verdi,
La Forza del Destino
Herva Nelli (Leonora),
Claramae Turner
(Preziosilla); Kurt
Baum/(10/27) Jan Peerce
(Don Alvaro), Robert Weede
(Don Carlo), (9/28) Nicola
Moscona/Nicola Rossi
Lemeni (Padre Guardiano)
Kurt Herbert Adler
    Sept. 28, Oct. 4
    Oct. 27 (Los Angeles)

Puccini, *Madama Butterfly*
Dorothy Kirsten (Cio-Cio-
San), Herta Glaz/Alice
Ostrowski (Suzuki); Eugene
Conley (Pinkerton); Francesco
Valentino (Sharpless)
Nicola Rescigno
    Sept. 29
    Oct. 27 (Los Angeles)

Mussorgsky,
Boris Godunov (in Italian)
Blanche Thebom/(10/7)
Claramae Turner (Marina);
Nicola Rossi Lemeni**
(Boris), Walter
Fredericks (Dimitri),
Nicola Moscona/(10/7)
Lorenzo Alvary (Pimen),
Alessio De Paolis (Shuisky),
Desiré Ligeti (Rangoni)
Erich Leinsdorf
    Oct. 2, 7m
    Oct. 24 (Los Angeles)

Verdi, *La Traviata*
Lily Pons (Violetta);
Jan Peerce/(10/11)
Eugene Conley (Alfredo),
Giuseppe Valdengo/(10/23)
Robert Weede (Germont)
Fausto Cleva
    Oct. 5, 11
    Oct. 23 (Los Angeles)

Puccini, *La Bohème*
Bidú Sayão (Mimi),
Uta Graf/Lois Hartzell
(Musetta); Jussi Bjoerling
(Rodolfo), Giuseppe
Valdengo (Marcello),
Nicola Moscona/Nicola
Rossi Lemeni (Colline)
Paul Breisach
    Oct. 8, 14m

Dorothy Kirsten/Bidú
Sayão (Mimi), Uta Graf/
Lois Hartzell (Musetta);
Jussi Bjoerling (Rodolfo),
Francesco Valentino/
Ralph Herbert (Marcello),
Nicola Moscona/Nicola
Rossi Lemeni (Colline)
Paul Breisach
    Oct. 22 (Fresno)
    Oct. 26 (Los Angeles)

Puccini, *Tosca*
Dorothy Kirsten (Tosca);
(10/12) Jussi Bjoerling/
Jan Peerce (Cavaradossi),
Robert Weede/(10/18)
Ralph Herbert (Scarpia)
Fausto Cleva
    Oct. 12, 18
    Oct. 31 (Los Angeles)

Wagner, *Parsifal*
Astrid Varnay (Kundry);
Set Svanholm (Parsifal),
Herbert Janssen (Amfortas),
Dezso Ernster (Gurnemanz),
Ralph Herbert (Klingsor)
Erich Leinsdorf
    Oct. 13
    Oct. 28 (Los Angeles)

Massenet, *Manon*
Bidú Sayão (Manon);
Frans Vroons (des Grieux),
Francesco Valentino
(Lescaut)
Fausto Cleva
    Oct. 16, 21m
    Nov. 2 (Los Angeles)

Beethoven, *Fidelio*
Astrid Varnay (Leonore),
Uta Graf (Marzelline);
Set Svanholm (Florestan),
Herbert Janssen (Pizarro),
Dezso Ernster (Rocco)
Alfred Wallenstein
    Oct. 19
    Oct. 25 (Los Angeles)

Verdi, *Rigoletto*
Lily Pons (Gilda),
Herta Glaz (Maddalena);
Robert Weede (Rigoletto),
Jussi Bjoerling (Duke),
Lorenzo Alvary/Dezso
Ernster (Sparafucile)
Pietro Cimara
    Oct. 20
    Nov. 3 (Los Angeles)

1952

Puccini, *Tosca*
Dorothy Kirsten (Tosca);
Mario Del Monaco/
Eugene Conley/Ferruccio
Tagliavini (Cavaradossi),
Robert Weede (Scarpia)
Fausto Cleva
    Sept. 16, 21m
    Oct. 25 (Los Angeles)

Verdi, *Rigoletto*
Lily Pons (Gilda), Claramae
Turner (Maddalena);
Giuseppe Valdengo/Robert
Weede (Rigoletto), Jan
Peerce/Eugene Conley
(Duke), Nicola Moscona/
Lorenzo Alvary (Sparafucile)
Pietro Cimara
    Sept. 17
    Nov. 1 (Los Angeles)

Boito, *Mefistofele*
Bidú Sayão (Margherita),
Jean Fenn (Elena); Nicola
Rossi Lemeni (Mefistofele),
Ferruccio Tagliavini/(10/11)
Mario del Monaco (Faust)
Fausto Cleva
    Sept. 20, 24, Oct. 11m
    Oct. 28 (Los Angeles)

Verdi, *Aida*
Mary Curtis/Herva Nelli
(Aida), Blanche Thebom
(Amneris); Mario Del
Monaco (Radames), Giuseppe
Valdengo (Amonasro)
Kurt Herbert Adler
    Sept. 23, 28m

Herva Nelli (Aida),
Fedora Barbieri/Blanche
Thebom (Amneris); Mario
Del Monaco (Radames),
Giuseppe Valdengo/
Frank Guarrera (Amonasro)
Kurt Herbert Adler
    Oct. 4
    Oct. 20 (Fresno)
    Oct. 26 (Los Angeles)

Puccini, *Il Tabarro*
Brenda Lewis (Giorgetta);
Mario Del Monaco/
Walter Fredericks (Luigi),

Robert Weede (Michele)
Glauco Curiel
    and
Puccini, *Suor Angelica*
Mary Curtis (Angelica),
Claramae Turner (Princess)
Kurt Herbert Adler
    and
Puccini, *Gianni Schicchi*
Dorothy Warenskjold
(Lauretta); Italo
Tajo (Schicchi), Eugene
Conley (Rinuccio)
Karl Kritz
    Sept. 26, Oct. 1

Il Tabarro
Brenda Lewis (Giorgetta);
Walter Fredericks (Luigi),
Robert Weede (Michele)
Glauco Curiel
    and
Suor Angelica
Mary Curtis (Angelica),
Claramae Turner (Princess)
Kurt Herbert Adler
    and
Gianni Schicchi
Dorothy Warenskjold
(Lauretta); Italo
Tajo (Schicchi), Eugene
Conley (Rinuccio)
Karl Kritz
    Oct. 31 (Los Angeles)

Strauss, *Der Rosenkavalier*
(in English)
Blanche Thebom (Octavian),
Brenda Lewis (Marschallin),
Dorothy Warenskjold
(Sophie); Lorenzo Alvary
(Ochs), Ernest Lawrence/
(10/29) Walter Fredericks
(Italian Singer), Ralph
Herbert (Faninal)
Paul Breisach
    Sept. 30, Oct. 5m
    Oct. 29 (Los Angeles)

Verdi, *Il Trovatore*
Herva Nelli/(10/8) Mary
Curtis (Leonora), (10/3)
Claramae Turner/Fedora
Barbieri (Azucena); Mario
Del Monaco (Manrico), Frank
Guarrera (Count Di Luna)
Paul Breisach
    Oct. 3, 8
    Oct. 24 (Los Angeles)

Verdi, *La Traviata*
Lily Pons (Violetta);
Eugene Conley/(10/20)
Jan Peerce (Alfredo), (10/4)
Robert Weede/Francesco
Valentino (Germont)
Pietro Cimara
    Oct. 4
    Oct. 20 (Fresno)
    Oct. 26 (Los Angeles)

Donizetti,
La Fille du Régiment
Lily Pons (Marie),
Claramae Turner (Marquise);
Ernest Lawrence (Tonio),

Salvatore Baccaloni (Sulpice)
Pietro Cimara
    Oct. 7, 12m
    Oct. 23 (Los Angeles)

Puccini, *La Bohème*
Bidú Sayão/Dorothy
Warenskjold (Mimi),
Jean Fenn/Brenda
Lewis (Musetta); Jan
Peerce/Ferruccio Tagliavini
(Rodolfo), Francesco
Valentino/Giuseppe Valdengo
(Marcello), Italo Tajo,
Nicola Moscona (Colline)
Gaetano Merola/Karl Kritz
    Oct. 10, 15

Dorothy Kirsten (Mimi),
Jean Fenn/Brenda
Lewis (Musetta); Ferruccio
Tagliavini/Jan Peerce
(Rodolfo), Giuseppe Valdengo/
Francesco Valentino
(Marcello), Nicola Moscona/
Italo Tajo (Colline)
Karl Kritz/Gaetano Merola
    Oct. 11 (Sacramento)
    Oct. 21 (San Diego)

Bidú Sayão (Mimi),
Jean Fenn (Musetta);
Ferruccio Tagliavini
(Rodolfo), Giuseppe
Valdengo (Marcello),
Italo Tajo (Colline)
Gaetano Merola
    Oct. 22 (Los Angeles)

Mozart, *Don Giovanni*
Mary Curtis (Anna),
Brenda Lewis (Elvira),
Bidú Sayão (Zerlina);
Nicola Rossi Lemeni
(Giovanni), Jan Peerce/
Eugene Conley (Ottavio),
Italo Tajo (Leporello)
Paul Breisach
    Oct. 14, 19m
    Nov. 2 (Los Angeles)

Mascagni,
Cavalleria Rusticana
Fedora Barbieri (Santuzza);
Jan Peerce (Turiddu),
Ralph Herbert (Alfio)
Kurt Herbert Adler
    and
Leoncavallo, *Pagliacci*
Bidú Sayão (Nedda);
Mario Del Monaco (Canio),
Frank Guarrera (Tonio),
Francesco Valentino (Silvio)
Karl Kritz
    Oct. 16
    Oct. 30 (Los Angeles)

Montemezzi,
L'Amore dei Tre Re
Dorothy Kirsten (Fiora);
Brian Sullivan (Avito), Robert
Weede (Manfredo), Nicola
Rossi Lemeni (Archibaldo)
Fausto Cleva
    Oct. 17
    Oct. 21 (Los Angeles)

1953

Boito, Mefistofele
Licia Albanese (Margherita), Beverly Sills (Elena); Nicola Rossi Lemeni (Mefistofele), Jan Peerce (Faust)
Fausto Cleva
Sept. 15, 20m
Oct. 19 (Los Angeles)

Puccini, La Bohème
Dorothy Kirsten/Licia Albanese (Mimi), Lois Hartzell (Musetta); David Poleri/Jan Peerce (Rodolfo), Cesare Bardelli/Enzo Mascherini (Marcello), Italo Tajo (Colline)
Glauco Curiel
Sept. 16, Oct. 17

Dorothy Warenskjold (Mimi), Lois Hartzell (Musetta); Jan Peerce (Rodolfo), Enzo Mascherini (Marcello), Italo Tajo (Colline)
Glauco Curiel
Oct. 31 (Los Angeles)

Massenet, Werther
Giulietta Simionato** (Charlotte), Dorothy Warenskjold (Sophie); Cesare Valletti** (Werther), John Lombardi (Albert)
Tullio Serafin
Sept. 19
Oct. 26 (Los Angeles)

Verdi, La Traviata
(9/22) Dorothy Kirsten/Licia Albanese (Violetta); David Poleri/(10/14) Jan Peerce (Alfredo), Enzo Mascherini (Germont)
Fausto Cleva
Sept. 22, Oct. 14
Oct. 22 (Los Angeles)

Mozart, Don Giovanni
Ellen Faull (Anna), Beverly Sills (Elvira), Barbara Gibson (Zerlina); Nicola Rossi Lemeni (Giovanni), Jan Peerce (Ottavio), Italo Tajo (Leporello)
Tullio Serafin
Sept. 23
Oct. 25 (Los Angeles)

Beethoven, The Creatures of Prometheus (Ballet)
Gordon Paxman (Prometheus); Virginia Johnson (Fire)
Glauco Curiel
and
Strauss, Elektra
Inge Borkh** (Elektra), Ellen Faull (Chrysothemis), Margarete Klose** (Klytemnestra); Ludwig Suthaus** (Aegisth), Paul Schoeffler (Orest)

Georg Solti**
Sept. 25, 30
Oct. 20 (Los Angeles)

Bizet, Carmen
Claramae Turner (Carmen), Dorothy Warenskjold (Micaëla); David Poleri/Brian Sullivan (Don José), Frank Guarrera (Escamillo)
Fausto Cleva
Sept. 26
Oct. 27 (Los Angeles)

Puccini, Madama Butterfly
Licia Albanese (Cio-Cio-San), Margaret Roggero (Suzuki); Brian Sullivan (Pinkerton), Cesare Bardelli/John Lombardi (Fresno, Sharpless)
Kurt Herbert Adler
Sept. 27m
Oct. 2 (Los Angeles)
Nov. 2 (Fresno)

Mussorgsky, Boris Godunov (in Italian)
Giulietta Simionato (Marina); Nicola Rossi Lemeni (Boris), Brian Sullivan (Dimitri), Lorenzo Alvary (Pimen), Alessio De Paolis (Shuisky), Cesare Bardelli (Rangoni)
Tullio Serafin
Sept. 29, Oct. 4m
Oct. 21 (Los Angeles)

Wagner, Tristan und Isolde
Gertrude Grob-Prandl** (Isolde), Margarete Klose (Brangäne); Ludwig Suthaus (Tristan), Paul Schoeffler (Kurwenal), Dezso Ernster/Desiré Ligeti (King Marke)
Georg Solti
Oct. 2, 7
Oct. 23 (Los Angeles)

Puccini, Turandot
Inge Borkh (Turandot), Licia Albanese/(10/11) Dorothy Warenskjold (Liù); Roberto Turrini (Calaf), Italo Tajo/(10/30) Desiré Ligeti (Timur)
Fausto Cleva
Oct. 6, 11m
Oct. 30 (Los Angeles)

Rossini, Il Barbiere di Siviglia
Giulietta Simionato (Rosina); Frank Guarrera (Figaro), Cesare Valletti (Almaviva), (10/9, 10) Nicola Rossi Lemeni/Italo Tajo (Basilio), Salvatore Baccaloni (Bartolo)
Tullio Serafin
Oct. 9
Oct. 10 (Sacramento)
Oct. 29 (San Diego)
Oct. 31 (Los Angeles)

Wagner, Die Walküre
Gertrude Grob-Prandl (Brünnhilde), Inge Borkh (Sieglinde), Margarete Klose (Fricka); Ludwig Suthaus (Siegmund), Paul Schoeffler (Wotan), Dezso Ernster (Hunding)
Georg Solti
Oct. 13, 18m
Nov. 1 (Los Angeles)

Verdi, Un Ballo in Maschera
Gertrude Grob-Prandl (Amelia), Margarete Klose (Ulrica), Barbara Gibson (Oscar); Roberto Turrini (Riccardo), Enzo Mascherini/Cesare Bardelli (Renato)
Tullio Serafin
Oct. 16
Oct. 28 (Los Angeles)

1954

Verdi, Rigoletto
Mado Robin** (Gilda), Claramae Turner/Rosalind Nadell (Maddalena); |Leonard Warren (Rigoletto), Richard Tucker/Brian Sullivan (Duke), Nicola Moscona/Desiré Ligeti (Sparafucile)
Fausto Cleva/Karl Kritz
Sept. 17, 26m

Mado Robin** (Gilda), Rosalind Nadell/Claramae Turner (Maddalena); Leonard Warren (Rigoletto), Jan Peerce (Duke), Nicola Moscona (Sparafucile)
Karl Kritz
Oct. 9 (Sacramento)
Oct. 22 (Los Angeles)

Puccini, Madama Butterfly
Licia Albanese (Cio-Cio-San), Rosalind Nadell (Suzuki); Giacinto Prandelli (Pinkerton), Ralph Herbert (Sharpless)
Karl Kritz/Leo Mueller
Sept. 18
Oct. 29 (Los Angeles)

Puccini, La Bohème
Rosanna Carteri** (Mimi), Franca Duval/Yola Casselle (Musetta); Jan Peerce/Brian Sullivan (Rodolfo), Frank Guarrera (Marcello), Nicola Moscona (Colline)
Leo Mueller
Sept. 19m
Oct. 24 (Los Angeles)

Verdi, La Forza del Destino
Carla Martinis (Leonora), Claramae Turner (Preziosilla); Richard Tucker/(9/30) Roberto Turrini (Don Alvaro), Leonard Warren (Don Carlo), Cesare Siepi (Padre Guardiano)
Fausto Cleva
Sept. 21, 30
Oct. 25 (Los Angeles)

Donizetti, Lucia di Lammermoor
Mado Robin (Lucia); Jan Peerce (Edgardo), Frank Guarrera (Enrico), Nicola Moscona (Raimondo), Ernesto Barbini
Sept. 23
Oct. 31 (Los Angeles)

Cherubini, Osteria Portoghese** (The Portuguese Inn)
Rosanna Carteri (Donna Gabriela); Lorenzo Alvary (Rodrigo), Ralph Herbert (Roselbo)
Glauco Curiel
and
Strauss, Salome
Inge Borkh (Salome), Claramae Turner (Herodias); Charles Kullman (Herod), Alexander Welitsch** (Jokanaan)
Eugen Szenkar**
Sept. 24, Oct. 7
Oct. 26 (Los Angeles)

Massenet, Manon
Dorothy Kirsten/(10/3) Rosanna Carteri (Manon); Giacinto Prandelli (des Grieux), Ralph Herbert (Lescaut)
Pierre Monteux
Sept. 28, Oct. 3m
Oct. 24 (Los Angeles)

Puccini, Tosca
Dorothy Kirsten/Licia Albanese (Tosca); Jan Peerce/Richard Tucker (Cavaradossi), Robert Weede (Scarpia)
Fausto Cleva
Oct. 1, 20

Dorothy Kirsten (Tosca); Brian Sullivan/(11/5) Roberto Turrini (Cavaradossi), Robert Weede/(11/5) Ralph Herbert (Scarpia)
Ernesto Barbini
Oct. 30 (Los Angeles)
Nov. 2 (San Diego)
Nov. 5 (Fresno)

Wagner, Der Fliegende Holländer
Inge Borkh (Senta); Hans Hotter (Dutchman), Brian Sullivan (Erik), Lorenzo Alvary (Daland)
Eugen Szenkar
Oct. 5, 10m
Oct. 28 (Los Angeles)

Puccini, Turandot
Carla Martinis/Inge Borkh (Turandot), Licia Albanese/(10/14) Dorothy Warenskjold (Liù); Roberto Turrini (Calaf), Nicola Moscona/(10/23) Desiré Ligeti (Timur)
Fausto Cleva
Oct. 8, 14
Oct. 23 (Los Angeles)

Mozart, Le Nozze di Figaro
Rosanna Carteri (Susanna), Licia Albanese (Countess), Dorothy Warenskjold (Cherubino); Cesare Siepi (Figaro), Hans Hotter (Count)
Eugen Szenkar
Oct. 12, 17m
Nov. 3 (Pasadena)

Puccini, Il Tabarro
Carla Martinis (Giorgetta); Brian Sullivan/(10/27) Roberto Turrini (Luigi), Robert Weede (Michele)
Glauco Curiel
and
Honegger, Joan of Arc at the Stake
Dorothy McGuire** (Joan), Franca Duval (Virgin); Lee Marvin** (Friar Dominic), Charles Kullman (Porcus)
Pierre Monteux
Oct. 15, 21
Oct. 27 (Los Angeles)

A Gala Night at the Opera
Salvatore Baccaloni, Rosanna Carteri, Dorothy Kirsten, Carla Martinis, Mado Robin, Cesare Siepi, Richard Tucker, Leonard Warren, Robert Weede et al.
Conductors: Fausto Cleva, Karl Kritz, Pierre Monteux, Leo Mueller
Oct. 16

Beethoven, Fidelio
Inge Borkh (Leonora), Dorothy Warenskjold (Marzelline); Roberto Turrini (Florestan), Hans Hotter (Pizarro), Lorenzo Alvary (Rocco)
Pierre Monteux
Oct. 19
Oct. 30 (Los Angeles)

1955

Verdi, Aida
Renata Tebaldi (Aida), Claramae Turner/(9/22) Nell Rankin (Amneris); Roberto Turrini (Radames), Leonard Warren (Amonasro)
Fausto Cleva
Sept. 15, 22, Oct. 16m
Oct. 26 (Los Angeles)

Bizet, Carmen
Nell Rankin (Carmen), Rosanna Carteri/(11/2) Dorothy Warenskjold (Micaëla); Richard Lewis** (Don José), Cornell MacNeil (Escamillo)
Jean Morel/(11/7) Leo Mueller
Sept. 17
Nov. 2 (Los Angeles)
Nov. 7 (Fresno)

Strauss, Der Rosenkavalier
Frances Bible (Octavian), Elisabeth Schwarzkopf** (Marschallin), Dorothy Warenskjold (Sophie); Otto Edelmann (Ochs), (9/20) Raymond Manton/Walter Fredericks (Italian Singer), Ralph Herbert (Faninal)
Erich Leinsdorf
Sept. 20, 24
Oct. 28 (Los Angeles)

Charpentier, Louise
Dorothy Kirsten (Louise), Claramae Turner (Mother); Brian Sullivan (Julien), Ralph Herbert (Father)
Jean Morel
Sept. 23, 29
Oct. 25 (Los Angeles)

Verdi, Macbeth
Inge Borkh (Lady Macbeth); Robert Weede (Macbeth), Walter Fredericks (Macduff), Giorgio Tozzi (Banquo)
Fausto Cleva
Sept. 27, Oct. 1
Nov. 1 (Los Angeles)

Mozart, Don Giovanni
Licia Albanese (Anna), Elisabeth Schwarzkopf (Elvira), Rosanna Carteri (Zerlina); Cesare Siepi (Giovanni), Jan Peerce (Ottavio), Lorenzo Alvary (Leporello)
Erich Leinsdorf
Sept. 30, Oct. 6
Nov. 5 (Los Angeles)

Giordano, Andrea Chénier
Renata Tebaldi (Maddalena); Richard Tucker (Chénier), Leonard Warren (Gérard)
Fausto Cleva
Oct. 4, 8
Oct. 21 (Los Angeles)

Walton, Troilus and Cressida**
Dorothy Kirsten (Cressida); Richard Lewis (Troilus), Robert Weede (Diomede), Giorgio Tozzi (Calkas)
Erich Leinsdorf
Oct. 7, 13
Nov. 4 (Los Angeles)

Gounod, Faust
Rosanna Carteri (Marguerite), Frances Bible (Siebel); (10/9) Brian Sullivan (Faust), Cornell MacNeil (Valentin), Cesare Siepi (Méphistophélès)
Jean Morel
Oct. 9 (Sacramento)
Oct. 18
Oct. 29 (Los Angeles)

Licia Albanese (Marguerite), Margaret Roggero (Siebel); Jan Peerce (Faust), Cornell MacNeil (Valentin), Cesare Siepi (Méphistophélès)
Jean Morel
Nov. 3 (San Diego)

Rimsky-Korsakov, The Golden Cockerel
Mattiwilda Dobbs** (Queen of Shemakha), Ruth Roehr (Voice of the Cockerel); Lorenzo Alvary (King Dodon), Raymond Manton (Astrologer), Walter Fredericks (Prince Guidon)
Erich Leinsdorf
and
Leoncavallo, Pagliacci
Licia Albanese (Nedda); Roberto Turrini (Canio), Leonard Warren/(10/15) Robert Weede (Tonio), (10/11) Cornell MacNeil/Heinz Blankenburg (Silvio)
Ernesto Barbini
Oct. 11, 15
Oct. 30m (Los Angeles)

Wagner, Lohengrin
Inge Borkh (Elsa), Nell Rankin (Ortrud); Brian Sullivan (Lohengrin), Alexander Welitsch (Telramund), Otto Edelmann (Heinrich)
Fausto Cleva
Oct. 14, 20
Oct. 23m (Los Angeles)

Puccini, Tosca
Renata Tebaldi/Dorothy Kirsten (Tosca); Richard Tucker/Roberto Turrini (Cavaradossi), Robert Weede (Scarpia)
Glauco Curiel
Oct. 19
Oct. 22 (Los Angeles)

Gala Performance
Licia Albanese, Rosanna Carteri, George Cehanovsky, Jan Peerce, Ralph Herbert, Giorgio Tozzi, Robert Weede and others.
Conductors: Ernesto Barbini, Glauco Curiel, Leo Mueller
Oct. 27 (Pasadena)

Puccini, Madama Butterfly
Dorothy Kirsten (Cio-Cio-San), Margaret Roggero (Suzuki); Richard Lewis (Pinkerton), Cornell MacNeil (Sharpless)
Glauco Curiel
Nov. 6m (Los Angeles)

1956

Puccini, Manon Lescaut
Dorothy Kirsten (Manon); Jussi Bjoerling (des Grieux), Louis Quilico/(10/19) Frank Guarrera (Lescaut)

Oliviero de Fabritiis**
Sept. 13, 20
Oct. 19 (Los Angeles)

Puccini, *Tosca*
Renata Tebaldi (Tosca);
(9/15) Richard Martell/
Jussi Bjoerling (Cavaradossi),
(9/15) Leonard Warren/
Anselmo Colzani (Scarpia)
Glauco Curiel
Sept. 15, 23m
Sept. 30 (Sacramento)

Renata Tebaldi (Tosca);
Richard Martell
(Cavaradossi), Anselmo
Colzani (Scarpia)
Glauco Curiel
Oct. 24 (Los Angeles)

Verdi, *Il Trovatore*
Eileen Farrell (Leonora),
Oralia Dominguez**
(Azucena); Jussi Bjoerling/
Roberto Turrini (Manrico),
Anselmo Colzani**
(Count Di Luna)
Oliviero de Fabritiis
Sept. 16m
Oct. 27 (Los Angeles)

Wagner,
Der Fliegende Holländer
Leonie Rysanek** (Senta);
Hans Hotter (Dutchman),
Ludwig Suthaus (Erik),
Lorenzo Alvary (Daland)
William Steinberg
Sept. 18, 22
Oct. 26 (Los Angeles)

Verdi, *Falstaff*
Elisabeth Schwarzkopf
(Alice), Audrey
Schuh (Nannetta),
Oralia Dominguez (Quickly),
Margaret Roggero (Meg);
Leonard Warren (Falstaff),
Giuseppe Campora (Fenton),
Frank Guarrera (Ford)
William Steinberg
Sept. 21, 27
Oct. 23 (Los Angeles)

Mussorgsky,
Boris Godunov (in Russian)
(Rimsky-Korsakov version)
Oralia Dominguez (Marina);
Boris Christoff** (Boris),
Richard Lewis (Dimitri),
Nicola Moscona (Pimen),
Cesare Curzi** (Shuisky),
Hans Hotter (Rangoni)
William Steinberg
Sept. 25, 29
Oct. 30 (Los Angeles)

Zandonai,
Francesca da Rimini
Leyla Gencer** (Francesca);
Richard Martell (Paolo),
Anselmo Colzani (Giovanni),
Cesare Curzi (Malatestino)
Oliviero de Fabritiis
Sept. 28, Oct. 4
Oct. 31 (Los Angeles)

Mozart, *Così fan tutte*
Elisabeth Schwarzkopf
(Fiordiligi), Nell
Rankin (Dorabella),
Patrice Munsel (Despina);
Richard Lewis (Ferrando),
Frank Guarrera (Guglielmo),
Lorenzo Alvary (Alfonso)
Hans Schwieger
Oct. 2, 6, 14m
Oct. 25 (San Diego)
Nov. 2 (Los Angeles)

Wagner, *Die Walküre*
Birgit Nilsson**
(Brünnhilde), Leonie
Rysanek (Sieglinde),
Nell Rankin (Fricka);
Ludwig Suthaus (Siegmund),
Hans Hotter (Wotan),
(10/5) Nicola Moscona/
Lorenzo Alvary (Hunding)
Hans Schwieger
Oct. 5, 11
Nov. 4m (Los Angeles)

Puccini, *Madama Butterfly*
(10/7) Licia Albanese/
Dorothy Kirsten (Cio-Cio-
San), Margaret Roggero
(Suzuki); Giuseppe
Campora (Pinkerton),
Louis Quilico (Sharpless)
Karl Kritz
Oct. 7m
Nov. 1 (San Diego)
Nov. 3 (Los Angeles)

Verdi, *Simon Boccanegra*
Renata Tebaldi (Amelia);
Leonard Warren (Simon),
Roberto Turrini (Gabriele),
Boris Christoff (Fiesco)
Oliviero de Fabritiis
Oct. 9, 13
Oct. 20 (Los Angeles)

Donizetti, *L'Elisir d'Amore*
Patrice Munsel (Adina);
Giuseppe Campora
(Nemorino),
Louis Quilico (Belcore),
Italo Tajo (Dulcamara)
Glauco Curiel
Oct. 12, 18
Oct. 29 (Pasadena)

Puccini, *La Bohème*
Licia Albanese (Mimi),
Mary Gray (Musetta);
Jan Peerce (Rodolfo),
Louis Quilico (Marcello),
Italo Tajo (Colline)
Karl Kritz
Oct. 16
Oct. 21m (Los Angeles)

Verdi, *Aida*
Leonie Rysanek (Aida),
Nell Rankin (Amneris);
Richard Martell (Radames),
Anselmo Colzani (Amonasro)
Oliviero de Fabritiis
Oct. 17
Oct. 28m (Los Angeles)

1957

Puccini, *Turandot*
Leonie Rysanek (Turandot),
Licia Albanese/(11/5)
Leyla Gencer (Liù);
Eugene Tobin** (Calaf),
Nicola Moscona (Timur)
Francesco Molinari-
Pradelli**
Sept. 17, 21
Sept. 29m (Berkeley)
Nov. 5 (Los Angeles)

Verdi, *La Traviata*
Leyla Gencer/(10/20)
Licia Albanese (Violetta);
Gianni Raimondi** (Alfredo),
Robert Merrill/(10/20)
Umberto Borghi (Germont)
Glauco Curiel
Sept. 19, Oct. 20m
Oct. 6 (Sacramento)

Leyla Gencer (Violetta);
Jon Crain (Alfredo),
Robert Merrill (Germont)
Glauco Curiel
Oct. 31 (San Diego)
Nov. 9 (Los Angeles)

Poulenc, *Dialogues of the*
*Carmelites*** (in English)
Dorothy Kirsten (Blanche),
Leontyne Price** (Mme.
Lidoine), Claramae Turner
(Mme. Croissy), Blanche
Thebom (Mother Marie),
Sylvia Stahlman (Constance)
Erich Leinsdorf
Sept. 20, 26, Oct. 16
Oct. 29 (Los Angeles)

Verdi,
Un Ballo in Maschera
Leonie Rysanek/(11/2)
Herva Nelli (Amelia),
Claramae Turner (Ulrica),
Sylvia Stahlman (Oscar);
Jan Peerce (Riccardo),
Robert Merrill (Renato)
William Steinberg
Sept. 24, 28
Nov. 2 (Los Angeles)

Donizetti,
Lucia di Lammermoor
Leyla Gencer (Lucia);
Gianni Raimondi/
Jan Peerce (Edgardo),
Umberto Borghi
(Enrico), Lorenzo Alvary/
Nicola Moscona (Raimondo)
Francesco Molinari-Pradelli
Sept. 27, Oct. 5

Leyla Gencer (Lucia);
Jan Peerce/Gianni
Raimondi (Edgardo),
Giuseppe Taddei (Enrico),
Nicola Moscona/Lorenzo
Alvary (Raimondo)
Francesco Molinari-Pradelli
Oct. 25, Nov. 10m (Los
Angeles)

Strauss, *Der Rosenkavalier*
Frances Bible (Octavian),
Elisabeth Schwarzkopf
(Marschallin), Rita Streich**
(Sophie); Otto Edelmann
(Ochs), Jon Crain/Eugene
Tobin (Italian Singer),
Ralph Herbert (Faninal)
Erich Leinsdorf
Oct. 1, 3

Frances Bible (Octavian),
Elisabeth Schwarzkopf
(Marschallin), Sylvia
Stahlman/Rita Streich
(Sophie); Otto Edelmann
(Ochs), Raymond
Manton (Italian Singer),
Ralph Herbert (Faninal)
Erich Leinsdorf
Oct. 13m
Oct. 27m (Los Angeles)

Strauss, *Ariadne auf Naxos*
Leonie Rysanek (Prima
Donna, Ariadne), Rita
Streich (Zerbinetta), Helen
George (Composer); Richard
Lewis (Tenor, Bacchus)
William Steinberg
Oct. 8, 12
Nov. 1 (Los Angeles)

Puccini, *Madama Butterfly*
Licia Albanese (Cio-Cio-San),
Katherine Hilgenberg
(Suzuki); Gianni Raimondi/
Richard Lewis (Pinkerton),
Umberto Borghi (Sharpless)
Karl Kritz/Glauco Curiel
Oct. 10
Nov. 3m (Los Angeles)

Verdi, *Macbeth*
Leonie Rysanek (Lady
Macbeth); Giuseppe
Taddei** (Macbeth),
Jon Crain (Macduff),
Lorenzo Alvary (Banquo)
Francesco Molinari-Pradelli
Oct. 11, 17
Oct. 30 (Los Angeles)

Puccini, *Tosca*
Dorothy Kirsten (Tosca);
Jan Peerce/Jon Crain/Gianni
Raimondi (Cavaradossi),
Giuseppe Taddei (Scarpia)
Erich Leinsdorf
Oct. 15, 19
Nov. 8 (Los Angeles)

Verdi, *Aida*
Leontyne Price/(10/21)
Leonie Rysanek (Aida),
Blanche Thebom/(10/21)
Claramae Turner (Amneris);
Eugene Tobin (Radames),
Robert Merrill (Amonasro)
Francesco Molinari-Pradelli
Oct. 18, 21, 23

Leontyne Price/
Herva Nelli (Aida),
Blanche Thebom (Amneris);
Eugene Tobin (Radames),
Robert Merrill/

Umberto Borghi (Amonasro)
Francesco Molinari-Pradelli
Oct. 26 (Los Angeles)
Nov. 7 (San Diego)

Mozart, *Così fan tutte*
Elisabeth Schwarzkopf
(Fiordiligi), Nan
Merriman (Dorabella),
Rita Streich (Despina);
Richard Lewis (Ferrando),
Heinz Blankenburg
(Guglielmo), Lorenzo
Alvary (Don Alfonso)
Erich Leinsdorf
Oct. 22, 24
Nov. 6 (Los Angeles)

Puccini, *La Bohème*
Dorothy Kirsten (Mimi),
Jan McArt (Musetta);
Gianni Raimondi (Rodolfo),
Ralph Herbert (Marcello),
Nicola Moscona (Colline)
Kurt Herbert Adler
Nov. 3 (Pasadena)

1958

Cherubini, *Medea*
Eileen Farrell (Medea),
Sylvia Stahlman (Glauce),
Claramae Turner (Neris);
Richard Lewis (Jason),
Giuseppe Modesti** (Creon)
Jean Fournet**
Sept. 12, 18
Sept. 28m (Berkeley)
Nov. 7 (Los Angeles)

Rossini,
Il Barbiere di Siviglia
Eugenia Ratti** (Rosina);
Rolando Panerai** (Figaro),
Richard Miller** (Count),
Giorgio Tozzi/Lorenzo
Alvary (Basilio), Salvatore
Baccaloni (Bartolo)
Glauco Curiel
Sept. 13
Oct. 26m (Los Angeles)

Verdi, *Don Carlo*
Leyla Gencer (Elisabetta),
Irene Dalis (Eboli);
Pier Miranda Ferraro/(11/4)
Jussi Bjoerling (Don Carlo),
Frank Guarrera (Rodrigo),
Giorgio Tozzi (Philip II),
Giuseppe Modesti (Inquisitor)
Georges Sebastian
Sept. 16, 20
Nov. 4 (Los Angeles)

Christel Goltz (Elisabetta),
Grace Hoffman (Eboli);
Pier Miranda Ferraro
(Don Carlo), Frank
Guarrera (Rodrigo),
Arnold Van Mill (Philip II),
Lorenzo Alvary (Inquisitor)
Georges Sebastian
Oct. 19m

Puccini, *La Bohème*
Lisa Della Casa (Mimi),
Eugenia Ratti (Musetta);
Gianni Raimondi/(10/2)

Umberto Borghi (Amonasro)
Francesco Molinari-Pradelli
Oct. 26 (Los Angeles)
Nov. 7 (San Diego)

Jussi Bjoerling (Rodolfo),
Rolando Panerai (Marcello),
Lorenzo Alvary/(10/2)
Giorgio Tozzi (Colline)
Jean Fournet
Sept. 19, 27, Oct. 2

Lisa Della Casa/
Dorothy Kirsten (Mimi),
Sylvia Stahlman/
Eugenia Ratti (Musetta);
Gianni Raimondi (Rodolfo),
Frank Guarrera/Rolando
Panerai (Marcello), Lorenzo
Alvary/Giorgio Tozzi (Colline)
Jean Fournet
Oct. 24 and Nov. 1 (Los
Angeles)

Verdi, *Rigoletto*
Leyla Gencer (Gilda), Cecilia
Ward/(10/20) Claramae
Turner (Maddalena);
Robert Weede (Rigoletto),
Gianni Raimondi/(11/8)
Jussi Bjoerling (Duke),
Lorenzo Alvary (Sparafucile)
Jean Fournet
Sept. 25, Oct. 20
Nov. 8 (Los Angeles)

Verdi, *Il Trovatore*
Leontyne Price (Leonora),
Claramae Turner/(10/11)
Irene Dalis (Azucena);
Jussi Bjoerling/(10/11) Pier
Miranda Ferraro (Manrico),
Louis Quilico (Count Di Luna)
Georges Sebastian
Sept. 26, Oct. 11
Oct. 5 (Sacramento)

Eileen Farrell (Leonora),
Irene Dalis (Azucena);
Jussi Bjoerling (Manrico),
Louis Quilico (Count Di Luna)
Georges Sebastian
Nov. 2m (Los Angeles)

Smetana,
The Bartered Bride
Elisabeth Schwarzkopf
(Marie); Richard Lewis
(Jenik), Howard Fried
(Vasek), Giorgio Tozzi (Kecal)
Leopold Ludwig**
Sept. 30, Oct. 4, 12m
Nov. 5 (Los Angeles)

Orff, *The Wise*
*Maiden*** (Die Kluge)
Leontyne Price (Peasant's
Daughter); Lawrence
Winters (King), Raymond
Manton (Donkey Man),
Eugene Green (Muleteer)
Leopold Ludwig
and

Orff, *Carmina Burana*
Elaine Malbin
(Burgundian Lady);
Frank Guarrera (Troubadour,
Old Poet, Drinker)
Leopold Ludwig
Oct. 3, 9
Oct. 28 (Los Angeles)

Verdi,
La Forza del Destino
Leonie Rysanek (Leonora),
Cecilia Ward (Preziosilla);
Pier Miranda Ferraro
(Don Alvaro), Robert
Weede (Don Carlo), Giuseppe
Modesti/Giorgio Tozzi/Arnold
Van Mill (Padre Guardiano)
Georges Sebastian
Oct. 7
Oct. 31 (Los Angeles)
Nov. 6 (San Diego)

Puccini, *Gianni Schicchi*
Sylvia Stahlman (Lauretta);
Giuseppe Taddei (Schicchi),
Richard Miller (Rinuccio)
Glauco Curiel
and

Strauss, *Elektra*
Christel Goltz (Elektra),
Lisa Della Casa
(Chrysothemis), Claramae
Turner/(10/16) Irene Dalis
(Klytemnestra); Sebastian
Feiersinger** (Aegisth),
Arnold Van Mill** (Orest)
Leopold Ludwig
Oct. 10, 16
Oct. 29 (Los Angeles)

Wagner, *Tannhäuser*
Leonie Rysanek (Elisabeth),
Grace Hoffman (Venus);
Sebastian Feiersinger
(Tannhäuser), Lawrence
Winters (Wolfram), Arnold
Van Mill (Hermann)
Leopold Ludwig
Oct. 14, 18, 22
Oct. 25 (Los Angeles)

Massenet, *Manon*
Leyla Gencer (Manon);
Richard Lewis (des Grieux),
Louis Quilico (Lescaut)
Jean Fournet
Oct. 17
Oct. 27 (San Diego)
Nov. 2 (Pasadena)

Mozart, *Le Nozze di Figaro*
Eugenia Ratti (Susanna),
Elisabeth Schwarzkopf
(Countess), Cecilia
Ward (Cherubino);
Rolando Panerai (Figaro),
Giuseppe Modesti (Count)
Kurt Herbert Adler
Oct. 21, 23
Oct. 30 (San Diego)
Nov. 9m (Los Angeles)

1959

Montemezzi,
L'Amore dei Tre Re
Dorothy Kirsten (Fiora);
Giuseppe Zampieri** (Avito),
Frank Guarrera (Manfredo),
Giorgio Tozzi (Archibaldo)
Francesco Molinari-Pradelli
Sept. 3 (Portland)
Sept. 17, Oct. 9
Nov. 2 (San Diego)
Nov. 4 (Los Angeles)

Puccini, *La Bohème*
Licia Albanese/Dorothy Kirsten (Mimì), Mary Costa (Musetta); Giuseppe Gismondo (Rodolfo), Mario Zanasi/Louis Quilico (Marcello), Mark Elyn/Giorgio Tozzi (Colline) Silvio Varviso**
  Sept. 4 and 7m (Portland)

Licia Albanese (Mimì), Mary Costa (Musetta); Giuseppe Gismondo (Rodolfo), Theodore Uppman/ Louis Quilico (Marcello), Lorenzo Alvary (Colline) Silvio Varviso
  Oct. 19
  Oct. 24 (Los Angeles)

Leoncavallo, *Pagliacci*
Lucine Amara (Nedda); Jon Vickers (Canio), Robert Weede (Tonio), Louis Quilico (Silvio) Arturo Basile
  and

Orff, *Carmina Burana*
Mary Costa (Burgundian Lady); Frank Guarrera (Troubadour, Old Poet, Drinker) Silvio Varviso
  Sept. 5 (Portland)

Pagliacci
Lucine Amara/Dolores Mari (Nedda); Jon Vickers/ Mario Del Monaco (Canio), Robert Weede (Tonio), Louis Quilico/ Theodor Uppman (Silvio) Arturo Basile
  and
Carmina Burana
Mary Costa (Burgundian Lady); Frank Guarrera (Troubadour, Old Poet, Drinker) Silvio Varviso
  Sept. 19
  Oct. 28 (Los Angeles)

Gluck, *Orfeo ed Euridice*
Blanche Thebom (Orfeo), Lucine Amara/(11/6) Mary Costa (Euridice), Joan Marie Moynagh (Amore) Silvio Varviso
  Sept. 6 (Portland)
  Sept. 15, 26
  Nov. 6 (Los Angeles)

Verdi, *Aida*
Leontyne Price (Aida), Irene Dalis (Amneris); Jon Vickers (Radames), Robert Weede/Lawrence Winters (Amonasro) Francesco Molinari-Pradelli
  Sept. 11, 24

Lucine Amara/ Leontyne Price (Aida), Irene Dalis (Amneris); Mario Del Monaco/

Jon Vickers (Radames), Louis Quilico/Lawrence Winters (Amonasro) Francesco Molinari-Pradelli
  Oct. 2
  Nov. 1m (Los Angeles)

Leontyne Price (Aida), Irene Dalis (Amneris), Jon Vickers (Radames), Giorgio Tozzi/George London (Amonasro) Francesco Molinari-Pradelli
  Oct. 11m (Berkeley)
  Nov. 7 (Los Angeles)

Puccini, *Madama Butterfly*
(9/7) Licia Albanese/Dorothy Kirsten (Cio-Cio-San), Edith Evans (Suzuki); Giuseppe Zampieri (Pinkerton), Mario Zanasi (Sharpless) Arturo Basile
  Sept. 7 (Portland)
  Oct. 18 (Sacramento)
  Nov. 10 (Los Angeles)

Dorothy Kirsten/Sena Jurinac** (Cio-Cio-San), Edith Evans (Suzuki); Giuseppe Gismondo/Giuseppe Zampieri (Pinkerton), Mario Zanasi (Sharpless) Arturo Basile
  Sept. 12, 22

Strauss,
*Die Frau ohne Schatten***
Edith Lang** (Empress), Marianne Schech (Dyer's Wife), Irene Dalis (Nurse); Sebastian Feiersinger (Emperor), Mino Yahia** (Barak) Leopold Ludwig
  Sept. 18, Oct. 15
  Nov. 9 (Los Angeles)

Giordano, *Andrea Chénier*
Gabriella Tucci** (Maddalena); Mario Del Monaco (Chénier), Robert Weede (Gérard) Francesco Molinari-Pradelli
  Sept. 25, Oct. 10
  Oct. 31 (Los Angeles)

Bizet, *Carmen*
Gloria Lane (Carmen), Lucine Amara/Mary Costa (Micaëla); Jon Vickers (Don José), Frank Guarrera/ Mario Zanasi (Escamillo) Arturo Basile
  Sept. 29, Oct. 1

Gloria Lane (Carmen), Lucine Amara/Mary Costa (Micaëla); Jon Vickers/ Richard Lewis (Don José), Frank Guarrera/Mario Zanasi (Escamillo) Arturo Basile
  Oct. 23 and Nov. 8m (Los Angeles)

Gloria Lane (Carmen), Mary Costa (Micaëla);

Jon Vickers (Don José), Frank Guarrera (Escamillo) Arturo Basile
  Oct. 29 (San Diego)

Mozart, *Don Giovanni*
Sena Jurinac/(11/3) Gabriella Tucci (Anna), Leontyne Price (Elvira), Pierrette Alarie (Zerlina); (10/3) Mino Yahia/George London (Giovanni), Richard Lewis (Ottavio), Lorenzo Alvary (Leporello) Leopold Ludwig
  Oct. 3, 20
  Nov. 3 (Los Angeles)

Wagner, *Die Meistersinger*
Sena Jurinac (Eva), Katherine Hilgenberg (Magdalene); Sebastian Feiersinger (Walther), Paul Schoeffler (Hans Sachs), Geraint Evans** (Beckmesser), (10/6) Giorgio Tozzi/Mino Yahia (Pogner), Cesare Curzi (David) Leopold Ludwig
  Oct. 6, 8, 21
  Oct. 30 (Los Angeles)

Stravinsky, *Danses Concertantes* (Ballet)
Nancy Johnson, Roderick Drew Earl Murray
  and

Strauss, *Ariadne auf Naxos*
Eileen Farrell (Prima Donna, Ariadne), Rita Streich (Zerbinetta), Sena Jurinac (Composer); Richard Lewis (Tenor, Bacchus) Leopold Ludwig
  Oct. 13, 17
  Oct. 27 (Los Angeles)

Verdi, *Otello*
Gabriella Tucci (Desdemona); Mario Del Monaco (Otello), Mario Zanasi (Iago) Francesco Molinari-Pradelli
  Oct. 16, 22
  Oct. 25m (Los Angeles)
  Nov. 5 (San Diego)

1960

Puccini, *Tosca*/
Dorothy Kirsten/ Lucine Amara (Tosca); Giuseppe Zampieri (Cavaradossi), Tito Gobbi/ Mario Zanasi (Scarpia) Silvio Varviso
  Sept. 16, 22

Floriana Cavalli**/ Dorothy Kirsten (Tosca); Giuseppe Zampieri (Cavaradossi), Tito Gobbi/ Robert Weede (Scarpia) Silvio Varviso
  Nov. 4 and 13m (Los Angeles)

Dorothy Kirsten (Tosca); Giuseppe Zampieri (Cavaradossi), Mario Zanasi (Scarpia) Silvio Varviso
  Nov. 10 (San Diego)

Bizet, *Carmen*
Jean Madeira (Carmen), Mary Costa (Micaëla); Jon Vickers (Don José), Mario Zanasi (Escamillo) Francesco Molinari-Pradelli
  Sept. 17
  Nov. 6m (Los Angeles)

Jean Madeira (Carmen), Lucine Amara/Mary Costa (Micaëla); Jon Vickers/Giuseppe Zampieri (Don José), Mario Zanasi (Escamillo) Francesco Molinari-Pradelli
  Oct. 16m (Berkeley)
  Oct. 23 (Sacramento)

Strauss,
Die Frau ohne Schatten
Leonie Rysanek (Empress), Marianne Schech (Barak's Wife), Irene Dalis (Nurse); Ticho Parly (Emperor), Paul Schoeffler (Barak) Leopold Ludwig
  Sept. 20, 24
  Nov. 16 (Los Angeles)

Puccini,
La Fanciulla del West
Dorothy Kirsten (Minnie); Sandor Konya** (Johnson), Tito Gobbi (Rance) Francesco Molinari-Pradelli
  Sept. 23, Oct. 1
  Nov. 2 (Los Angeles)

Verdi, *Simon Boccanegra*
Lucine Amara/(10/29) Floriana Cavalli (Amelia); Tito Gobbi (Simon), Giuseppe Zampieri (Gabriele), Giorgio Tozzi (Fiesco) Leopold Ludwig
  Sept. 27, Oct. 6
  Oct. 29 (Los Angeles)

Verdi, *Aida*
Leonie Rysanek/(10/24) Floriana Cavalli** (Aida), Irene Dalis (Amneris); (9/30) Jon Vickers/ Sandor Konya (Radames), (9/30) Robert Weede/ Mario Zanasi (Amonasro) Francesco Molinari-Pradelli
  Sept. 30, Oct. 24
  Nov. 14 (Los Angeles)

Berg, *Wozzeck* (in English)
Marilyn Horne (Marie); Geraint Evans (Wozzeck), Ticho Parly (Drum Major), Richard Lewis (Captain), Lorenzo Alvary (Doctor) Leopold Ludwig
  Oct. 4, 8, 26
  Nov. 11 (Los Angeles)

Strauss, *Der Rosenkavalier*
(9/29) Frances Bible/ Hertha Toepper** (Octavian), Elisabeth Schwarzkopf (Marschallin), Sylvia Stahlman (Sophie); Kurt Boehme (Ochs), (9/29) Raymond Manton (Italian Singer), Richard Wentworth (Faninal) Silvio Varviso
  Sept. 29, Oct. 7, 16
  Nov. 3 (San Diego)
  Nov. 5 (Los Angeles)

Bellini, *La Sonnambula*
Anna Moffo (Amina); Nicola Monti (Elvino), Giorgio Tozzi/(San Diego) Ferruccio Mazzoli (Rodolfo) Francesco Molinari-Pradelli
  and

Glazunov,
Variations de Ballet
Jocelyn Vollmar, Roderick Drew Ottavio de Rosa
  Oct. 11, 13
  Oct. 31 (Los Angeles)
  Nov. 17 (San Diego)

Puccini, *La Bohème*
Lucine Amara (Mimì), Mary Costa (Musetta); Sandor Konya/Jan Peerce (Rodolfo), Mario Zanasi (Marcello), Lorenzo Alvary (Colline) Silvio Varviso
  Oct. 14, 22

Floriana Cavalli/Anna Moffo (Mimì), Mary Costa (Musetta); Giuseppe Zampieri/ Sandor Konya (Rodolfo), Mario Zanasi (Marcello), Lorenzo Alvary (Colline) Silvio Varviso
  Nov. 1 & 12 (Los Angeles)

Mozart, *Così fan tutte*
Elisabeth Schwarzkopf (Fiordiligi), Katherine Hilgenberg (Dorabella), Mary Costa (Despina); Richard Lewis (Ferrando), Frank Guarrera (Guglielmo), Paul Schoeffler (Don Alfonso) Kurt Herbert Adler
  Oct. 15, 18
  Nov. 9 (Los Angeles)

Wagner, *Lohengrin*
Ingrid Bjoner** (Elsa), Irene Dalis (Ortrud); Sandor Konya (Lohengrin), Robert Anderson (Telramund), Kurt Boehme (Heinrich) Francesco Molinari-Pradelli
  Oct. 21, 27
  Oct. 30m (Los Angeles)

Verdi, *La Traviata*
Mary Costa/Anna Moffo (Violetta); Giuseppe Zampieri/ Jan Peerce (Alfredo),

Robert Weede (Germont) Silvio Varviso
  Oct. 20, 25

Anna Moffo/Mary Costa (Violetta); Jan Peerce/ Giuseppe Zampieri (Alfredo), Robert Weede (Germont) Silvio Varviso
  Oct. 28 and Nov. 15 (Los Angeles)

Puccini, *Madama Butterfly*
Leontyne Price (Cio-Cio-San), Katherine Hilgenberg (Suzuki); Giuseppe Zampieri (Pinkerton), Mario Zanasi (Sharpless) Kurt Herbert Adler
  Nov. 8 (Los Angeles)

1961

Donizetti,
Lucia di Lammermoor
(9/15) Anna Moffo/ Joan Sutherland (Lucia); Renato Cioni (Edgardo), Vladimir Ruzdak**/(10/25) Claude Heater (Enrico), (9/15) Kieth Engen**/ Giorgio Tozzi (Raimondo) Francesco Molinari-Pradelli
  Sept. 15, 23, Oct. 25

Joan Sutherland (Lucia); Renato Cioni (Edgardo), Vladimir Ruzdak (Enrico), Plinio Clabassi/(11/2) Kieth Engen (Raimondo) Francesco Molinari-Pradelli
  Oct. 29m and Nov. 4 (Los Angeles)
  Nov. 2 (San Diego)

Puccini, *Turandot*
Lucille Udovick (Turandot), Leontyne Price/(11/7, 17) Eva Likova (Liù); Sandor Konya (Calaf), Plinio Clabassi (Timur) Francesco Molinari-Pradelli
  Sept. 16, 26
  Nov. 7 and 17 (Los Angeles)

Dello Joio, *Blood Moon****
Mary Costa (Ninette), Irene Dalis (Cleo); Albert Lance** (Raymond), Kieth Engen (Dumas) Leopold Ludwig
  Sept. 18, Oct. 7
  Nov. 8 (Los Angeles)

Mussorgsky,
Boris Godunov (in English) (Rimsky-Korsakov version)
Irene Dalis/(10/13) Marilyn Horne (Marina); Giorgio Tozzi (Boris), Albert Lance (Dimitri), Joshua Hecht (Pimen), Herbert Handt (Shuisky), Plinio Clabassi (Rangoni) Leopold Ludwig
  Sept. 21, Oct. 13
  Nov. 1 (Los Angeles)

Puccini, *Madama Butterfly*
Leontyne Price/(11/19) Licia Albanese (Cio-Cio-San), Mildred Miller (Suzuki); Sandor Konya (Pinkerton), Vladimir Ruzdak (Sharpless) Kurt Herbert Adler
  Sept. 22, 28
  Nov. 19m (Los Angeles)

Mozart, *Le Nozze di Figaro*
Graziella Sciutti** (Susanna), Lisa Della Casa (Countess), Mildred Miller (Cherubino); Geraint Evans (Figaro), Kieth Engen (Count) Silvio Varviso
  Sept. 29, Oct. 14
  Nov. 5m (Los Angeles)

Verdi, *Rigoletto*
Mary Costa (Gilda), Margarethe Bence**/ Mildred Miller (Maddalena); Cornell MacNeil/Ettore Bastianini (Rigoletto), Renato Cioni/Giuseppe Zampieri (Duke), Plinio Clabassi (Sparafucile) Silvio Varviso
  Sept. 30, Oct. 18

Mary Costa (Gilda), Mildred Miller/Margarethe Bence (Maddalena); Ettore Bastianini/Cornell MacNeil (Rigoletto), Renato Cioni/Giuseppe Zampieri (Duke), Plinio Clabassi/Joshua Hecht (Sparafucile) Silvio Varviso
  Nov. 6 and 18 (Los Angeles)

Mary Costa (Gilda), Mildred Miller (Maddalena); Cornell MacNeil (Rigoletto), Giuseppe Zampieri (Duke), Plinio Clabassi (Sparafucile) Silvio Varviso
  Nov. 16 (San Diego)

Beethoven, *Fidelio*
Gré Brouwenstijn (Leonore), Marilyn Horne (Marzelline); Fritz Uhl** (Florestan), Paul Schoeffler (Pizarro), (10/5, 8) William Wildermann/Otto von Rohr (Rocco) Leopold Ludwig
  Oct. 5, 24
  Oct. 8m (Berkeley)
  Nov. 9 (San Diego)
  Nov. 15 (Los Angeles)

Verdi, *Nabucco*
Lucille Udovick (Abigaille), Margarethe Bence (Fenena); Cornell MacNeil (Nabucco), Giorgio Tozzi (Zaccaria), Giuseppe Zampieri/ Renato Cioni (Ismaele) Francesco Molinari-Pradelli
  Oct. 6, 19

Lucille Udovick (Abigaille),
Janis Martin (Fenena);
Ettore Bastianini (Nabucco),
Giorgio Tozzi (Zaccaria),
Renato Cioni (Ismaele)
Francesco Molinari-Pradelli
    Oct. 23

Lucille Udovick (Abigaille),
Margarethe Bence (Fenena);
Cornell MacNeil/
Ettore Bastianini (Nabucco),
Giorgio Tozzi (Zaccaria),
Giuseppe Zampieri/Renato
Cioni (Ismaele)
Francesco Molinari-Pradelli
    Oct. 30 and Nov. 10 (Los
    Angeles)

Britten, *A Midsummer
Night's Dream***
Mary Costa (Tytania),
Marguerite Gignac (Helena),
Marilyn Horne (Hermia);
Russell Oberlin (Oberon),
David Thaw (Lysander),
Claude Heater (Demetrius)
Silvio Varviso
    Oct. 10, 26
    Oct. 31 (Los Angeles)

Verdi,
Un Ballo in Maschera
Gré Brouwenstijn (Amelia),
Margarethe Bence (Ulrica),
Graziella Sciutti (Oscar);
Giuseppe Zampieri (Gustavo),
Ettore Bastianini
(Anckarstrom)
Francesco Molinari-Pradelli
    Oct. 12, 20
    Oct. 27 (Los Angeles)

Gré Brouwenstijn (Amelia),
Janis Martin/Katherine
Hilgenberg (Ulrica),
Graziella Sciutti (Oscar);
Albert Lance/Giuseppe
Zampieri (Gustavo),
Cornell MacNeil
(Anckarstrom)
Francesco Molinari-Pradelli
    Oct. 22 (Sacramento)
    Nov. 11 (Los Angeles)

Wagner, *Die Meistersinger*
Lisa Della Casa (Eva),
Katherine Hilgenberg
(Magdalene); Fritz
Uhl (Walther),
Paul Schoeffler (Sachs),
Geraint Evans (Beckmesser),
(10/17) Giorgio Tozzi/
Otto von Rohr** (Pogner),
David Thaw (David)
Leopold Ludwig
    Oct. 17, 21
    Oct. 28 and Nov. 12m (Los
    Angeles)

Verdi, *Aida*
Gré Brouwenstijn/
Elinor Ross (Aida),
Irene Dalis (Amneris);
Sandor Konya (Radames),
Ettore Bastianini/

Vladimir Ruzdak (Amonasro)
Francesco Molinari-Pradelli
    Nov. 3 and 14 (Los
    Angeles)

1962

Puccini, *La Bohème*
Dorothy Kirsten/(10/22)
Victoria de los Angeles
(Mimi), (9/14) Mary Costa/
Marilyn Horne (Musetta),
Renato Cioni (Rodolfo),
Thomas Tipton (Marcello),
Giorgio Tozzi/(9/29)
John Macurdy (Colline)
Francesco Molinari-Pradelli
    Sept. 14, 22, 29

Victoria de los
Angeles (Mimi),
Marilyn Horne (Musetta);
Sandor Konya/Renato
Cioni (Rodolfo), Ettore
Bastianini/Thomas Tipton
(Marcello), Giorgio Tozzi/
John Macurdy (Colline)
Francesco Molinari-Pradelli
    Oct. 26 and Nov. 16 (Los
    Angeles)

Berg, *Wozzeck* (in English)
Marilyn Horne (Marie);
Geraint Evans (Wozzeck),
Brian Sullivan (Drum Major),
Richard Lewis (Captain),
Michael Langdon** (Doctor)
Leopold Ludwig
    Sept. 15, 21
    Nov. 12 (Los Angeles)

Verdi, *Don Carlo*
Consuelo Rubio (Elisabetta),
Irene Dalis (Eboli);
Sandor Konya (Don Carlo),
Thomas Stewart (Rodrigo),
Giorgio Tozzi (Philip II),
Michael Langdon (Grand
Inquisitor)
Francesco Molinari-Pradelli
    Sept. 18, 22
    Oct. 30 (Los Angeles)

Bizet, *Carmen*
Sona Cervena** (Carmen),
Wilma Lipp (Micaëla);
Mario Del Monaco (Don
José), Thomas Stewart/
(10/27, 11/2) Ettore
Bastianini (Escamillo)
Janis Ferencsik**
    Sept. 20, Oct. 5
    Oct. 27 and Nov. 2 (Los
    Angeles)

Gounod, *Faust*
Mary Costa (Marguerite),
Kerstin Meyer (Siebel);
Albert Lance (Faust),
Thomas Stewart/(11/11)
Frank Guarrera (Valentin),
Giorgio Tozzi
(Méphistophélès)
Oliviero De Fabritiis
    Sept. 25, 28
    Nov. 3 and 11m (Los
    Angeles)

Strauss, *Der Rosenkavalier*
Kerstin Meyer (Octavian),
Elisabeth Schwarzkopf
(Marschallin), Wilma
Lipp (Sophie); Michael
Langdon (Ochs), Glade
Peterson (Italian Singer),
Thomas Tipton (Faninal)
Janis Ferencsik
    Sept. 27, Oct. 12
    Nov. 7 (Los Angeles)

Verdi, *Il Trovatore*
Elinor Ross (Leonora),
Giulietta Simionato/(11/8,
10) Sona Cervena (Azucena);
James McCracken (Manrico),
Ettore Bastianini/
(10/14) Thomas Stewart
(Count Di Luna)
Francesco Molinari-Pradelli
    Oct. 2, 6
    Oct. 14m (Berkeley)
    Nov. 4m and Nov. 10 (Los
    Angeles)
    Nov. 8 (San Diego)

Donizetti,
La Figlia del Reggimento
Jolanda Meneguzzer**
(Marie), Sona
Cervena (Marquise);
Renato Cioni (Tonio),
Salvatore Baccaloni (Sulpice)
Oliviero De Fabritiis
    Oct. 4
    Nov. 13 (Los Angeles)

Verdi, *Otello*
Victoria de los Angeles/
(10/18) Raina
Kabaivanska** (Desdemona);
James McCracken (Otello),
Tito Gobbi (Iago)
Francesco Molinari-Pradelli
    Oct. 9, 18
    Nov. 14 (Los Angeles)

Verdi, *Falstaff*
Wilma Lipp (Alice), Jolanda
Meneguzzer (Nannetta),
Giulietta Simionato/(11/5)
Sona Cervena (Quickly),
Kerstin Meyer (Meg);
Geraint Evans (Falstaff),
Glade Peterson (Fenton),
Thomas Stewart (Ford)
Janis Ferencsik
    Oct. 11, 23
    Nov. 5 (Los Angeles)

Leoncavallo, *Pagliacci*
(10/13) Marilyn Horne/Wilma
Lipp (Nedda); Mario
Del Monaco (Canio),
Ettore Bastianini (Tonio),
Russell Christopher (Silvio)
Oliviero De Fabritiis
    and
Mascagni,
Cavalleria Rusticana
(10/13) Irene Dalis/
Giulietta Simionato
(Santuzza); (10/13, 31)
Renato Cioni/Brian
Sullivan (Turiddu),

Thomas Tipton (Alfio)
Oliviero De Fabritiis
    Oct. 13, 24
    Oct. 21 (Sacramento)
    Oct. 31 (Los Angeles)

Pagliacci
Wilma Lipp (Nedda);
Sandor Konya (Canio),
Geraint Evans (Tonio),
Russell Christopher (Silvio)
Oliviero De Fabritiis
    and
Cavalleria Rusticana
Irene Dalis (Santuzza);
Glade Peterson (Turiddu),
Thomas Tipton (Alfio)
Oliviero De Fabritiis
    Nov. 15 (San Diego)
    Nov. 17 (Los Angeles)

Mozart, *Don Giovanni*
Victoria de los Angeles
(Anna), Elisabeth
Schwarzkopf (Elvira),
Jolanda Meneguzzer
(Zerlina); Giorgio Tozzi
(Giovanni), Richard
Lewis (Ottavio), Geraint
Evans (Leporello)
Leopold Ludwig
    Oct. 16, 20
    Oct. 28m and Nov. 9 (Los
    Angeles)
    Nov. 1 (San Diego)

Stravinsky,
The Rake's Progress
Mary Costa (Anne Trulove),
Kerstin Meyer (Baba
the Turk), Sona
Cervena (Mother Goose);
Richard Lewis (Tom
Rakewell), Thomas
Tipton (Nick Shadow)
Leopold Ludwig
    Oct. 19, 25
    Oct. 29 (Los Angeles)

Puccini, *Tosca*
Dorothy Kirsten (Tosca);
Renato Cioni (Cavaradossi),
Ettore Bastianini/
Tito Gobbi (Scarpia)
Francesco Molinari-Pradelli
    Nov. 6 and 18m (Los
    Angeles)

1963

Verdi, *Aida*
Leontyne Price (Aida),
Regina Resnik/(10/18)
Sandra Warfield (Amneris);
Sandor Konya/(10/18)
James McCracken
(Radames), John
Shaw**/(10/18) Julien
Haas (Amonasro)
Francesco Molinari-Pradelli
    Sept. 13, 21
    Oct. 18

Leontyne Price (Aida),
Regina Resnik/Nell Rankin
(Amneris); Sandor Konya
(Radames), John Shaw/

Julien Haas (Amonasro)
Francesco Molinari-Pradelli
    Nov. 5 and 10m (Los
    Angeles)

Bellini, *La Sonnambula*
Joan Sutherland (Amina);
Renato Cioni (Elvino),
Richard Cross (Rodolfo)
Richard Bonynge
    Sept. 14, 17, 22m
    Nov. 2 and 4 (Los Angeles)

Boito, *Mefistofele*
Mary Costa
(Margherita, Elena);
Giorgio Tozzi (Mefistofele),
Sandor Konya (Faust)
Francesco Molinari-Pradelli
    Sept. 19, 24
    Nov. 17m (Los Angeles)

Rossini,
Il Barbiere di Siviglia
Reri Grist (Rosina); Hermann
Prey (Figaro), Cesare
Valletti (Almaviva), Peter
Van Der Bilt** (Basilio),
Elfego Esparza** (Bartolo)
Janis Ferencsik
    Sept. 20, 28, Oct. 6m
    Nov. 3m and 9 (Los
    Angeles)

Saint-Saëns,
Samson et Dalila
Sandra Warfield/(11/19)
Nell Rankin (Dalila);
James McCracken (Samson),
Julien Haas** (Priest)
Georges Prêtre
    Sept. 26, Oct. 11
    Nov. 19 (Los Angeles)

Puccini, *Tosca*
Leontyne Price (Tosca);
Sandor Konya (Cavaradossi),
John Shaw (Scarpia)
Georges Prêtre
    Sept. 27, Oct. 3
    Nov. 1 (Los Angeles)

Leontyne Price (Tosca);
Renato Cioni (Cavaradossi),
Julien Haas (Scarpia)
Georges Prêtre
    Oct. 13m
    Oct. 28 (Sacramento)
    Nov. 13 (Los Angeles)

Tchaikovsky, *The Queen
of Spades* (in English)
Dorothy Kirsten (Lisa),
Regina Resnik (Countess),
Janis Martin (Paulina);
James McCracken
(Gherman), Thomas
Stewart (Yeletsky),
Hermann Prey (Olivier),
John Shaw (Tomsky)
Leopold Ludwig
    Oct. 1, 5, 27m
    Nov. 14 (San Diego)
    Nov. 22 (Los Angeles -
    Performance cancelled)

Verdi, *La Traviata*
Mary Costa (Violetta);
Renato Cioni/(11/23)

Glade Peterson (Alfredo),
Thomas Stewart (Germont)
Francesco Molinari-Pradelli
    Oct. 4, 17
    Nov. 15 and 23 (Los
    Angeles)

Verdi,
La Forza del Destino
Leontyne Price (Leonora);
James McCracken
(Don Alvaro), Julien
Haas (Don Carlo), Walter
Kreppel** (Padre Guardiano)
Francesco Molinari-Pradelli
    Oct. 8, 24
    Nov. 16 (Los Angeles)

Wagner, *Die Walküre*
Amy Shuard (Brünnhilde),
Siw Ericsdotter**
(Sieglinde), Regina Resnik
(Fricka); Jon Vickers
(Siegmund), Leonardo
Wolovsky**/(11/21)
Otto Edelmann (Wotan),
Walter Kreppel (Hunding)
Leopold Ludwig
    Oct. 10, 15
    Nov. 18 (Los Angeles)
    Nov. 21 (San Diego)

Verdi, *Falstaff*
Mary Costa (Alice), Jolanda
Meneguzzer (Nannetta),
Sona Cervena (Quickly),
Janis Martin (Meg);
Geraint Evans (Falstaff),
Glade Peterson (Fenton),
Thomas Stewart (Ford)
Janis Ferencsik
    Oct. 12
    Oct. 20m (Berkeley)
    Nov. 7 (San Diego)

Poulenc, *The Dialogues
of the Carmelites*
Lee Venora (Blanche), Siw
Ericsdotter (Mme. Lidoine),
Regina Resnik (Mme.
Croissy), Sandra Warfield
(Mother Marie), Reri Grist
(Constance)
Leopold Ludwig
    Oct. 22, 26
    Nov. 12 (Los Angeles)

Strauss, *Capriccio*
Elisabeth Schwarzkopf
(Countess), Sona
Cervena (Clairon);
Cesare Valletti (Flamand),
Thomas Stewart (Count),
Hermann Prey (Olivier),
Leonardo Wolovsky
(La Roche)
Georges Prêtre
    Oct. 25, 31
    Nov. 6 (Los Angeles)

Mozart, *Così fan tutte*
Elisabeth Schwarzkopf
(Fiordiligi), Helen
Vanni (Dorabella),
Reri Grist (Despina);
Cesare Valletti (Ferrando),
Hermann Prey (Guglielmo),

Leonardo Wolovsky
(Don Alfonso)
Janos Ferencsik
    Oct. 19, 29
    Nov. 8 (Los Angeles)

Puccini, *La Bohème*
Lee Venora (Mimi),
Mary Costa (Musetta);
Renato Cioni (Rodolfo),
Julien Haas (Marcello),
Joshua Hecht (Colline)
Francesco Molinari-Pradelli
    Nov. 20 and 24m (Los
    Angeles)

1964

Verdi, *Otello*
Pilar Lorengar**
(Desdemona);
James McCracken (Otello),
Tito Gobbi/(11/2, 24)
Chester Ludgin (Iago)
Francesco Molinari-Pradelli
    Sept. 11, 19, 25
    Nov. 2 (Sacramento)
    Nov. 17 (Los Angeles)
    Nov. 24 (San Diego)

Wagner, *Parsifal*
Irene Dalis (Kundry); Sandor
Konya (Parsifal), Eberhard
Waechter (Amfortas),
Giorgio Tozzi (Gurnemanz),
Joshua Hecht (Klingsor)
Georges Prêtre
    Sept. 12, 18, 20m
    Nov. 22m (Los Angeles)

Bizet, *Carmen*
Regina Resnik (Carmen),
Mary Costa/Pilar
Lorengar (Micaëla);
Richard Martell (Don José),
Joshua Hecht (Escamillo)
Georges Prêtre/Ferdinand
Leitner
    Sept. 14, Oct. 1

Regina Resnik (Carmen),
Pilar Lorengar (Micaëla),
Jon Vickers (Don José),
Joshua Hecht (Escamillo)
Ferdinand Leitner
    Oct. 9
    Nov. 19 (San Diego)

Regina Resnik (Carmen),
Lee Venora/Mary Costa
(Micaëla); Jon Vickers/
Richard Martell (Don José),
Joshua Hecht (Escamillo)
Ferdinand Leitner/
Georges Prêtre
    Nov. 16 and 25 (Los
    Angeles)

Mozart, *Le Nozze di Figaro*
Reri Grist (Susanna),
Pilar Lorengar (Countess),
Lee Venora (Cherubino);
Geraint Evans (Figaro),
Eberhard Waechter (Count)
Ferdinand Leitner**
    Sept. 17, Oct. 3
    Nov. 21 (Los Angeles)

Strauss, *Der Rosenkavalier*
Irmgard Seefried (Octavian), Elisabeth Schwarzkopf/ (11/26) Hildegard Hillebrecht** (Marschallin), Reri Grist (Sophie), Otto Edelmann (Ochs), André Montal (Italian Singer), Chester Ludgin (Faninal) Ferdinand Leitner
Sept. 22, 24, 27m
Nov. 26 (Los Angeles)

Strauss,
Die Frau ohne Schatten
Ella Lee (Empress), Gladys Kuchta (Dyer's Wife), Irene Dalis (Nurse); Richard Martell (Emperor), Eberhard Waechter (Barak) Leopold Ludwig
Sept. 26, Oct. 30
Nov. 18 (Los Angeles)

Verdi, *Il Trovatore*
Ella Lee (Leonora), Regina Resnik/(10/24, 29, 11/7) Sandra Warfield (Azucena); James McCracken (Manrico), Raymond Wolansky (Count Di Luna) Francesco Molinari-Pradelli
Sept. 29, Oct. 16, 24, 29
Nov. 7 and 29m (Los Angeles)

Puccini, *Gianni Schicchi*
Lee Venora (Lauretta); Tito Gobbi (Schicchi), Glade Peterson (Rinuccio) Ferdinand Leitner
and

Orff, *Carmina Burana*
(10/2) Reri Grist/Mary Costa (Burgundian Lady); Raymond Wolansky (Troubadour, Drinker) Ferdinand Leitner
Oct. 2, 10
Nov. 12 (San Diego)
Nov. 20 (Los Angeles)

Verdi, *Nabucco*
Gladys Kuchta (Abigaille), Janis Martin (Fenena); Tito Gobbi (Nabucco), Giorgio Tozzi (Zaccaria), Franco Tagliavini** (Ismaele) Francesco Molinari-Pradelli
Oct. 6, 15
Oct. 18m (Berkeley)
Nov. 14 (Los Angeles)

Smetana,
The Bartered Bride
Mary Costa (Marie); Glade Peterson (Jenik), Howard Fried (Vashek), Geraint Evans (Kecal) Leopold Ludwig
Oct. 8, 11m
Nov. 15m (Los Angeles)

Beethoven, *Fidelio*
Birgit Nilsson (Leonore), Lee Venora (Marzelline); Jon Vickers (Florestan), Geraint Evans (Pizarro), Andrew Foldi (Rocco) Leopold Ludwig
Oct. 13, 17
Nov. 9 (Los Angeles)

Puccini, *Turandot*
Birgit Nilsson (Turandot), Pilar Lorengar (Liù); Franco Tagliavini (Calaf), Giorgio Tozzi (Timur) Francesco Molinari-Pradelli
Oct. 20, 22, 25m
Nov. 6 and 11 (Los Angeles)

Shostakovich, *Katerina Ismailova*** (in English)
Marie Collier** (Katerina); Jon Vickers (Sergei), Chester Ludgin (Boris), Richard Martell (Zinovy), Giorgio Tozzi (Old Convict) Leopold Ludwig
Oct. 23, 31
Nov. 23 (Los Angeles)

Leoncavallo, *Pagliacci*
Mary Costa (Nedda); James McCracken/ Jon Vickers (Canio), Robert Weede (Tonio), Raymond Wolansky (Silvio) Francesco Molinari-Pradelli
and

Orff, *Carmina Burana*
Reri Grist (Burgundian Lady); Raymond Wolansky (Troubadour, Drinker) Francesco Molinari-Pradelli
Oct. 27
Nov. 28 (Los Angeles)

Verdi, *La Traviata*
Joan Sutherland (Violetta); Robert Ilosfalvy** (Alfredo), Eberhard Waechter (Germont) Richard Bonynge
Nov. 1m, 3, 5
Nov. 8m and 10 (Los Angeles)

Verdi, *Aida*
Ella Lee (Aida), Irene Dalis (Amneris); Jon Vickers/James McCracken (Radames), Chester Ludgin (Amonasro) Francesco Molinari-Pradelli
Nov. 13 and 27 (Los Angeles)

1965

Giordano, *Andrea Chénier*
Renata Tebaldi (Maddalena); Richard Tucker/(10/2) Giovanni Gibin/(11/16) Franco Corelli (Chénier), Ettore Bastianini (Gérard) Francesco Molinari-Pradelli
Sept. 10, 16, Oct. 2
Nov. 16 (Los Angeles)

Wagner, *Die Meistersinger*
Pilar Lorengar/(10/3) Lucine Amara (Eva), Claramae Turner (Magdalene); Jess Thomas (Walther), Heinz Imdahl** (Hans Sachs), Toni Blankenheim** (Beckmesser), Thomas O'Leary (Pogner), Alexander Young (David) Leopold Ludwig
Sept. 11, 17, Oct. 3m
Nov. 12 (Los Angeles)

Strauss, J.,
Die Fledermaus (in English)
Mary Costa (Rosalinda), Reri Grist/(11/24) Patricia Brooks (Adele), Sona Cervena (Orlofsky); Richard Lewis (Eisenstein), Brian Sullivan (Alfred) (9/14, 18, 24, 30) Leopold Ludwig/Horst Stein
Sept. 14, 18, 24, 30, Oct. 10m
Nov. 15, 21m, 27 (Los Angeles)
Nov. 24 (San Diego)

Puccini, *La Bohème*
Renata Tebaldi (Mimi), (9/19) Jolanda Meneguzzer/ Marie Collier (Musetta); Sandor Konya/(9/29) Renato Cioni (Rodolfo), Raymond Wolansky (Marcello), Joshua Hecht (Colline) Piero Bellugi
Sept. 19m, 23, 29
Nov. 20 and 25 (Los Angeles)

Puccini,
La Fanciulla del West
Marie Collier (Minnie), (9/21, 26) Giovanni Gibin/ Franco Corelli (Johnson), Chester Ludgin (Rance) Francesco Molinari-Pradelli
Sept. 21, 26m
Nov. 10 (San Diego)
Nov. 13 (Los Angeles)

Berg, *Lulu* (in English)
Evelyn Lear (Lulu), Sona Cervena (Geschwitz); Ramon Vinay (Dr. Schön), Brian Sullivan (Painter), Richard Lewis (Alwa) Leopold Ludwig
Sept. 25, Oct. 1
Nov. 18 (Los Angeles)

Verdi,
La Forza del Destino
Leontyne Price (Leonora), Annamaria Bessel** (Preziosilla); Sandor Konya (Don Alvaro), Raymond Wolansky (Don Carlo), Ugo Trama (Padre Guardiano) Francesco Molinari-Pradelli
Sept. 28, Oct. 5, 9
Nov. 11, 14m (Los Angeles)

Rossini,
Il Barbiere di Siviglia
Reri Grist/(10/24, 11/28) Jolanda Meneguzzer (Rosina); Richard Fredricks/(10/24) Heinz Blankenburg (Figaro), Alexander Young (Almaviva), Ugo Trama (Basilio), Ramon Vinay (Bartolo) Piero Bellugi
Oct. 7, 8, 24m
Nov. 28m

Wagner, *Lohengrin*
Hildegard Hillebrecht (Elsa), Annamaria Bessel (Ortrud); Jess Thomas (Lohengrin), Chester Ludgin (Telramund), Thomas O'Leary (Heinrich) Horst Stein**
Oct. 12, 14
Oct. 17m (Berkeley)
Nov. 1 (Sacramento)
Nov. 6 and 22 (Los Angeles)
Nov. 17 (San Diego)

Mozart, *Don Giovanni*
Claire Watson** (Elisabetta), Marilyn Horne (Eloira); Jon Vickers (Don Carlo), Peter Glossop (Rodrigo), Giorgio Tozzi (Philip II), Chester Ludgin (Grand Inquisitor) Francesco Molinari-Pradelli
Sept. 22, 27, Oct. 1

Strauss, *Elektra*
Amy Shuard (Elektra), Enriqueta Tarrés** (Chrysothemis), Regina Resnik (Klytemnestra); Richard Cassilly (Aegisth), Thomas Stewart (Orest) Horst Stein
Sept. 24, 30, Oct. 6
Oct. 9m (Berkeley)

Montemezzi,
L'Amore dei Tre Re
Dorothy Kirsten (Fiora); Giuseppe Campora (Avito), Raymond Wolansky (Manfredo), Nicola Ghiuselev (Archibaldo) Francesco Molinari-Pradelli
Oct. 4, 7, 15

Mussorgsky, *Boris Godunov* (in English)
(Shostakovich orchestration) Janis Martin (Marina); Chester Ludgin (Boris), Richard Cassilly (Dimitri), Ara Berberian (Pimen), Howard Fried (Shuisky), Morley Meredith (Rangoni) Horst Stein
Oct. 11, 14, 20, 23m

Verdi, *Rigoletto*
Reri Grist (Gilda), Joyce Blackham (Maddalena); Peter Glossop (Rigoletto),

Horst Stein
Oct. 23, 26
Nov. 19 (Los Angeles)

Debussy,
Pelléas et Mélisande
Pilar Lorengar (Mélisande), Claramae Turner (Geneviève); André Jobin** (Pelléas), Thomas Stewart (Golaud), Thomas O'Leary (Arkel) Jean Martinon
Oct. 29, Nov. 3
Nov. 9 (Los Angeles)

1966

Bellini, *I Puritani*
Joan Sutherland (Elvira); Alfredo Kraus (Arturo), Raymond Wolansky (Riccardo), Nicola Ghiuselev (Giorgio) Richard Bonynge
Sept. 20, 23, 29, Oct. 2m, 8
Oct. 5 (Sacramento)

Verdi, *Don Carlo*
Claire Watson** (Elisabetta), Marilyn Horne (Eboli); Jon Vickers (Don Carlo), Peter Glossop (Rodrigo), Giorgio Tozzi (Philip II), Chester Ludgin (Grand Inquisitor) Francesco Molinari-Pradelli
Sept. 22, 27, Oct. 1

Strauss, *Elektra*
Amy Shuard (Elektra), Enriqueta Tarrés** (Chrysothemis), Regina Resnik (Klytemnestra); Richard Cassilly (Aegisth), Thomas Stewart (Orest) Horst Stein
Sept. 24, 30, Oct. 6
Oct. 9m (Berkeley)

Montemezzi,
L'Amore dei Tre Re
Dorothy Kirsten (Fiora); Giuseppe Campora (Avito), Raymond Wolansky (Manfredo), Nicola Ghiuselev (Archibaldo) Francesco Molinari-Pradelli
Oct. 4, 7, 15

Mussorgsky, *Boris Godunov* (in English)
(Shostakovich orchestration) Janis Martin (Marina); Chester Ludgin (Boris), Richard Cassilly (Dimitri), Ara Berberian (Pimen), Howard Fried (Shuisky), Morley Meredith (Rangoni) Horst Stein
Oct. 11, 14, 20, 23m

Verdi, *Rigoletto*
Reri Grist (Gilda), Joyce Blackham (Maddalena); Peter Glossop (Rigoletto),

Alfredo Kraus (Duke), Walter Kreppel (Sparafucile) Francesco Molinari-Pradelli
Oct. 13, 16m, 21

Lee Venora (Gilda), Janis Martin (Maddalena); Chester Ludgin (Rigoletto), Ottavio Garaventa (Duke), Federico Davià** (Sparafucile) Francesco Molinari-Pradelli
Nov. 5

Wagner, *Tannhäuser*
Régine Crespin (Elisabeth), Janis Martin (Venus); Jess Thomas (Tannhäuser), Thomas Stewart (Wolfram), Walter Kreppel (Hermann) Horst Stein
Oct. 18, 22, 27, 30m

Puccini, *Madama Butterfly*
Teresa Stratas/(11/13, 26) Dorothy Kirsten (Cio-Cio-San), Dorothy Krebill/ (11/13, 26) Janis Martin (Suzuki); Ottavio Garaventa (Pinkerton), Chester Ludgin (Sharpless) Francesco Molinari-Pradelli
Oct. 25, 28, Nov. 3
Nov. 13m, 26

Mozart, *Le Nozze di Figaro*
Reri Grist (Susanna), Claire Watson (Countess), Lee Venora (Cherubino); Geraint Evans (Figaro), Thomas Stewart (Count) Jascha Horenstein
Oct. 29, Nov. 1, 6m, 10

Berlioz, *Les Troyens*
Régine Crespin (Cassandre, Didon), Sona Cervena (Anna), Dorothy Krebill (Ascagne); Jon Vickers (Enée), David Thaw (Iopas), Ara Berberian (Narbal), Clifford Grant (Panthée) Jean Périsson**
Nov. 4, 8, 12

Verdi, *Falstaff*
Raina Kabaivanska (Alice), Lee Venora (Nannetta), Sona Cervena (Quickly), Janis Martin (Meg); Ramon Vinay (Falstaff), Ottavio Garaventa (Fenton), Frank Guarrera (Ford) Francesco Molinari-Pradelli
Nov. 11, 17, 20m

Bizet, *Carmen*
Grace Bumbry (Carmen), Carol Todd (Micaëla); Jon Vickers (Don José), Frank Guarrera (Escamillo) Jean Périsson
Nov. 15, 18, 24, 27m

Janáček,
*The Makropulos Case***
Marie Collier (Emilia Marty); Gregory Dempsey**

(Albert Gregor), Chester Ludgin (Baron Prus) Jascha Horenstein
Nov. 19, 22, 25

1967

Ponchielli, *La Gioconda*
Leyla Gencer (Gioconda), Grace Bumbry (Laura), Maureen Forrester (La Cieca); Renato Cioni (Enzo), Chester Ludgin (Barnaba), Ara Berberian (Alvise) Giuseppe Patanè
Sept. 19, 22, 27, Oct. 1m
Sept. 24 (Sacramento)

Mozart, *The Magic Flute*
Jane Marsh (Pamina), Jeanette Scovotti (Queen of the Night); Stuart Burrows** (Tamino), Geraint Evans (Papageno), Thomas O'Leary (Sarastro) Horst Stein
Sept. 20, 23, 26, 29, Oct. 8m

Charpentier, *Louise*
Arlene Saunders (Louise), Sona Cervena (Mother); John Alexander (Julien), Nicola Rossi Lemeni (Father) Jean Périsson
Sept. 30, Oct. 3, 13

Strauss, *Der Rosenkavalier*
Sylvia Anderson (Octavian), Régine Crespin (Marschallin), Reri Grist (Sophie); Josef Greindl (Ochs), Robert Ilosfalvy (Italian Singer), John Modenos (Faninal) Horst Stein
Oct. 4, 7, 10, 15m

Verdi, *Macbeth*
Grace Bumbry (Lady Macbeth); Chester Ludgin (Macbeth), Daniele Barioni (Macduff), Thomas O'Leary (Banquo) Giuseppe Patanè
Oct. 6, 11, 17
Oct. 22m (Berkeley)

Puccini, *Manon Lescaut*
Dorothy Kirsten (Manon); Robert Ilosfalvy (des Grieux), Delme Bryn-Jones** (Lescaut) Herbert Grossman
Oct. 14, 20, 24

Wagner, *Tristan und Isolde*
Irene Dalis (Isolde), Mignon Dunn (Brangäne); Jess Thomas (Tristan), Chester Ludgin (Kurwenal), Josef Greindl (King Marke) Horst Stein
Oct. 18, 27, 31, Nov. 5m

Donizetti, *L'Elisir d'Amore*
Reri Grist (Adina); Alfredo Kraus (Nemorino), Ingvar Wixell** (Belcore),

Sesto Bruscantini (Dulcamara)
Giuseppe Patanè
Oct. 21, 25, 29m

Schuller, *The Visitation*
Felicia Weathers (Teena), Jeanette Scovotti (Miss Hampton); Simon Estes (Carter Jones), Ragnar Ulfung (Chuck), Ingvar Wixell (Held)
Gunther Schuller
Oct. 28, Nov. 3, 8

Gounod, *Faust*
Arlene Saunders (Marguerite), Sylvia Anderson (Siebel); Alfredo Kraus (Faust), Ingvar Wixell (Valentin), Nicolai Ghiaurov (Méphistophélès)
Jean Périsson
Nov. 1, 4, 7, 10, 12m

Puccini, *La Bohème*
Mirella Freni (Mimì), Jeanette Scovotti (Musetta); Luciano Pavarotti (Rodolfo), Ingvar Wixell (Marcello), Simon Estes (Colline)
Mario Bernardi**
Nov. 11, 15, 19m, 21, 24

Verdi,
Un Ballo in Maschera
Leontyne Price (Amelia), Mignon Dunn (Ulrica), Reri Grist (Oscar); Ragnar Ulfung (Gustavo), Cornell MacNeil (Renato)
Mario Bernardi
Nov. 14, 18, 23, 26m

Wagner, *Das Rheingold*
Irene Dalis (Fricka), Mignon Dunn (Erda); David Ward (Wotan), Jess Thomas (Loge), John Modenos (Alberich)
Leopold Ludwig
Nov. 17, 22, 25

1968

Verdi, *Ernani*
Leontyne Price (Elvira); Renato Cioni (Ernani), Peter Glossop (Don Carlo), Ezio Flagello (Silva)
Giuseppe Patanè
Sept. 13, 18, 22m, 28

Rossini,
Il Barbiere di Siviglia
Teresa Berganza (Rosina); Ingvar Wixell (Figaro), Pietro Bottazzo (Almaviva), Nicola Rossi Lemeni (Basilio), Renato Capecchi (Bartolo)
Aldo Faldi
Sept. 14, 17, 20, 25, 29m

Berlioz, *Les Troyens*
Régine Crespin (Cassandre, Didon), Margarita Lilova**(Anna), Sylvia Anderson (Ascanius); Guy Chauvet (Enée),

Rico Serbo (Iopas), Ara Berberian (Narbal), Richard J. Clark (Pantheas) Jean Périsson
Sept. 15m, 21, 24
Oct. 6m (Berkeley)

Wagner, *Die Walküre*
Nadezda Kniplova (Brünnhilde), Régine Crespin (Sieglinde), Margarita Lilova (Fricka); Jess Thomas (Siegmund), Hubert Hofmann (Wotan), William Wildermann (Hunding)
Sept. 27, 30, Oct. 9, 12

Puccini, *Madama Butterfly*
Jeannette Pilou/(11/9) Dorothy Kirsten (Cio-Cio-San), Sylvia Anderson (Suzuki); Nicholas Di Virgilio (Pinkerton), Ingvar Wixell (Sharpless) Aldo Faldi
Oct. 4, 19, 27m, Nov. 9, 29
Oct. 16 (Sacramento)

Triple Bill:
Weill/Schuller, *Royal Palace**** (in German)
Carol Todd (Dejanira), Sheila Marks (Soprano); Vahan Khanzadian (Tenor)
Gunther Schuller
and
Schoenberg, *Erwartung*
Marie Collier (Woman)
Gunther Schuller
and
Milhaud,
Christopher Columbus (The Discovery of America)
Carol Todd (Isabella), Shigemi Matsumoto (Soprano); Thomas Tipton (Columbus I), Allan Monk (Columbus II), William Wildermann (Explicator)
Gunther Schuller
Oct. 5, 8, 13m

Verdi, *Il Trovatore*
Radmila Bakocevic (Leonora), Margarita Lilova (Azucena); Robert Ilosfalvy (Manrico), Victor Braun**/(11/2) Louis Quilico (Count Di Luna)
Giuseppe Patanè
Oct. 11, 15, 20m, 23, Nov. 2

Berg, *Wozzeck* (in English)
Evelyn Lear (Marie); Geraint Evans (Wozzeck), Ticho Parly (Drum Major), Richard Lewis (Captain), Herbert Beattie (Doctor)
Leopold Ludwig
Oct. 18, 22, 26

Donizetti,
Lucia di Lammermoor
Margherita Rinaldi (Lucia);

Luciano Pavarotti/ (11/6) Nicholas Di Virgilio (Edgardo), Victor Braun (Enrico), Clifford Grant (Raimondo)
Giuseppe Patanè
Oct. 25, 29, Nov. 3m, 6, 9

Strauss, *Salome*
Anja Silja** (Salome), Sona Cervena (Herodias); Richard Lewis (Herod), Franz Mazura** (Jokanaan)
Horst Stein
Nov. 1, 5, 10m, 16

Mozart, *Don Giovanni*
Enriqueta Tarrés (Anna), Teresa Zylis-Gara** (Elvira), Jeannette Pilou (Zerlina); Cesare Siepi (Giovanni), William Holley (Ottavio), Ugo Trama (Leporello)
Horst Stein
Nov. 8, 12, 17m, 20, 23

Puccini, *Turandot*
Amy Shuard (Turandot), Jane Marsh (Liù); Ludovic Spiess** (Calaf), Ara Berberian (Timur)
Giuseppe Patanè
Nov. 15, 19, 24m, 27, 30

Auber, *Fra Diavolo* (in English)
Mary Costa (Zerlina), Sylvia Anderson (Lady Pamela); Nicolai Gedda (Fra Diavolo), Herbert Beattie (Lord Plimpton)
Mario Bernardi
Nov. 22, 26, Dec. 1m

1969 LOS ANGELES SEASON

Puccini, *Turandot*
Amy Shuard (Turandot), Jane Marsh (Liù); Ludovic Spiess (Calaf), Ara Berberian (Timur)
Giuseppe Patanè
March 1, 7

Rossini,
Il Barbiere di Siviglia
Mary Costa (Rosina); Enzo Sordello (Figaro), Pietro Bottazzo (Almaviva), Nicola Rossi Lemeni (Basilio), Ramon Vinay (Bartolo)
Aldo Faldi
March 2m, 15

Verdi, *Il Trovatore*
Radmila Bakocevic (Leonora), Margarita Lilova (Azucena); Robert Ilosfalvy (Manrico), Victor Braun (Count Di Luna)
Giuseppe Patanè
March 5, 9m

Donizetti,
Lucia di Lammermoor
Margherita Rinaldi (Lucia); Renato Cioni (Edgardo),

Delme Bryn-Jones (Enrico), Clifford Grant (Raimondo)
Giuseppe Patanè
March 8, 23m

Verdi, *Ernani*
Leontyne Price (Elvira); Renato Cioni (Ernani), Peter Glossop (Don Carlo), Giorgio Tozzi (Silva)
Giuseppe Patanè
March 14, 19

Wagner, *Das Rheingold*
Sona Cervena (Fricka), Margarita Lilova (Erda); Franz Mazura (Wotan), Glade Peterson (Loge), Rudolf Knoll (Alberich)
Horst Stein
March 28

Mozart, *Don Giovanni*
Enriqueta Tarrés (Anna), Teresa Zylis-Gara (Elvira), Jeannette Pilou (Zerlina); Cesare Siepi (Giovanni), William Holley (Ottavio), Ugo Trama (Leporello)
Horst Stein
March 16m, 22

Berlioz, *Les Troyens*
Régine Crespin (Cassandre, Didon), Margarita Lilova (Anna), Sylvia Anderson (Ascagne); Guy Chauvet (Enée), Rico Serbo (Iopas), Ara Berberian (Narbal), Richard J. Clark (Panthée)
Jean Périsson
March 21

Puccini, *Madama Butterfly*
Jeannette Pilou/Dorothy Kirsten (Cio-Cio-San), Sylvia Anderson (Suzuki); Nicholas Di Virgilio (Pinkerton), Delme Bryn-Jones (Sharpless)
Aldo Faldi
March 12, 30m

Wagner, *Die Walküre*
Nadezda Kniplova (Brünnhilde), Régine Crespin (Sieglinde), Margarita Lilova (Fricka); Jon Vickers (Siegmund), David Ward (Wotan), William Wildermann (Hunding)
Leopold Ludwig
March 26, 29

1969 SAN FRANCISCO SEASON

Verdi, *La Traviata*
Jeannette Pilou (Violetta); Franco Bonisolli (Alfredo), Ingvar Wixell (Germont)
Giuseppe Patanè
Sept. 16, 19, 24, 28m, Oct. 4

Strauss, *Ariadne auf Naxos*
Ludmila Dvorakova (Prima Donna, Ariadne), Reri Grist/(9/26)

Colette Boky (Zerbinetta), Janis Martin (Composer); Jess Thomas/(9/21) James King (Tenor, Bacchus)
Gunther Schuller
Sept. 17, 21m, 26

Puccini, *La Bohème*
Dorothy Kirsten (Mimì), Colette Boky/(10/1, 12) Margot Moser (Musetta); Luciano Pavarotti (Rodolfo), Sesto Bruscantini/(10/1, 12) Ingvar Wixell (Marcello), Ara Berberian (Colline)
Anton Coppola
Sept. 20, 23, Oct. 1, 12m

Lucine Amara/
Dorothy Kirsten (Mimì), Margot Moser (Musetta); Placido Domingo/ John Alexander (Rodolfo), James Farrar (Marcello), Ara Berberian (Colline)
Jean Périsson
Nov. 15, 28

Beethoven, *Fidelio*
Gwyneth Jones (Leonore), Sheila Marks (Marzelline); James King (Florestan), Franz Mazura (Pizarro), Peter Lagger** (Rocco)
Sixten Ehrling
Sept. 27, 30, Oct. 3, 8

Donizetti, *L'Elisir d'Amore*
Reri Grist (Adina); Luciano Pavarotti (Nemorino), Ingvar Wixell (Belcore), Sesto Bruscantini (Dulcamara)
Giuseppe Patanè
Oct. 7, 10, 15, 19m

Wagner, *Götterdämmerung*
Amy Shuard (Brünnhilde), Janis Martin (Gutrune); Jess Thomas (Siegfried), Franz Mazura (Gunther), Peter Lagger (Hagen)
Otmar Suitner**
Oct. 11, 14, 17, 26m

Verdi, *Aida*
Gwyneth Jones (Aida), Margarita Lilova (Amneris); Guy Chauvet (Radames), James Farrar (Amonasro)
Jean Périsson
Oct. 18, 21, 24, 29

Ljiljana Molnar-Talajic** (Aida), Margarita Lilova (Amneris); Jon Vickers (Radames), James Farrar (Amonasro)
Jean Périsson
Nov. 23 (Sacramento)
Nov. 26, 30m

Mozart, *The Magic Flute*
Margaret Price** (Pamina), Cristina Deutekom (Queen of the Night); Stuart Burrows (Tamino), Geraint Evans (Papageno), David Ward/(10/31, 11/2)

Peter Lagger (Sarastro)
Charles Mackerras
Oct. 22, 25, 28, 31
Nov. 2m (Berkeley)

Verdi,
La Forza del Destino
Nancy Tatum (Leonora), Sylvia Anderson (Preziosilla); Carlo Bergonzi (Don Alvaro), Ingvar Wixell (Don Carlo), Giorgio Tozzi (Padre Guardiano)
Giuseppe Patanè
Nov. 1, 4, 7, 9m, 12

Rossini, *La Cenerentola*
Teresa Berganza (Angelina); Pietro Bottazzo (Don Ramiro), Renato Capecchi (Dandini), Paolo Montarsolo (Don Magnifico)
Charles Mackerras
Nov. 5, 8, 11, 16m

Debussy,
Pelléas et Mélisande
Jeannette Pilou (Mélisande), Margarita Lilova (Geneviève); Henri Gui** (Pelléas), Frantz Petri** (Golaud), Giorgio Tozzi (Arkel)
Jean Périsson
Nov. 14, 18, 22

Janáček, *Jenůfa* (in English)
Felicia Weathers (Jenůfa), Irene Dalis (Kostelnička); Glade Peterson (Laca), Ragnar Ulfung (Števa)
Bohumil Gregor**
Nov. 21, 25, 29

1970

Puccini, *Tosca*
Dorothy Kirsten/(9/26, 10/4) Régine Crespin/(10/9) Jeannine Crader (Tosca); Ludovic Spiess (Cavaradossi), Cornell MacNeil (Scarpia)
Carlo Felice Cillario
Sept. 18, 23, 26, Oct. 4m, 9

Dorothy Kirsten (Tosca); Placido Domingo (Cavaradossi), Louis Quilico (Scarpia)
James Levine
Nov. 22m, 28

Verdi, *Falstaff*
Mary Costa (Alice), Margaret Price (Nannetta), Lily Chookasian (Quickly), Sylvia Anderson (Meg); Geraint Evans (Falstaff), Stuart Burrows (Fenton), Dan Richardson** (Ford)
Bruno Bartoletti
Sept. 19, 25, 29, Oct. 7

Wagner, *Siegfried*
Berit Lindholm (Brünnhilde), Sheila Nadler (Erda); Jess Thomas (Siegfried), Dan Richardson (Alberich),

Ragnar Ulfung (Mime), Thomas Stewart (Wanderer)
Otmar Suitner
Sept. 22, 27m, Oct. 2

Bizet, *Carmen*
Brigitte Fassbaender** (Carmen), Jane Marsh (Micaëla); Guy Chauvet (Don José), José Van Dam (Escamillo)
Jean Périsson
Sept. 30, Oct. 3, 6, 11m, 16

Joy Davidson (Carmen), Shigemi Matsumoto/ Jane Marsh (Micaëla); Glade Peterson/ Placido Domingo (Don José), Allan Monk (Escamillo)
Jean Périsson
Nov. 16 (Sacramento)
Nov. 26

Verdi, *Nabucco*
Marion Lippert (Abigaille), Sylvia Anderson (Fenena); Cornell MacNeil (Nabucco), Rolf Bjoerling** (Ismaele), Giorgio Tozzi (Zaccaria)
Carlo Felice Cillario
Oct. 10, 13, 18m, 21

Mozart, *Così fan tutte*
Margaret Price (Fiordiligi), Teresa Berganza/(10/23, 28) Rosalind Elias (Dorabella), Graziella Sciutti (Despina); Ryland Davies** (Ferrando), Alberto Rinaldi (Guglielmo), Renato Capecchi (Don Alfonso)
John Pritchard
Oct. 17, 20, 23, 28

Strauss, *Salome*
Anja Silja (Salome), Sona Cervena (Herodias); Ragnar Ulfung (Herod), Gerd Nienstedt (Jokanaan)
Bohumil Gregor
Oct. 24, 27, 30

Wagner, *Tristan und Isolde*
Birgit Nilsson (Isolde), Janis Martin (Brangäne); Wolfgang Windgassen (Tristan), William Dooley (Kurwenal), Giorgio Tozzi (King Marke)
Otmar Suitner
Oct. 31, Nov. 6, 10, 15m, 18

Gounod, *Faust*
Judith Beckman** (Marguerite), Sylvia Anderson/(11/21)Joyce Castle (Siebel); Alain Vanzo** (Faust), Dominic Cossa (Valentin), Roger Soyer** (Méphistophélès)
Jean Périsson
Nov. 3, 8m, 13, 21, 25

Verdi, *Otello*
Raina Kabaivanska (Desdemona);

James McCracken (Otello),
Kostas Paskalis (Iago)
Bohumil Gregor
Nov. 7, 11, 20, 24, 29m

Stravinsky,
The Rake's Progress
Jane Marsh (Anne),
Sylvia Anderson (Baba),
Donna Petersen (Mother
Goose); Gregory Dempsey
(Tom Rakewell), William
Dooley (Nick Shadow),
Clifford Grant (Trulove)
Gunther Schuller
Nov. 14, 17, 27

1971

Massenet, *Manon*
Beverly Sills (Manon);
Nicolai Gedda (des Grieux),
Allan Monk (Lescaut)
Jean Périsson
Sept. 10, 19m, 25, 29,
Oct. 3m, 8

Strauss, *Der Rosenkavalier*
Christa Ludwig (Octavian),
Sena Jurinac (Marschallin),
Helen Donath(Sophie);
Manfred Jungwirth** (Ochs),
Nicolai Gedda/(9/14, 26)
Kenneth Riegel
(Italian Singer), Raymond
Wolansky (Faninal)
Silvio Varviso
Sept. 11, 14, 17, 22, 26m

Puccini, *Madama Butterfly*
Teresa Kubiak (Cio-Cio-
San), Helen Vanni (Suzuki);
Stuart Burrows (Pinkerton),
Bruce Yarnell (Sharpless)
James Levine
Sept. 12m, 15, 18, 21, 24,
Oct. 2, 24m

Wagner, *Die Meistersinger*
Arlene Saunders (Eva),
Helen Vanni (Magdalene);
James King (Walther),
Theo Adam (Hans Sachs),
Geraint Evans (Beckmesser),
Ezio Flagello (Pogner),
John Walker (David)
Otmar Suitner
Oct. 1, 6, 9, 12, 17m

Britten, *A Midsummer
Night's Dream* (English
Opera Group)
Jennifer Vyvyan (Tytania),
April Cantelo (Helena),
Carolyn Maia/Maureen
Morelle (Hermia);
James Bowman (Oberon),
Robert Tear/(10/15)
Neville Williams (Lysander),
Benjamin Luxon (Demetrius),
Owen Brannigan (Bottom)
Steuart Bedford
Oct. 5, 10m, 15

Tchaikovsky,
Eugene Onegin (in English)
Evelyn Lear (Tatiana),
Edna Garabedian (Olga);

Thomas Stewart (Onegin),
Stuart Burrows (Lensky),
Ara Berberian (Gremin)
Charles Mackerras
Oct. 13, 16, 19, 22, 31m

Verdi, *Il Trovatore*
Leontyne Price (Leonora),
Margarita Lilova (Azucena);
James King/(10/26) Placido
Domingo (Manrico), Raymond
Wolansky (Count Di Luna)
Carlo Felice Cillario
Oct. 23, 26, 29, Nov. 3

Ljiljana Molnar-Talajic
(Leonora), (11/8)
Margarita Lilova/Irene
Dalis (Azucena); James
King (Manrico), Raymond
Wolansky (Count Di Luna)
Carlo Felice Cillario
Nov. 8 (Sacramento)
Nov. 13

Ljiljana Molnar-Talajic
(Leonora), Irene
Dalis (Azucena); James
McCracken (Manrico), Louis
Quilico/Raymond Wolansky
(Count Di Luna)
Charles Wilson
Nov. 25, 28m

Verdi,
Un Ballo in Maschera
Martina Arroyo (Amelia),
Irene Dalis (Ulrica),
Helen Donath (Oscar);
Luciano Pavarotti (Riccardo),
Franco Bordoni (Renato)
Charles Mackerras
Oct. 27, 30, Nov. 2, 5, 7m

Berg, *Lulu*
Anja Silja (Lulu),
Sona Cervena (Geschwitz);
John Reardon (Dr. Schoen),
Josef Hopferwieser** (Alwa),
Ragnar Ulfung (Painter)
Christoph von Dohnányi
Nov. 6, 9, 14m, 19

Donizetti, *Maria Stuarda*
Joan Sutherland (Mary
Stuart), Huguette
Tourangeau (Elizabeth I),
Ariel Bybee (Anna);
Stuart Burrows (Leicester),
Ara Berberian (Cecil),
Cornelis Opthof (Talbot)
Richard Bonynge
Nov. 12, 16, 21m, 24, 27

Puccini, *Il Tabarro*
Leontyne Price (Giorgetta);
Aldo Bottion (Luigi),
Gabriel Bacquier (Michele)
Nino Sanzogno
and
Orff, *Carmina Burana*
Shigemi Matsumoto
(Burgundian Lady); Raymond
Wolansky (Troubadour,
Old Poet, Drinker)
Nino Sanzogno
Nov. 17, 20, 23, 26

1972

Bellini, *Norma*
Joan Sutherland (Norma),
Huguette Tourangeau
(Adalgisa); John
Alexander (Pollione),
Clifford Grant (Oroveso)
Richard Bonynge
Sept. 15, 20, 24m, 30,
Oct. 6

Mozart, *Le Nozze di Figaro*
Judith Blegen (Susanna),
Kiri Te Kanawa (Countess),
Frederica von Stade
(Cherubino); Geraint
Evans (Figaro), Ingvar
Wixell (Count)
Reynald Giovaninetti
Sept. 16, 19, 22, 27,
Oct. 1m

Verdi, *Aida*
Teresa Kubiak (Aida),
Ruza Baldani/(10/14)
Shirley Verrett (Amneris);
Carlo Cossutta (Radames),
Bruce Yarnell (Amonasro)
Nino Sanzogno
Sept. 23, 29, Oct. 4, 8m,
14

Marina Krilovici (Aida),
Irina Arkhipova (Amneris);
Richard Cassilly (Radames),
Norman Mittelmann
(Amonasro)
Jesus Lopez-Cobos
Nov. 16, 21, 24

Wagner, *Das Rheingold*
Margarita Lilova (Fricka),
Edna Garabedian (Erda);
Thomas Stewart (Wotan),
Richard Holm (Loge),
Marius Rintzler** (Alberich)
Otmar Suitner
Sept. 26, Oct. 7, 17

Wagner, *Die Walküre*
(10/3) Berit Lindholm/
Birgit Nilsson (Brünnhilde),
(10/3) Marita Napier**/
Berit Lindholm (Sieglinde),
Margarita Lilova (Fricka);
Jess Thomas (Siegmund),
Thomas Stewart (Wotan),
Clifford Grant (Hunding)
Otmar Suitner
Oct. 3, 20, 28

Wagner, *Siegfried*
Berit Lindholm/(11/1)
Birgit Nilsson (Brünnhilde),
Margarita Lilova (Erda);
Jess Thomas (Siegfried),
Marius Rintzler (Alberich),
Wolf Appel (Mime);
Thomas Stewart (Wanderer)
Otmar Suitner
Oct. 10, 22m, Nov. 1

Wagner, *Götterdämmerung*
(10/13) Berit Lindholm/
Birgit Nilsson (Brünnhilde),
Marita Napier (Gutrune);
Jess Thomas (Siegfried),

Thomas Stewart (Gunther),
Clifford Grant (Hagen)
Otmar Suitner
Oct. 13, 24, Nov. 4

Puccini, *Tosca*
Hana Janku (Tosca);
Placido Domingo
(Cavaradossi), Ingvar
Wixell (Scarpia)
Nino Sanzogno
Oct. 15, 18, 21, 27, 29m

Dorothy Kirsten (Tosca);
Wieslaw Ochman
(Cavaradossi), Kostas
Paskalis (Scarpia)
Byron Dean Ryan
Nov. 19 (Sacramento)
Nov. 22, 25

Von Einem, *The Visit
of the Old Lady***
Regina Resnik (Claire
Zachanassian); Raymond
Wolansky (Alfred Ill),
Richard Cassilly (Mayor),
Bruce Yarnell (Priest)
Maurice Peress
Oct. 25, 31, Nov. 5m, 10

Meyerbeer, *L'Africaine*
Shirley Verrett (Selika),
Evelyn Mandac (Inès);
Placido Domingo (Vasco
da Gama), Norman
Mittelmann (Nelusko),
Simon Estes (Don Pedro)
Jean Périsson
Nov. 3, 7, 12m, 15, 18

Donizetti,
Lucia di Lammermoor
Beverly Sills (Lucia); Luciano
Pavarotti (Edgardo),
Raymond Wolansky (Enrico),
Clifford Grant/(11/17, 23)
Simon Estes (Raimondo)
Jesus Lopez-Cobos**
Nov. 8, 11, 14, 17, 23, 26m

1973

Donizetti, *La Favorita*
Maria Luisa Nave/(9/21, 26,
29) Gwendolyn Killebrew
(Leonora); Luciano
Pavarotti (Fernando),
Renato Bruson (Alfonso),
Bonaldo Giaiotti (Baldassare)
Carlo Felice Cillario
Sept. 7, 12, 16m, 21, 26,
29

Strauss, J. Jr.,
Die Fledermaus (in English)
Joan Sutherland (Rosalinda),
Judith Blegen (Adele),
Huguette Tourangeau
(Orlofsky); Nolan Van
Way (Eisenstein), Ragnar
Ulfung (Alfred), Bruce
Yarnell (Dr. Falke),
Walter Slezak** (Frosch)
Richard Bonynge
Sept. 8, 11, 14, 19, 30m,
Oct. 2

Verdi, *Rigoletto*
Izabella Nawe** (Gilda),
Silvana Mazzieri**
(Maddalena); Sherrill
Milnes (Rigoletto),
Giacomo Aragall (Duke),
Clifford Grant (Sparafucile)
Kazimierz Kord
Sept. 15, 18, 23m, 28,
Oct. 3, 7m

Mozart, *Così fan tutte*
Evelyn Lear (Fiordiligi),
Frederica von Stade
(Dorabella), Evelyn
Mandac (Despina);
Ryland Davies (Ferrando),
Richard Stilwell (Guglielmo),
Geraint Evans (Don Alfonso)
John Pritchard
Sept. 22, 25, Oct. 5, 10,
14m

Wagner, *Tannhäuser*
Leonie Rysanek (Elisabeth),
Marita Napier (Venus);
Jess Thomas (Tannhäuser),
Thomas Stewart (Wolfram),
Clifford Grant (Hermann)
Otmar Suitner
Oct. 6, 9, 12, 17, 21m

Mussorgsky,
Boris Godunov
(Original version, Lamm
edition; in Russian)
(10/13, 16) Gwendolyn
Killebrew/Evelyn Lear
(Marina); Martti Talvela
(Boris), Alberto Remedios**
(Dimitri), Philip
Booth (Pimen), Ragnar
Ulfung (Shuisky)
Kazimierz Kord
Oct. 13, 16, 19, 24, 28m

Strauss, *Elektra*
Ingrid Steger** (Elektra),
Marita Napier/(10/23)
Leonie Rysanek
(Chrysothemis), Irene
Dalis (Klytemnestra);
Ragnar Ulfung (Aegisth),
Thomas Stewart (Orest)
Otmar Suitner
Oct. 20, 23, 26, Nov. 3

Britten, *Peter Grimes*
Ava June** (Ellen),
Sheila Nadler (Auntie),
Donna Petersen (Mrs.
Sedley); Jess Thomas
(Peter Grimes), Geraint
Evans (Capt. Balstrode)
John Pritchard
Oct. 27, 30, Nov. 4m, 9

Verdi, *La Traviata*
Beverly Sills (Violetta);
Wieslaw Ochman (Alfredo),
(11/2) Gian Piero Mastromei/
(11/10) Norman Mittelmann/
Guillermo Sarabia (Germont)
Kurt Herbert Adler
Nov. 2, 7, 10, 20, 22, 25m

Verdi, *Don Carlo*
Gwyneth Jones (Elisabetta),
Josephine Veasey (Eboli);
Alberto Remedios (Carlo),
Norman Mittelmann
(Rodrigo), Martti
Talvela (Philip II), Michael
Langdon (Grand Inquisitor)
Silvio Varviso
Nov. 8, 11m, 14, 17, 23

Puccini, *La Bohème*
Teresa Stratas (Mimi),
Ariel Bybee (Musetta);
José Carreras (Rodolfo),
Bruce Yarnell (Marcello),
Maurizio Mazzieri (Colline)
Jean Périsson
Nov. 13, 16, 18m, 21, 24

1974

Puccini, *Manon Lescaut*
Leontyne Price (Manon);
Giorgio Merighi (des Grieux),
Julian Patrick (Lescaut)
Reynald Giovaninetti
Sept. 13, 18, 21, 24, 27,
Oct. 6m

Wagner, *Parsifal*
Eva Randova** (Kundry);
Jess Thomas (Parsifal),
Thomas Stewart (Amfortas),
Kurt Moll (Gurnemanz),
Peter Van Ginkel (Klingsor)
Otmar Suitner
Sept. 14, 17, 20, 25, 29m

Strauss, *Salome*
Leonie Rysanek (Salome),
Astrid Varnay (Herodias);
Hans Hopf (Herod),
Siegmund Nimsgern
(Jokanaan)
Otmar Suitner
Sept. 22m, 28, Oct. 1, 4,
12

Puccini, *Madama Butterfly*
Renata Scotto (Cio-Cio-
San), Judith Forst (Suzuki);
Giorgio Merighi/(10/5)
Giacomo Aragall/(10/18)
José Carreras (Pinkerton),
Julian Patrick (Sharpless)
Kurt Herbert Adler
Oct. 2, 5, 8, 13m, 18

Pilar Lorengar (Cio-Cio-San),
Sandra Walker (Suzuki);
(11/23) Sandor Konya/
Barry Morell (Pinkerton),
Frank Guarrera (Sharpless)
Kurt Herbert Adler
Nov. 23m, 27, 30

Wagner, *Tristan und Isolde*
Birgit Nilsson (Isolde),
Yvonne Minton (Brangäne);
Jess Thomas (Tristan),
Jef Vermeersch**
(Kurwenal), Kurt
Moll (King Marke)
Silvio Varviso
Oct. 11, 15, 19, 24, 27m

Rossini, *La Cenerentola*
Frederica von Stade
(Angelina); Ugo Benelli
(Don Ramiro), Paolo
Montarsolo (Don Magnifico),
Renato Capecchi (Dandini)
John Pritchard
Oct. 16, 22, 26m, Nov. 1,
3m

Massenet, *Esclarmonde*
Joan Sutherland
(Esclarmonde),
Huguette Tourangeau
(Parséis); Giacomo
Aragall (Roland), Robert
Kerns (Bishop of Blois)
Richard Bonynge
Oct. 23, 26, 29, Nov. 2m, 8

Verdi, *Otello*
Pilar Lorengar (Desdemona);
James King (Otello),
Wassili Janulako** (Iago)
Jesus Lopez-Cobos
Oct. 30, Nov. 2, 5, 10m, 15

Mozart, *Don Giovanni*
Anna Tomowa-Sintow**
(Anna), Rachel
Yakar** (Elvira),
Carol Malone** (Zerlina);
Roger Soyer (Giovanni),
Gösta Winbergh** (Ottavio),
Stafford Dean (Leporello)
John Pritchard
Nov. 6, 9, 12, 17m, 22,
30m

Verdi, *Luisa Miller*
Katia Ricciarelli (Luisa);
Luciano Pavarotti (Rodolfo),
Louis Quilico (Miller),
Giorgio Tozzi (Walter),
Dieter Weller** (Wurm)
Jesus Lopez-Cobos
Nov. 13, 16, 19, 24m, 29

Donizetti, *The Daughter
of the Regiment*
Beverly Sills (Marie),
Claramae Turner (Marquise),
Hermione Gingold**
(Duchess); William
Harness (Tonio), Spiro
Malas (Sulpice)
Anton Guadagno
Nov. 20, 23, 26, 28,
Dec. 1m

1975

Verdi, *Il Trovatore*
Joan Sutherland (Leonora),
Elena Obraztsova/(9/17, 21m)
Shirley Verrett (Azucena);
Luciano Pavarotti (Manrico),
Ingvar Wixell (Di Luna)
Richard Bonynge
Sept. 12, 17, 21m, 27, 30,
Oct. 3

Renata Scotto (Leonora),
Bianca Berini (Azucena);
Juan Lloveras** (Manrico),
Louis Quilico (Di Luna)
Kurt Herbert Adler
Nov. 22m, 26, 29

Monteverdi,
L'Incoronazione di Poppea
(Leppard edition)
Tatiana Troyanos (Poppea),
Carol Malone (Drusilla),
Beverly Wolff (Ottavia);
Eric Tappy** (Nerone),
Richard Stilwell (Ottone),
Peter Meven** (Seneca)
Raymond Leppard
Sept. 13, 16, 19, 24, 28m

Wagner,
Der Fliegende Holländer
Marita Napier (Senta);
Theo Adam (Dutchman),
William Lewis (Eric,
Steersman), Marius
Rintzler (Daland)
Kenneth Schermerhorn
Sept. 20, 23, 26, Oct. 1,
5m

Donizetti, *L'Elisir d'Amore*
Judith Blegen (Adina);
José Carreras (Nemorino),
Ingvar Wixell (Belcore),
Paolo Montarsolo
(Dulcamara)
Carlo Felice Cillario
Oct. 4, 7, 10, 12m, 17

Bellini, *Norma*
Rita Hunter/(10/22, 25m, 31)
Cristina Deutekom (Norma),
Tatiana Troyanos (Adalgisa);
Robleto Merolla** (Pollione),
Clifford Grant (Oroveso)
Carlo Felice Cillario
Oct. 11, 14, 19m, 22,
25m, 31

Tchaikovsky,
Pikovaya Dama
Galina Vishnevskaya (Lisa),
Anita Terzian** (Paulina),
Regina Resnik (Countess);
Peter Gougaloff**
(Gherman), Ryan
Edwards (Yeletsky)
Mstislav Rostropovich**
Oct. 15, 18, 21, 24, 26m,
Nov. 1m

Massenet, *Werther*
Heather Harper (Charlotte),
Carol Malone (Sophie);
Giacomo Aragall (Werther),
Ronald Hedlund (Albert)
Elyakum Shapirra
Oct. 25, 28, Nov. 2m, 7,
15m

Verdi, *Simon Boccanegra*
Kiri Te Kanawa (Amelia);
Ingvar Wixell (Simon),
Giorgio Merighi (Gabriele),
Martti Talvela (Fiesco)
Paolo Peloso**
Oct. 29, Nov. 1, 4, 9m, 14

Giordano, *Andrea Chénier*
Josella Ligi** (Maddalena);
Placido Domingo (Chénier),
Cornell MacNeil (Gérard)
Emerson Buckley
Nov. 5, 8, 11, 16m, 21

Puccini, *Il Tabarro*
Brenda Roberts/(11/12)
Clarice Carson (Giorgetta);
Robleto Merolla (Luigi),
Guillermo Sarabia (Michele)
Elyakum Shapirra
and
Puccini, *Gianni Schicchi*
Irem Poventud (Lauretta);
Donald Gramm (Schicchi),
Edoardo Gimenez (Rinuccio)
Elyakum Shapirra
Nov. 12, 15, 18, 23m, 28

Mozart, *The Magic Flute*
Kiri Te Kanawa (Pamina),
Zdzislawa Donat** (Queen);
William Harness (Tamino),
Alan Titus (Papageno),
Robert Lloyd** (Sarastro)
Kurt Herbert Adler
Nov. 19, 22, 25, 27, 30m

1976

Massenet, *Thaïs*
Beverly Sills (Thaïs); Sherrill
Milnes (Athanaël), Claes
Ahnsjö** (Nicias), Alexander
Malta** (Palémon)
John Pritchard
Sept. 10, 15, 19m, 25, 28,
Oct. 1

Wagner, *Die Walküre*
Roberta Knie (Brünnhilde),
(9/11, 14, 17)Leonie
Rysanek/Janis
Martin (Sieglinde),
Ruth Hesse (Fricka);
Jon Vickers (Siegmund),
Hans Sotin (Wotan),
Clifford Grant (Hunding)
Otmar Suitner
Sept. 11, 14, 17, 22, 26m,
Oct. 2m

Verdi,
La Forza del Destino
Anna Tomowa-Sintow
(Leonora), Susanne Marsee
(Preziosilla); Barry Morell/
(9/29, 10/3) Bruno Prevedi
(Don Alvaro), Renato Bruson
(Don Carlo), Paul Plishka
(Padre Guardiano)
Kurt Herbert Adler
Sept. 18, 21, 24, 29,
Oct. 3m

Raina Kabaivanska
(Leonora), Susanne
Marsee (Preziosilla);
Robert Ilosfalvy (Don
Alvaro), Garbis Boyagian**
(Don Carlo), Kolos
Kovats** (Padre Guardiano)
Kurt Herbert Adler
Nov. 7m, 13m, 19

Puccini, *Tosca*
(10/2) Leonie Rysanek/Janis
Martin (Tosca); Giacomo
Aragall (Cavaradossi),
Ingvar Wixell (Scarpia)
Paolo Peloso
Oct. 2, 5, 8, 10m, 16, 23m

Britten, *Peter Grimes*
Heather Harper (Ellen),
Sheila Nadler (Auntie),
Donna Petersen (Mrs.
Sedley); Jon Vickers
(Peter Grimes), Geraint
Evans (Capt. Balstrode)
John Pritchard
Oct. 6, 9, 13, 17m, 22

Strauss,
Die Frau ohne Schatten
Leonie Rysanek (Empress),
Ursula Schröder-Feinen
(Barak's Wife), Ruth
Hesse (Nurse); Matti
Kastu** (Emperor),
Walter Berry (Barak)
Karl Böhm
Oct. 15, 19, 24m, 30,
Nov. 2

Janáček,
The Makropulos Case
Anja Silja (Emilia Marty);
William Lewis
(Albert Gregor), Geraint
Evans (Baron Prus)
Christoph von Dohnányi
Oct. 20, 23, 26, 29, 31m

Mascagni,
Cavalleria Rusticana
Tatiana Troyanos (Santuzza);
Placido Domingo (Turiddu),
Wassili Janulako (Alfio)
Kenneth Schermerhorn
and
Leoncavallo, *Pagliacci*
Noelle Rogers (Nedda);
Placido Domingo (Canio),
Ingvar Wixell (Tonio),
Brent Ellis (Silvio)
Kenneth Schermerhorn
Oct. 27, 30m, Nov. 5, 10

Cavalleria Rusticana
Régine Crespin (Santuzza);
(11/13, 16) Placido
Domingo/Juan Lloveras
(Turiddu), Wassili
Janulako (Alfio)
Kenneth Schermerhorn
and
Pagliacci
(11/13, 16) Noelle
Rogers/Raina Kabaivanska
(Nedda); (11/13, 16)
Placido Domingo /
Bruno Prevedi (Canio),
(11/13, 16) Ingvar
Wixell/Peter Glossop (Tonio),
Brent Ellis (Silvio)
Kenneth Schermerhorn
Nov. 13, 16, 21m, 24, 27

Imbrie, *Angle of Repose* ***
Nancy Shade (Susan),
Susanne Marsee (Shelly),
Donna Petersen (Ada);
William Lewis (Frank),
Dale Duesing** (Oliver),
Chester Ludgin (Lyman)
John Mauceri
Nov. 6, 9, 14m, 18, 26

Rossini,
Il Barbiere di Siviglia
Frederica von Stade
(Rosina); Timothy
Nolen/(11/23, 25, 28m)
Vicente Sardinero (Figaro),
John Brecknock (Almaviva),
Giorgio Tozzi (Basilio),
Renato Capecchi (Bartolo)
Silvio Varviso
Nov. 12, 17, 20, 23, 25,
28m

1977

Cilea,
Adriana Lecouvreur
Renata Scotto (Adriana),
Elena Obraztsova (Princess);
Giacomo Aragall (Maurizio),
Giuseppe Taddei (Michonnet)
Gianandrea Gavazzeni
Sept. 9, 13, 16, 24, 28,
Oct. 2m

Mozart, *Idomeneo*
Christiane Eda-Pierre (Ilia),
Carol Neblett (Elettra),
Maria Ewing (Idamante);
Eric Tappy (Idomeneo),
George Shirley (High Priest)
John Pritchard
Sept. 10, 14, 18m, 20, 23

Janáček, *Katya Kabanova*
Elisabeth Söderström
(Katya), Susanne
Marsee (Barbara),
Beverly Wolff (Kabanikha);
William Lewis (Boris),
Barry McCauley (Vanya),
William Cochran (Tikhon),
Chester Ludgin (Dikoy)
Rafael Kubelik
Sept. 17, 21, 25m, 27, 30

Wagner, *Das Rheingold*
Hanna Schwarz** (Fricka),
Patricia Payne**/(10/12,
16, 22) Jocelyne Taillon
(Erda); Franz-Ferdinand
Nentwig** (Wotan),
Ragnar Ulfung (Loge),
Joszef Dene** (Alberich)
Heinrich Hollreiser
Oct. 1, 4, 7, 12, 16m, 22

Gounod, *Faust*
Nancy Shade (Marguerite),
Susanne Marsee (Siebel);
Giacomo Aragall (Faust),
Giorgio Zancanaro (Valentin),
Giorgio Tozzi
(Méphistophélès)
Jean Périsson
Oct. 5, 8, 11, 14, 23m

Carol Todd (Marguerite),
Gwendolyn Jones (Siebel);
Barry McCauley (Faust),
Lawrence Cooper (Valentin),
James Courtney
(Méphistophélès)
Richard Bradshaw**
Nov. 26m

1978

Verdi, *Otello*
Katia Ricciarelli
(Desdemona);
Placido Domingo (Otello),
Guillermo Sarabia (Iago)
Giuseppe Patanè
Sept. 8, 13, 17m, 22, 26,
30

Bellini, *Norma*
Shirley Verrett (Norma),
Alexandrina Milcheva
(Adalgisa); Nunzio
Todisco** (Pollione),
Clifford Grant (Oroveso)
Paolo Peloso
Sept. 9, 12, 15, 20, 24m,
30m

Verdi, *Aida*
Maria Parazzini** (Aida),
Fiorenza Cossotto (Amneris);
James McCracken
(Radames), Norman
Mittelmann (Amonasro)
Gianandrea Gavazzeni
Oct. 15, 18, 21, 24, 30m,
Nov. 5m

Eva Marton (Aida),
Tatiana Troyanos (Amneris);
Gianfranco Cecchele
(Radames), Ingvar
Wixell (Amonasro)
Gianandrea Gavazzeni
Nov. 18, 24, 26

Strauss, *Ariadne auf Naxos*
Leontyne Price (Prima
Donna, Ariadne), Ruth
Welting (Zerbinetta), Tatiana
Troyanos (Composer);
Allen Cathcart (Bacchus)
Janos Ferencsik
Oct. 19, 22, 25, 28,
Nov. 6m

Puccini, *Turandot*
Montserrat Caballé
(Turandot), Leona Mitchell
(Liù); Luciano Pavarotti
(Calaf), Giorgio Tozzi (Timur)
Riccardo Chailly
Oct. 29, Nov. 1, 4, 9, 13m,
16, 19m

Bellini, *I Puritani*
Beverly Sills (Elvira);
Cesar-Antonio Suarez
(Arturo), Giorgio
Zancanaro (Riccardo),
Bonaldo Giaiotti (Giorgio)
Paolo Peloso
Nov. 2, 5, 8, 11, 20m, 23

Verdi,
Un Ballo in Maschera
Katia Ricciarelli (Amelia),
Kathleen Battle (Oscar),
Patricia Payne (Ulrica);
José Carreras (Gustavo),
Yuri Mazurok (Renato)
Kurt Herbert Adler
Nov. 12, 15, 19, 22, 25,
27m

Britten, *Billy Budd*
Dale Duesing (Billy), Richard
Lewis (Capt. Vere), Forbes
Robinson** (Claggart)
David Atherton**
Sept. 16, 19, 23, 28,
Oct. 1m

Wagner, *Lohengrin*
Anne Evans (Elsa),
Janis Martin (Ortrud);
(9/29, 10/3, 6) Guy
Chauvet/William Neill
(Lohengrin), Raimund
Herincx (Telramund),
Gwynne Howell (Heinrich)
Kurt Herbert Adler
Sept. 29, Oct. 3, 6, 11,
14m, 22

Mozart, *Don Giovanni*
Olivia Stapp (Anna),
Ellen Shade (Elvira),
Ruth Welting (Zerlina);
Justino Diaz (Giovanni),
David Rendall (Ottavio),
Walter Berry (Leporello)
Hans Drewanz**
Oct. 4, 7, 10, 13, 15m, 21m

Puccini, *Tosca*
Montserrat Caballé/(10/29)
Gwyneth Jones (Tosca);
Luciano Pavarotti
(Cavaradossi) Giuseppe
Taddei (Scarpia)
Paolo Peloso
Oct. 14, 17, 20, 23, 25,
29m

Magda Olivero (Tosca);
Juan Lloveras (Cavaradossi),
Giorgio Tozzi (Scarpia)
Paolo Peloso
Nov. 22, 25

Massenet, *Werther*
Maria Ewing (Charlotte),
Kathleen Battle (Sophie);
José Carreras (Werther),
Allan Monk (Albert)
Antonio de Almeida
Oct. 18, 21, 28, 31,
Nov. 3, 5m

Strauss, *Der Rosenkavalier*
Hanna Schwarz (Octavian),
Leonie Rysanek
(Marschallin), Carol
Malone (Sophie); Walter
Berry (Ochs), Jerome Pruett
(Italian Singer), Chester
Ludgin (Faninal)
Janos Ferencsik
Oct. 27, Nov. 4, 6, 12m,
14, 17

Puccini, *La Bohème*
Ileana Cotrubas (Mimi),
Julia Migenes (Musetta);
Giacomo Aragall (Rodolfo),
Brent Ellis (Marcello),
Samuel Ramey (Colline)
Silvio Varviso/(11/23, 26)
Calvin Simmons
Nov. 1, 4m, 7, 10, 13, 18,
23, 26m

Carol Vaness (Mimi),
Pamela South (Musetta);
Barry McCauley (Rodolfo),
Lawrence Cooper (Marcello),
Paul Hudson (Colline)
Calvin Simmons
Nov. 25m

Beethoven, *Fidelio*
Gwyneth Jones (Leonore),
Sheri Greenawald
(Marzelline); Spas Wenkoff**
(Florestan), Siegmund
Nimsgern (Pizarro),
Marius Rintzler (Rocco)
Günther Wich**
Nov. 11, 15, 18m, 21, 24

1979

Ponchielli, *La Gioconda*
Renata Scotto (Gioconda),
Stefania Toczyska** (Laura),
Margarita Lilova (La Cieca);
Luciano Pavarotti (Enzo),
Norman Mittelmann
(Barnaba), Ferruccio
Furlanetto (Alvise)
Dancers: Martine van Hamel,
Christian Holder, Gary Chryst
Bruno Bartoletti
Sept. 7, 12, 16m, 21, 25,
29

Debussy,
Pelléas et Mélisande
Maria Ewing (Mélisande),
Gwendolyn Jones
(Geneviève); Dale
Duesing (Pelléas),
Michael Devlin (Golaud),
John Macurdy (Arkel)
Julius Rudel
Sept. 8, 11, 14, 19, 23m

Verdi, *Don Carlo*
Anna Tomowa-Sintow
(Elisabetta), Livia
Budai** (Eboli); Giacomo
Aragall (Don Carlo),
Wolfgang Brendel (Rodrigo),
Evgeny Nesterenko**
(Philip II), Stefan Elenkov**
(Grand Inquisitor)
Silvio Varviso
Sept. 15, 18, 22m, 26,
30m, Oct. 5

Strauss, *Elektra*
Danica Mastilovic (Elektra),
Leonie Rysanek
(Chrysothemis), Anny
Schlemm** (Klytemnestra);
William Neill (Aegisth),
Franz Mazura (Orest)
Berislav Klobučar
Sept. 28, Oct. 2, 7m,
11, 13

Dallapiccola, *Il Prigioniero*
(In English)
Janis Martin (Mother);
Michael Devlin (Prisoner),
Werner Götz** (Jailer,
Grand Inquisitor)
Reynald Giovaninetti
and

Poulenc, *La Voix humaine*
Magda Olivero (The Woman)
Reynald Giovaninetti
and
Puccini, *Gianni Schicchi*
Sheri Greenawald (Lauretta),
Fedora Barbieri (Zita);
Giuseppe Taddei
(Gianni Schicchi), Yordi
Ramiro** (Rinuccio)
Reynald Giovaninetti
Oct. 3, 6, 9, 14m, 19

Wagner,
Der Fliegende Holländer
Marita Napier (Senta); Simon
Estes (Dutchman), William
Lewis (Erik, Steersman),
Marius Rintzler (Daland)
Christof Perick**
Oct. 12, 16, 21m, 25, 27,
Nov. 3m

Puccini,
La Fanciulla del West
Carol Neblett (Minnie);
Placido Domingo
(Dick Johnson), Benito
di Bella** (Rance)
Giuseppe Patanè
Oct. 17, 20, 23, 27m, 31,
Nov. 2

Donizetti,
Roberto Devereux
(10/26) Montserrat Caballé/
Ellen Kerrigan (Elizabeth),
Stefania Toczyska (Sara);
Carlo Bini (Roberto),
Juan Pons (Nottingham)
Gianfranco Masini
Oct. 26, 30, Nov. 4m, 7,
10, 15

Verdi,
La Forza del Destino
Leontyne Price (Leonora),
Judith Forst (Preziosilla);
Veriano Luchetti
(Don Alvaro), Guillermo
Sarabia/(11/6, 9) Renato
Bruson (Don Carlo), Martti
Talvela (Padre Guardiano)
Kurt Herbert Adler
Nov. 3, 6, 9, 14

Leontyne Price (Leonora),
Judith Forst (Preziosilla);
Carlo Bini (Don Alvaro),
Guillermo Sarabia
(Don Carlo), Martti
Talvela (Padre Guardiano)
Kurt Herbert Adler
Nov. 17m, 22, 25m

Mozart, *Così fan tutte*
Pilar Lorengar (Fiordiligi),
Anne Howells (Dorabella),
Danièle Perriers** (Despina);
Michael Cousins (Ferrando),
Dale Duesing (Guglielmo),
Thomas Stewart
(Don Alfonso)
John Pritchard
Nov. 10m, 13, 16, 18m,
21, 24

Rebecca Cook (Fiordiligi),
Susan Quittmeyer
(Dorabella), Pamela
South (Despina);
James Hoback (Ferrando),
Jake Gardner (Guglielmo),
Wayne Turnage (Don Alfonso)
David Agler
Nov. 24m

Rossini, *Tancredi*
(Stylized concert version)
Marilyn Horne (Tancredi),
Margherita Rinaldi
(Amenaide), Carmen
Balthrop (Roggiero);
Dalmacio Gonzalez (Argirio),
Nicola Zaccaria (Orbazzano)
Henry Lewis
Nov. 17, 20, 23

Puccini, *Tosca*
Eva Marton (Tosca); Placido
Domingo/(12/27) Giuseppe
Giacomini (Cavaradossi),
Justino Díaz (Scarpia)
Kurt Herbert Adler
Dec. 20, 22, 27 (Manila,
Philippines)

1980

Saint-Saëns,
Samson et Dalila
Shirley Verrett (Dalila);
Placido Domingo (Samson),
Wolfgang Brendel
(High Priest)
Julius Rudel
Sept. 5, 9, 13, 18, 21m, 24

Verdi, *Simon Boccanegra*
Margaret Price (Amelia);
Renato Bruson (Simon),
Giorgio Lamberti (Gabriele),
Cesare Siepi (Fiesco)
Lamberto Gardelli
Sept. 6, 11, 14m, 17, 23,
26

Strauss,
Die Frau ohne Schatten
Leonie Rysanek/(9/30)
Eva Marton (Empress),
Birgit Nilsson (Barak's Wife),
Ruth Hesse (Nurse);
James King (Emperor),
Gerd Feldhoff (Barak)
Berislav Klobučar
Sept. 10, 15, 20, 25, 30

Donizetti, *Don Pasquale*
Ruth Welting (Norina);
Geraint Evans (Pasquale),
David Rendall (Ernesto),
Timothy Nolen (Malatesta)
Uwe Mund**
Sept. 27, Oct. 3, 6, 8, 12m

(Performances in English)
Erie Mills (Norina),
Alexander Malta (Pasquale),
James Hoback (Ernesto),
John Brandstetter
(Malatesta)
David Agler
Nov. 22m, Dec. 3, 6

Janáček, *Jenůfa*
Elisabeth Söderström
(Jenůfa), Sena Jurinac
(Kostelnička); William
Lewis (Števa), Allen
Cathcart (Laca),
Albert Rosen
Oct. 1, 4, 7, 10, 14, 19m

Mozart, *The Magic Flute*
Sheri Greenawald (Pamina),
(10/11) Barbara Carter/
Rita Shane (Queen);
Perry Price (Tamino),
Dale Duesing (Papageno),
Ulrik Cold** (Sarastro)
Ulrich Weder**
Oct. 11, 15, 18, 21, 24,
26m, 31

Verdi, *La Traviata*
Valerie Masterson**/(11/8)
Barbara Daniels (Violetta);
Beniamino Prior (Alfredo),
Lorenzo Saccomani
(Germont)
Antonio de Almeida
Oct. 17, 22, 25, 28,
Nov. 2m, 5, 8

Strauss, *Arabella*
Kiri Te Kanawa (Arabella),
Barbara Daniels (Zdenka),
Erie Mills (Fiakermilli);
Ingvar Wixell (Mandryka),
William Lewis (Matteo),
Alexander Malta (Waldner)
Wolfgang Rennert
Oct. 29, Nov. 1, 4, 9m, 14,
17

Wagner, *Tristan und Isolde*
Gwyneth Jones (Isolde),
Ruza Baldani (Brangäne);
Spas Wenkoff (Tristan),
Thomas Stewart (Kurwenal),
Simon Estes (King Marke)
Kurt Herbert Adler
Nov. 7, 11, 16m, 21, 26, 29

Mascagni,
Cavalleria Rusticana
Tatiana Troyanos/(11/25, 28)
Olivia Stapp (Santuzza);
Michail Svetlev (Turiddu),
Benito di Bella (Alfio)
Nikša Bareza**
and
Leoncavallo, *Pagliacci*
Emily Rawlins (Nedda);
James King (Canio),
Benito di Bella (Tonio),
Lorenzo Saccomani (Silvio)
Nikša Bareza
Nov. 12, 15, 18, 23m,
25, 28

Puccini, *Madama Butterfly*
Yasuko Hayashi (Cio-Cio-
San), Judith Forst (Suzuki);
Luis Lima (Pinkerton),
Allan Monk (Sharpless)
Myung-Whun Chung
Nov. 19, 22, 27, 30m,
Dec. 2, 5

Reimann, *Lear* **
(in English)
Helga Dernesch (Goneril),
Rita Shane (Regan),
Emily Rawlins (Cordelia);
Thomas Stewart (Lear),
Chester Ludgin (Gloucester),
Timothy Noble (Albany),
David Knutson (Edgar),
Jacque Trussel (Edmund)
Gerd Albrecht**
June 12, 15, 18, 21m, 23

Mozart, *Don Giovanni*
Carol Vaness (Anna),
Lella Cuberli (Elvira),
Pamela South (Zerlina);
Cesare Siepi (Giovanni),
Gösta Winbergh (Ottavio),
Giuseppe Taddei (Leporello)
Ádám Fischer**
June 16, 19, 24, 28m,
July 2, 4

Wagner,
Die Meistersinger
Hannelore Bode (Eva),
Marvellee Cariaga
(Magdalene); William
Johns (Walther), Karl
Ridderbusch (Hans Sachs),
Gottfried Hornik**
(Beckmesser),
Kurt Rydl (Pogner),
David Gordon (David)
Kurt Herbert Adler
June 27, 30, July 3, 9,
13, 19m

Verdi, *Rigoletto*
Patricia Wise (Gilda),
Victoria Vergara
(Maddalena); (7/1,5)
Garbis Boyagian/Matteo
Manuguerra (Rigoletto),
Peter Dvorský (Duke),
Kurt Rydl (Sparafucile)
Nikša Bareza
July 1, 5m, 8, 11, 14, 17

Monteverdi,
L'Incoronazione di Poppea
Tatiana Troyanos (Poppea),
Pamela South (Drusilla),
Sarah Walker (Ottavia);
Eric Tappy (Nerone),
Wolfgang Brendel (Ottone),
John Macurdy (Seneca)
David Agler
July 7, 10, 12m, 15, 18

1981

Rossini, *Semiramide*
Montserrat Caballé
(Semiramide), Marilyn
Horne (Arsace);
Dalmacio Gonzalez (Idreno),
James Morris (Assur)
Richard Bonynge
Sept. 11, 16, 20m, 23, 26,
Oct. 1

Massenet, *Manon*
Reri Grist (Manon);
Stuart Burrows (des Grieux),

Dale Duesing (Lescaut)
Julius Rudel
Sept. 12, 15, 18, 24,
27m, 30

Shostakovich, *Lady
Macbeth of Mtsensk*
Anja Silja (Katerina),
Nelda Nelson (Sonyetka);
William Lewis (Sergei),
Chester Ludgin (Boris),
Jacque Trussel (Zinovy),
Kevin Langan (Old Convict)
Calvin Simmons
Sept. 19, 25, 29,
Oct. 8, 11m

Lehár, *The Merry Widow*
Joan Sutherland (Anna),
Judith Forst (Valencienne);
Anson Austin** (Camille),
Håkan Hagegård (Danilo)
Richard Bonynge
Oct. 3, 6, 9, 13, 16, 21,
25m, 28, 31

Bizet, *Carmen*
Teresa Berganza (Carmen),
Rebecca Cook (Micaëla);
Franco Bonisolli (Don José),
Simon Estes (Escamillo)
Kurt Herbert Adler
Oct. 10, 14, 18m, 22,
26, 30, Nov. 3

Hanna Schwarz (Carmen),
Leona Mitchell (Micaëla);
Placido Domingo (Don José),
Lenus Carlson (Escamillo)
Kurt Herbert Adler
Dec. 4, 7, 10, 13m

Massenet, *Le Cid*
(Stylized Concert Version)
Carol Neblett (Chimène),
Jennifer Ringo (Infanta);
William Lewis (Rodrigue),
Timothy Noble (King),
Ferruccio Furlanetto
(Don Diègue)
Julius Rudel
Oct. 15, 17, 19

Berg, *Wozzeck* (in English)
Janis Martin (Marie);
Geraint Evans (Wozzeck),
Jean Cox (Drum Major),
Richard Lewis (Captain),
Roderick Kennedy** (Doctor)
Wolfgang Rennert
Oct. 24, 27, Nov. 1m, 6, 11

Donizetti,
Lucia di Lammermoor
Ashley Putnam (Lucia);
Neil Shicoff (Edgardo),
Lenus Carlson (Enrico),
Ferruccio Furlanetto
(Raimondo)
David Agler
Nov. 4, 7, 9, 13, 17, 22m

Jennifer Ringo (Lucia);
Abram Morales (Edgardo),
Jake Gardner (Enrico),
Gregory Stapp (Raimondo)
Richard Bradshaw
Nov. 8m

Verdi, *Aida*
Margaret Price/(11/18)
Leontyne Price (Aida),
Stefania Toczyska (Amneris);
Luciano Pavarotti
(Radames), Simon
Estes (Amonasro)
García Navarro**
Nov. 12, 15m, 18, 21,
24, 27

Wagner, *Die Walküre*
Birgit Nilsson/(11/28,
12/6, 12) Eszter Kovács
(Brünnhilde), Leonie Rysanek
(Sieglinde), Nadine Denize
(Fricka); James King/(12/6)
Jess Thomas (Siegmund),
Manfred Schenk (Wotan),
Kurt Rydl (Hunding)
Otmar Suitner
Nov. 20, 25, 28,
Dec. 1, 6m, 12

Verdi, *Il Trovatore*
Leontyne Price (Leonora),
Fiorenza Cossotto (Azucena);
Giorgio Lamberti (Manrico),
Wolfgang Brendel (Di Luna)
Pinchas Steinberg**
Nov. 26, 29m, Dec. 2, 5,
8, 11

Handel, *Julius Caesar*
Tatiana Troyanos (Caesar),
Valerie Masterson
(Cleopatra), Sarah
Walker (Cornelia),
Delia Wallis (Sextus);
James Bowman (Ptolemy)
Charles Mackerras
May 28, June 2, 5, 8, 13m

Puccini, *Turandot*
Linda Kelm (Turandot),
Barbara Daniels (Liù);
Nicola Martinucci (Calaf),
Kevin Langan (Timur)
Myung-Whun Chung
June 3, 6m, 9, 12, 15, 18

Rossini,
Il Barbiere di Siviglia
Margarita Zimmermann/
(6/23, 27, 7/1) Kathleen
Kuhlmann (Rosina);
Dale Duesing (Figaro),
Dano Raffanti (Almaviva),
Cesare Siepi (Basilio),
Enrico Fissore (Bartolo)
Andrew Meltzer
June 11, 16, 19, 23, 27m,
July 1

Verdi, *Nabucco*
Olivia Stapp/(6/30, 7/3)
Judith Telep-Ehrlich
(Abigaille), Susan
Quittmeyer (Fenena); Matteo
Manuguerra (Nabucco),
Gordon Greer (Ismaele),
Paul Plishka (Zaccaria)
Kurt Herbert Adler
June 17, 20m, 22, 25, 30,
July 3

Stravinsky,
The Rake's Progress
Diana Soviero (Anne),
Mignon Dunn (Baba);
Dennis Bailey
(Tom Rakewell),
Donald Gramm (Nick),
Kevin Langan (Trulove)
David Agler
June 24, 26, 29,
July 2, 4m

1982

Verdi,
Un Ballo in Maschera
Montserrat Caballé/
(9/22, 25, 27) Rebecca
Cook (Amelia), Kathleen
Battle (Oscar), Ruža
Baldani (Ulrica); (9/10)
Luciano Pavarotti/
Vasile Moldoveanu/(9/27)
Ermanno Mauro (Gustavo),
Silvano Carroli/(9/22, 25, 27)
Pablo Elvira (Renato)
Kurt Herbert Adler
Sept. 10, 13, 16, 19m,
22, 25, 27

Bellini, *Norma*
Joan Sutherland (Norma),
Marilyn Horne (Adalgisa);
Ermanno Mauro (Pollione),
Ezio Flagello (Oroveso)
Richard Bonynge
Sept. 11, 14, 17, 21, 26m,
29, Oct. 2

Strauss, *Salome*
Josephine Barstow (Salome),
Helga Dernesch (Herodias);
Emile Belcourt (Herod),
Michael Devlin (Jokanaan)
Berislav Klobučar
Sept. 24, 28, Oct. 1, 6,
9, 12, 17m

Mozart, *Le Nozze di Figaro*
Lucia Popp (Susanna),
Helena Döse** (Countess),
Faith Esham (Cherubino);
Hermann Prey (Figaro),
Tom Krause (Count)
Silvio Varviso
Oct. 5, 8, 15, 20, 24m,
27, 30

Rossini, *La Cenerentola*
Marilyn Horne (Angelina);
Francisco Araiza**
(Don Ramiro), Paolo
Montarsolo (Don Magnifico),
Sesto Bruscantini (Dandini)
Mario Bernardi
Oct. 10m, 13, 16, 19,
22, 25, 31m

Poulenc, *Dialogues
of the Carmelites*
Carol Vaness (Blanche),
Leontyne Price
(Mme. Lidoine),
Régine Crespin (Mme.
de Croissy), Virginia
Zeani (Mother Marie),

173

Betsy Norden (Constance)
Henry Lewis
Oct. 23, 26, 29, Nov. 3,
6, 9, 14m

Tchaikovsky,
Pikovaya Dama
Teresa Zylis-Gara (Lisa),
Susan Quittmeyer (Paulina),
Regina Resnik (Countess);
Michail Svetlev (Gherman),
Stephen Dickson (Yeletsky),
Tom Krause (Tomsky)
David Agler
Nov. 4, 7m, 12, 15, 18,
22, 27

Massenet, *Cendrillon*
Sheri Greenawald (Lucette),
Ruth Welting (Fairy
Godmother), Maureen
Forrester (Mme. de la
Haltière), Delia Wallis
(Prince Charming); Donald
Gramm (Pandolfe)
Mario Bernardi
Nov. 10, 13, 20m, 25, 29,
Dec. 3, 6

Wagner, *Lohengrin*
Pilar Lorengar (Elsa),
Leonie Rysanek (Ortrud);
Peter Hofmann (Lohengrin),
Hermann Becht**
(Telramund), David
Ward (Heinrich)
Heinrich Hollreiser
Nov. 19, 23, 28m,
Dec. 1, 5m, 8, 11

Puccini, *Tosca*
Gwyneth Jones (Tosca);
Giacomo Aragall
(Cavaradossi), Justino
Díaz (Scarpia)
García Navarro
Nov. 24, 26, 30, Dec. 4,
7, 10, 12m

SUMMER 1983

Wagner, *Das Rheingold*
Hanna Schwarz (Fricka),
Reinhild Runkel** (Erda);
Michael Devlin (Wotan),
William Lewis (Loge),
Walter Berry (Alberich)
Edo de Waart
May 27, June 2, 5m,
10, 18

Wagner, *Die Walküre*
Jeannine Altmeyer/(6/12, 16)
Gwyneth Jones (Brünnhilde),
Leonie Rysanek (Sieglinde),
Helga Dernesch (Fricka);
Peter Hofmann (Siegmund),
Thomas Stewart (Wotan),
Hans Tschammer (Hunding)
Edo de Waart
May 28, June 3, 8,
12m, 16

Puccini, *La Bohème*
Ilona Tokody** (Mimi),
Mary Jane Johnson
(Musetta); Luis
Lima (Rodolfo),

J. Patrick Raftery (Marcello),
Kevin Langan (Colline)
García Navarro
June 4, 9, 11, 19m, 24, 27

Bizet, *Carmen*
Victoria Vergara (Carmen),
Barbara Daniels (Micaëla);
William Johns (Don José),
Michael Devlin (Escamillo)
Pierre Dervaux
June 17, 22, 26m, 29,
July 2

Mozart, *Così fan tutte*
Pilar Lorengar (Fiordiligi),
Tatiana Troyanos/
(7/3, Act II) Laura
Brooks Rice (Dorabella),
Ruth Ann Swenson
(Despina); Gösta
Winbergh (Ferrando),
Tom Krause (Guglielmo),
Geraint Evans (Don Alfonso)
Andrew Meltzer
June 23, 25, 28,
July 1, 3m

1983

Verdi, *Otello*
Margaret Price (Desdemona);
(9/9) Plácido Domingo/
(9/12, 15) Richard
Cassilly/Carlo
Cossutta (Otello),
Silvano Carroli (Iago)
Marek Janowski
Sept. 9, 12, 15, 18m,
23, 27, Oct. 1

Strauss, *Ariadne auf Naxos*
Rosalind Plowright/(9/25, 28,
10/2) Carmen Reppel**
(Prima Donna,
Ariadne), Kathleen Battle
(Zerbinetta), Susan
Quittmeyer (Composer);
(9/10, 13, 17) Dennis Bailey/
William Johns (Bacchus)
Christoph von Dohnányi
Sept. 10, 13, 17, 21,
25m, 28, Oct. 2m

Janáček, *Katya Kabanova*
(in English)
Anja Silja (Katya), Laura
Brooks Rice (Barbara),
Evelyn Lear (Kabanikha);
André Jobin (Boris),
Gregory Kunde (Vanya),
Emile Belcourt (Tikhon),
Michael Devlin (Dikoy)
Christoph von Dohnányi
Sept. 24, 30, Oct. 4, 7,
9m, 12

Verdi, *La Traviata*
(10/5) Nelly Miricioiu**/
(10/8, 11, 14) Winifred
Faix Brown/Katia
Ricciarelli (Violetta);
Alberto Cupido** (Alfredo),
Leo Nucci (Germont)
Richard Bradshaw
Oct. 5, 8, 11, 14, 18,
21, 27, 30m

Adriana Vanelli (Violetta);
Walter MacNeil (Alfredo),
Thomas Woodman (Germont)
Kathryn Cathcart
Oct. 22m

Tippett, *The Midsummer
Marriage***
Mary Jane Johnson
(Jenifer), Sheri
Greenawald (Bella),
Sheila Nadler (Sosostris);
Dennis Bailey (Mark), Ryland
Davies (Jack), Raimund
Herincx (King Fisher)
David Agler
Oct. 15, 19, 23m, 26, 29,
Nov. 1

Saint-Saëns,
Samson et Dalila
Marilyn Horne/(11/13)
Leslie Richards (Dalila);
Guy Chauvet (Samson),
Louis Quilico (High Priest),
Kevin Langan (Old Hebrew)
Jean Fournet
Oct. 20, 25, 28,
Nov. 2, 5, 9, 13m

Offenbach, *La Grande
Duchesse de Gérolstein*
Régine Crespin (Duchesse),
Kaaren Erickson (Wanda);
Tibère Raffalli** (Fritz),
Michel Trempont**
(General Boum)
Marc Soustrot**
Nov. 6m, 8, 12, 16, 19,
25m, Dec. 1, 6

Ponchielli, *La Gioconda*
Montserrat Caballé/(11/27,
30, 12/3) Maria Slatinaru**
(Gioconda), Mariana
Paunova (Laura),
Sheila Nadler (La Cieca);
Franco Bonisolli (Enzo),
Matteo Manuguerra
(Barnaba), Dimitri
Kavrakos (Alvise)
Andrew Meltzer
Nov. 11, 15, 20m, 24,
27m, 30, Dec. 3

Puccini, *Manon Lescaut*
Mirella Freni (Manon);
Ermanno Mauro (des
Grieux), Vicente
Sardinero (Lescaut)
Maurizio Arena
Nov. 17, 22, 25, 28,
Dec. 4m, 7, 10

Mussorgsky,
Boris Godunov
(original version, in Russian)
Stefka Mineva (Marina),
Nicolai Ghiaurov (Boris),
Wieslaw Ochman (Dimitri),
John Tomlinson (Pimen),
Emile Belcourt (Shuisky),
John Del Carlo (Rangoni)
Marek Janowski
Nov. 23, 26, Dec. 2, 5,
8, 11m

SUMMER 1984

Donizetti, *Don Pasquale*
Diana Soviero (Norina);
Paolo Montarsolo
(Don Pasquale),
Francesco Araiza (Ernesto),
Pablo Elvira (Malatesta)
Guido Ajmone-Marsan
May 25, 27m, June 1, 7,
9, 11

Wagner, *Siegfried*
Eva Marton (Brünnhilde),
Helga Dernesch (Erda);
René Kollo (Siegfried),
Stanley Wexler (Alberich),
Helmut Pampuch**/(6/8, 12)
Francis Egerton (Mime),
Thomas Stewart (Wanderer)
Edo de Waart
May 26, 31, June 3m,
8, 12

Verdi, *Aida*
Leontyne Price/(6/20, 23, 27,
30) Stefka Evstatieva (Aida),
Ruža Baldani (Amneris),
Franco Bonisolli (Radames),
Juan Pons (Amonasro)
Edo de Waart
June 2, 6, 10m, 15, 20,
23, 27, 30

Strauss, J. Jr.,
Die Fledermaus (in English)
Josephine Barstow
(Rosalinda), Deborah
Sasson (Adele),
Helga Dernesch (Orlofsky);
Peter Hofmann (Eisenstein),
Ragnar Ulfung (Alfred),
Michael Devlin (Dr. Falke)
Andrew Meltzer
June 16, 19, 22, 24m, 26,
28, July 1m

1984

Verdi, *Ernani*
Montserrat Caballé/(9/30)
Mary Jane Johnson (Elvira);
Nunzio Todisco/(9/26, 30)
Giuliano Ciannella (Ernani),
Sherrill Milnes (Don Carlo),
Paul Plishka (Silva)
Lamberto Gardelli
Sept. 7, 12, 15, 19, 22,
26, 30m

Bizet, *Carmen*
Alicia Nafé** (Carmen),
Kaaren Erickson (Micaëla);
Giuliano Ciannella/(9/27)
Luis Lima (Don José),
Lenus Carlson (Escamillo)
García Navarro
Sept. 8, 11, 14, 17, 20,
23m, 27

Bellini, *La Sonnambula*
Frederica von Stade (Amina);
Dennis O'Neill (Elvino),
Samuel Ramey (Rodolfo)
Nicola Rescigno
Sept. 18, 21, 25, 29,
Oct. 4, 7m, 12

Donizetti, *L'Elisir d'Amore*
Alida Ferrarini** (Adina);
Luis Lima (Nemorino),
Dale Duesing (Belcore),
John Del Carlo (Dulcamara)
David Agler
Oct. 2, 5, 9, 13, 17,
21m, 27

Puccini, *Madama Butterfly*
Veronika Kincses (Cio-Cio-
San), Laura Brooks
Rice (Suzuki); Miguel
Cortez (Pinkerton),
Tom Krause (Sharpless)
Richard Bradshaw
Oct. 6, 10, 14m, 16, 19,
24, 30, Nov. 2

Nikki Li Hartliep (Cio-Cio-
San), Donna Bruno (Suzuki);
Walter MacNeil (Pinkerton),
James Busterud (Sharpless)
James Johnson
Dec. 1m, 6

Strauss, *Elektra*
Janis Martin (Elektra),
Carol Neblett (Chrysothemis),
Viorica Cortez (Klytemnestra);
Dennis Bailey (Aegisth),
Peter Wimberger (Orest)
Jeffrey Tate
Oct. 18, 23, 26,
Nov. 1, 4m, 7, 10

Donizetti, *Anna Bolena*
Joan Sutherland (Anna),
(10/25) Livia Budai/
Judith Forst (Giovanna
Seymour), Rachel
Gettler (Smeton);
Rockwell Blake (Percy),
Kevin Langan (Henry VIII)
Richard Bonynge
Oct. 25, 28m, 31,
Nov. 3, 6, 9, 13

Mussorgsky,
Khovanshchina
Helga Dernesch (Marfa);
Matti Salminen (Khovansky),
William Lewis (Golitsin),
Dennis Bailey (Andrei),
Timothy Noble (Shaklovity),
Gwynne Howell (Dosifei)
Gerd Albrecht
Nov. 11m, 14, 18m, 24,
27, 30

Verdi, *Rigoletto*
Luciana Serra (Gilda),
Leslie Richards (Maddalena);
Ingvar Wixell (Rigoletto),
Dano Raffanti (Duke), James
Patterson (Sparafucile)
Kurt Herbert Adler
Nov. 17, 20, 23, 29,
Dec. 2m, 5, 8

Mozart, *Don Giovanni*
Rebecca Cook (Anna),
Pilar Lorengar (Elvira),
Margarita Zimmermann
(Zerlina); Wolfgang
Brendel (Giovanni), Keith
Lewis (Ottavio), Enrico

Fissore (Leporello), Matti
Salminen (Commendatore)
Myung-Whun Chung
Nov. 21, 25m, 28,
Dec. 1, 4, 7, 9m

SUMMER 1985 - The Ring

Wagner,
*Der Ring des Nibelungen
Das Rheingold*
Hanna Schwarz (Fricka),
Mariana Paunova (Erda);
James Morris (Wotan),
William Lewis (Loge),
Walter Berry (Alberich)
Edo de Waart
June 2, 7, 12

Die Walküre
Gwyneth Jones (Brünnhilde),
Jeannine Altmeyer
(Sieglinde), Helga
Dernesch (Fricka);
Peter Hofmann (Siegmund),
James Morris (Wotan),
John Tomlinson (Hunding)
Edo de Waart
June 4, 9m, 15

Siegfried
Eva Marton (Brünnhilde),
Hanna Schwarz (Erda);
René Kollo (Siegfried),
Walter Berry (Alberich),
Helmut Pampuch (Mime),
Thomas Stewart (Wanderer)
Edo de Waart
June 5, 11, 16m

Götterdämmerung
Eva Marton (Brünnhilde),
Kathryn Bouleyn (Gutrune),
René Kollo (Siegfried),
Michael Devlin (Gunther),
John Tomlinson (Hagen)
Edo de Waart
June 8, 13, 19

Weber, *Der Freischütz*
(Concert Performance)
Pilar Lorengar (Agathe),
Ruth Ann Swenson
(Aennchen); William
Johns (Max), Michael
Devlin (Kaspar)
Heinrich Hollreiser
June 14, 18, 21

1985

Cilea, *Adriana Lecouvreur*
Mirella Freni (Adriana),
Cleopatra Ciurca (Princess);
Ermanno Mauro (Maurizio),
Leo Nucci (Michonnet)
Maurizio Arena
Sept. 6, 10, 13, 16, 22m,
25, 28

Reimann, *Lear* (in English)
Helga Dernesch (Goneril),
Anja Silja (Regan), Sheri
Greenawald (Cordelia);
Thomas Stewart (Lear),
Chester Ludgin (Gloucester),
Timothy Noble (Albany),
David Knutson (Edgar),

Jacque Trussel (Edmund)
Friedemann Layer**
Sept. 7, 12, 15m, 17,
20, 27

Handel, *Orlando*
Marilyn Horne (Orlando),
Valerie Masterson (Angelica),
Ruth Ann Swenson
(Dorinda); Jeffrey
Gall (Medoro), Kevin
Langan (Zoroastro)
Charles Mackerras
Sept. 14, 18, 21, 24,
Oct. 3, 6m

Puccini, *Turandot*
Eva Marton/(10/9, 12, 15,
18) Linda Kelm (Turandot),
Adriana Anelli (Liù);
Franco Bonisolli (Calaf),
John Macurdy (Timur)
Berislav Klobučar
Sept. 26, 29m, Oct. 2, 5,
9, 12, 15, 18

Massenet, *Werther*
Renata Scotto (Charlotte),
Cheryl Parrish (Sophie);
Alfredo Kraus (Werther),
Stephen Dickson (Albert)
Michel Plasson
Oct. 4, 10, 13m, 16,
19, 22, 25

Verdi, *Falstaff*
Pilar Lorengar (Alice), Ruth
Ann Swenson (Nannetta),
Marilyn Horne (Quickly),
Susan Quittmeyer, (Meg);
Ingvar Wixell (Falstaff),
Walter MacNeil (Fenton),
Alan Titus (Ford)
Maurizio Arena
Oct. 20m, 23, 27m, 30,
Nov. 2, 5, 8

Nikki Li Hartliep (Alice),
Li-Chan Chen (Nannetta),
Dolora Zajic (Quickly),
Kathryn Cowdrick (Meg);
Richard Pendergraph
(Falstaff), James Schwisow
(Fenton), David Malis (Ford)
Richard Bradshaw
Nov. 25, 30m

Puccini, *Tosca*
Maria Slatinaru (Tosca);
Giuseppe Giacomini
(Cavaradossi), James
Morris (Scarpia)
Carlo Felice Cillario
Oct. 26, 29, Nov. 3m, 6,
9, 12, 15

Verdi,
Un Ballo in Maschera
Carol Neblett (Amelia),
Erie Mills (Oscar),
Fiorenza Cossotto (Ulrica);
Carlo Bergonzi/(12/1, 6)
Giacomo Aragall (Gustavo),
Silvano Carroli (Renato)
John Pritchard
Nov. 7, 10m, 13, 17m,
20, 23, Dec. 1m, 6

Britten, *Billy Budd*
Dale Duesing (Billy),
James King (Capt. Vere),
James Morris (Claggart)
Raymond Leppard
Nov. 14, 19, 22, 27, 30,
Dec. 3, 8m

Strauss,
Der Rosenkavalier
Brigitte Fassbaender
(Octavian), Kiri Te
Kanawa (Marschallin),
Cheryl Parrish (Sophie);
Kurt Moll (Ochs), Tonio
Di Paolo (Italian Singer),
Renato Capecchi (Faninal)
John Pritchard
Nov. 21, 24m, 26, 29,
Dec. 2, 4, 7

SUMMER 1986

Verdi, *Il Trovatore*
Ghena Dimitrova (Leonora),
Dolora Zajic (Azucena);
Franco Bonisolli (Manrico),
Silvano Carroli/(6/12, 15, 18)
Piero Cappuccilli (Luna)
Andrew Meltzer
May 24, 29, June 3, 6,
12, 15m, 18

Donizetti,
Lucia di Lammermoor
Gianna Rolandi (Lucia);
Barry McCauley
(Edgardo), Pablo Elvira
(Enrico), Konstantin
Sfiris** (Raimondo)
Carlo Felice Cillario
May 27, 31, June 5, 8m,
11, 20, 25

Mascagni,
Cavalleria Rusticana
Fiorenza Cossotto
(Santuzza); Ermanno
Mauro (Turiddu),
Piero Cappuccilli (Alfio)
Anton Guadagno/(6/22)
Carlo Felice Cillario
and
Leoncavallo, *Pagliacci*
Diana Soviero (Nedda);
Ermanno Mauro (Canio),
Piero Cappuccilli (Tonio),
David Malis (Silvio)
Anton Guadagno/(6/22)
Carlo Felice Cillario
June 1m, 4, 7, 10, 13,
17, 22m

Poulenc, *La Voix humaine*
Karan Armstrong
(The Woman)
James Johnson
and
Menotti, *The Medium*
Régine Crespin (Mme. Flora),
Li-Chan Chen (Monica)
Jérôme Kaltenbach**
June 19, 21, 24, 26, 29m

1986

Verdi, *Don Carlos*
Pilar Lorengar (Elisabeth),
Stefania Toczyska (Eboli);
Neil Shicoff (Carlos),
Alan Titus (Rodrigue), Robert
Lloyd (Philippe II), Joseph
Rouleau (Grand Inquisitor)
John Pritchard/(9/28, 10/1)
James Johnson
Sept. 5, 10, 13, 17, 20,
28m, Oct. 1

Mozart, *Le Nozze di Figaro*
Gianna Rolandi (Susanna),
Kiri Te Kanawa (Countess),
Susan Quittmeyer
(Cherubino); Samuel
Ramey (Figaro), Michael
Devlin (Almaviva)
Jeffrey Tate
Sept. 6, 9, 12, 16,
21m, 24, 26

Janáček, *Jenůfa*
Gabriela Beňačková
(Jenůfa), Leonie Rysanek
(Kostelnička); Neil
Rosenshein (Števa),
Wieslaw Ochman (Laca)
Charles Mackerras
Sept. 14m, 19, 23, 27,
Oct. 2, 5m

Verdi,
La Forza del Destino
Maria Slatinaru (Leonora),
Judith Forst (Preziosilla);
Carlo Cossutta (Don Alvaro),
Wolfgang Brendel
(Don Carlo), Paul
Plishka (Padre Guardiano)
Maurizio Arena
Sept. 25, 30, Oct. 4, 9,
12m, 15, 18

Gounod, *Faust*
Mary Jane Johnson
(Marguerite), Kathryn
Cowdrick (Siebel); (10/7, 10,
16) Alfredo Kraus/Luis
Lima (Faust), Alan
Titus (Valentin), (10/7)
Robert Lloyd/(10/10,16)
Paul Plishka/Justino
Díaz (Méphistophélès)
Jean Fournet
Oct. 7, 10, 16, 22, 25, 30,
Nov. 2m

Wagner, *Die Meistersinger*
Cheryl Studer (Eva),
Sandra Walker (Magdalene);
James King (Walther),
Hans Tschammer (Hans
Sachs), Michel
Trempont (Beckmesser),
Kurt Rydl (Pogner),
David Gordon (David),
Kurt Herbert Adler
Oct. 14, 19m, 23, 26m, 29,
Nov. 1, 7

Puccini, *La Bohème*
Nelly Miricioiu (Mimi),
Nancy Gustafson (Musetta);

Alberto Cupido/(11/6, 9, 12,
15) Luis Lima (Rodolfo),
Tom Krause (Marcello),
Kevin Langan (Colline)
Maurizio Arena
Oct. 24, 28, 31, Nov. 4, 6,
9m, 12, 15

Tchaikovsky,
Eugene Onegin (in Russian)
Mirella Freni (Tatiana),
Sandra Walker (Olga);
Thomas Allen (Onegin),
Dénes Gulyás (Lensky),
Nicolai Ghiaurov
(Prince Gremin)
Richard Bradshaw
Nov. 8, 11, 16m, 21,
26, 30m, Dec. 5

Massenet, *Manon*
Sheri Greenawald (Manon);
Francisco Araiza
(des Grieux), Gino
Quilico (Lescaut)
Jean Fournet
Nov. 14, 20, 23m, 28, 30,
Dec. 3, 6

Verdi, *Macbeth*
Shirley Verrett
(Lady Macbeth);
Timothy Noble (Macbeth),
Vladimir Popov (Macduff),
John Tomlinson (Banquo)
Kazimierz Kord
Nov. 19, 22, 25, 29,
Dec. 2, 4, 7m

1987

Rossini,
Il Barbiere di Siviglia
Susanne Mentzer (Rosina);
Leo Nucci (Figaro),
Patrick Power** (Almaviva),
Nicolai Ghiaurov (Basilio),
Renato Capecchi (Bartolo)
Alberto Zedda
Sept. 11, 16, 20m, 24,
26, 29, Oct. 2

Strauss, *Salome*
Gwyneth Jones (Salome),
Helga Dernesch (Herodias);
James King (Herod),
Michael Devlin (Jokanaan)
John Pritchard
Sept. 12, 15, 18, 23, 27m,
Oct. 3

Mozart, *Die Zauberflöte*
Etelka Csavlek** (Pamina),
Luciana Serra (Queen
of the Night); Francisco
Araiza (Tamino), David
Malis (Papageno),
Kevin Langan (Sarastro)
Friedemann Layer
Sept. 19, 22, 25, 30,
Oct. 6, 8, 11m

Puccini, *Tosca*
Olivia Stapp (Tosca);
Ermanno Mauro
(Cavaradossi),
Alain Fondary**/(10/25)
Juan Pons (Scarpia),

Richard Bradshaw
Oct. 4m, 7, 10, 16,
22, 25m

Beethoven, *Fidelio*
Elizabeth Connell (Leonore),
Cheryl Parrish (Marzelline);
James McCracken
(Florestan), Franz
Ferdinand Nentwig (Pizarro),
Paul Plishka (Rocco)
John Pritchard
Oct. 13, 18m, 21, 24,
27, 30, Nov. 5

Verdi, *La Traviata*
Nelly Miricioiu (Violetta);
Francisco Araiza (Alfredo),
Juan Pons (Germont)
Andrew Meltzer
Oct. 17, 20, 23, 28,
Nov. 1m, 4, 7m

Madelyn Renée/Susan
Patterson (Violetta);
Douglas Wunsch (Alfredo),
Thomas Potter (Germont)
John Fiore
Dec. 10, 12m

Verdi, *Nabucco*
Mara Zampieri**/(11/13, 19,
22) Grace Bumbry
(Abigaille), Leslie
Richards (Fenena);
Piero Cappuccilli (Nabucco),
Paul Plishka (Zaccaria),
Quade Winter (Ismaele)
Maurizio Arena
Oct. 31, Nov. 3, 7, 10,
13, 19, 22m

Offenbach,
Les Contes d'Hoffmann
Tracy Dahl (Olympia), Nancy
Gustafson (Antonia), Mary
Jane Johnson (Giulietta);
Susan Quittmeyer/(12/8, 11)
Donna Bruno (Nicklausse);
Plácido Domingo/(11/25)
Neil Shicoff/(12/8, 11)
John Alexander (Hoffmann),
James Morris/(12/8, 11) Tom
Krause (Lindorf, Coppélius,
Dapertutto, Dr. Miracle)
Michel Plasson
Nov. 11, 15m, 18, 21,
25, 28, Dec. 8, 11

Gounod, *Roméo et Juliette*
Ruth Ann Swenson (Juliette);
Alfredo Kraus/(11/24, 29,
12/4) John David de
Haan/(12/2) Fernando
De La Mora** (Roméo),
Stephen Dickson (Mercutio),
Gwynne Howell (Laurence)
Michel Plasson
Nov. 14, 17, 20, 24, 29m,
Dec. 2, 4

Tchaikovsky,
Pikovaya Dama
Stefka Evstatieva (Lisa),
Kathryn Cowdrick (Paulina),
Régine Crespin (Countess);
Wieslaw Ochman (Gherman),

Richard Bradshaw
Oct. 4m, 7, 10, 16,
22, 25m

J. Patrick Raftery (Yeletsky),
Timothy Noble (Tomsky)
Emil Tchakarov
Nov. 23, 27, Dec. 1, 5,
9, 13m

1988

Meyerbeer, *L'Africaine*
Shirley Verrett (Sélika), Ruth
Ann Swenson (Inès); Plácido
Domingo (Vasco da Gama),
Justino Díaz (Nélusko),
Michael Devlin (Don Pedro)
Maurizio Arena
Sept. 9, 13, 16, 18m,
21, 24, 27

Stravinsky,
The Rake's Progress
Susan Patterson (Anne),
Victoria Vergara (Baba the
Turk); Jerry Hadley (Tom),
William Shimell** (Nick),
James Patterson/(9/23)
Raymond Murcell (Trulove)
John Mauceri
Sept. 10, 15, 23, 28,
Oct. 2m, 4

Rossini, *Maometto II***
June Anderson (Anna),
Marilyn Horne (Calbo);
Simone Alaimo (Maometto),
Chris Merritt (Paolo)
Alberto Zedda
Sept. 17, 19, 25m, 30,
Oct. 6, 9m

Wagner,
Der Fliegende Holländer
(9/29) Deborah Polaski**/
(10/1, 5, 7) Janis Martin/
(10/11, 15, 23) Sophia
Larson** (Senta); José Van
Dam/(10/11) Monte Pederson
(Dutchman), Wieslaw
Ochman (Steersman/Erik),
Sergei Koptchak (Daland)
Jérôme Kaltenbach
Sept. 29, Oct. 1, 5, 7,
11, 15, 23m

Mozart, *Così fan tutte*
Etelka Csavlek (Fiordiligi),
Diana Montague (Dorabella);
Gianna Rolandi/(10/21,
Act II) Janet Williams
(Despina); Dénes Gulyás
(Ferrando), Stephen Dickson
(Guglielmo), Tom Krause/
(10/18 [Act II], 21, 27, 30
[Act II], 11/3) Renato
Capecchi (Don Alfonso)
Kazimierz Kord
Nov. 20m, 23, 27m,
Dec. 1, 3, 6, 10

Puccini, *Manon Lescaut*
Pilar Lorengar (Manon);
Peter Dvorský/(11/9
from the pit) William
Lewis (des Grieux),
Marcel Vanaud (Lescaut)
John Pritchard
Oct. 16m, 19, 26, 29,
Nov. 1, 4, 9

Wagner, *Parsifal*
Waltraud Meier (Kundry);
René Kollo (Parsifal),
Jorma Hynninen (Amfortas),
Kurt Moll (Gurnemanz),
Walter Berry (Klingsor)
John Pritchard
Oct. 22, 25, 28,
Nov. 2, 6m, 8

Shostakovich, *Lady
Macbeth of Mtsensk*
Josephine Barstow
(Katerina), Emily
Golden (Sonyetka);
Jacque Trussel (Sergei),
William Lewis (Zinovy),
Michael Devlin (Boris),
James Patterson
(Old Convict)
John Pritchard/
(12/4) Ian Robertson
Nov. 12, 19, 21, 25, 30,
Dec. 4m

Puccini, *La Bohème*
Mirella Freni (Mimi),
Sandra Pacetti (Musetta);
Luciano Pavarotti/(12/2, 8)
Luis Lima (Rodolfo),
Gino Quilico (Marcello),
Nicolai Ghiaurov (Colline)
Tiziano Severini**
Nov. 16, 19m, 22, 26, 29,
Dec. 2, 8

Cecilia Gasdia (Mimi),
Evelyn de la Rosa (Musetta);
Fernando De La Mora/
Luis Lima (Rodolfo),
David Malis (Marcello),
Kevin Langan (Colline)
John Fiore
Dec. 9, 11m

Nikki Li Hartliep (Mimi),
Janet Williams (Musetta);
Douglas Wunsch (Rodolfo),
Victor Ledbetter (Marcello),
Philip Skinner (Colline)
John Fiore
Dec. 10m

Ponchielli, *La Gioconda*
Eva Marton/(12/10)
Galina Savova (Gioconda),
Cleopatra Ciurca/(12/6)
Stefania Toczyska (Laura),
Katherine Ciesinski (Laura),
Sheila Nadler (La Cieca);
Vyacheslav Polozov (Enzo),
Cornelis Opthof (Barnaba),
Bonaldo Giaiotti (Alvise)
Kazimierz Kord
Nov. 20m, 23, 27m,
Dec. 1, 3, 6, 10

SUMMER 1989

Glass, *Satyagraha*
Claudia Cummings
(Mrs. Schlesen), Ann
Panagulias (Mrs. Naidoo),
Catherine Keen (Kasturbai);
Douglas Perry (Gandhi)
Bruce Ferden
June 3, 5, 7, 9, 11m

1989

Verdi, *Falstaff*
Pilar Lorengar (Alice),
Ruth Ann Swenson
(Nannetta), Marilyn
Horne (Quickly), Kathryn
Cowdrick (Meg); Thomas
Stewart (Falstaff), John
David De Haan (Fenton),
J. Patrick Raftery (Ford)
Kazimierz Kord
Sept. 8, 13, 17m, 21,
23, 26, 29

Patricia Racette (Alice),
Janet Williams (Nannetta),
Catherine Keen (Quickly),
Patricia Spence (Meg);
Timothy Noble (Falstaff),
Benoit Boutet (Fenton),
Victor Ledbetter (Ford)
Ian Robertson
Sept. 17

Berg, *Lulu*
Ann Panagulias (Lulu),
Evelyn Lear (Geschwitz);
Victor Braun (Dr. Schön),
Michael Myers (Painter),
Barry McCauley (Alwa),
Hans Hotter (Schigolch)
John Mauceri
Sept. 9, 12, 15, 20, 23m,
Oct. 1m

Boito, *Mefistofele*
Gabriela Beňačková
(Margherita, Elena);
Samuel Ramey (Mefistofele),
Dennis O'Neill (Faust)
Maurizio Arena
Sept. 16, 19, 22, 24m, 28,
Oct. 4, 8m, 10

Verdi, *Otello*
Katia Ricciarelli
(Desdemona);
Ermanno Mauro (Otello),
Brent Ellis (Iago)
Kazimierz Kord
Sept. 30, Oct. 3, 6, 12,
15m, 20 (at Masonic
Aud.), 24

Mozart, *Idomeneo*
Karita Mattila (Ilia),
Nancy Gustafson (Elettra);
Wieslaw Ochman (Idomeneo),
Hans Peter Blochwitz**
(Idamante), William
Lewis (Arbace)
John Pritchard
Oct. 7, 11, 14m, 17
(cancelled), 22m
(at Masonic Aud.), 25, 27

Verdi, *Aida*
Sharon Sweet**/(10/29)
Alessandra Marc (Aida),
Dolora Zajick (Amneris);
Vladimir Popov (Radames),
Timothy Noble (Amonasro)
Cal Stewart Kellogg
Oct. 21 (at Masonic Aud.),
26, 29m, Nov. 1, 4, 7,
12m, 14

Puccini, *Madama Butterfly*
Nikki Li Hartliep (Cio-Cio-San), Robynne Redmon (Suzuki); Vyacheslav Polozov (Pinkerton), Gaétan Laperrière (Sharpless)
John Fiore
Oct. 28, 31, Nov. 3, 5m, 10, 15, 18

Diana Soviero (Cio-Cio-San), Emily Manhart (Suzuki); Giacomo Aragall (Pinkerton), Brian Schexnayder (Sharpless)
John Fiore
Dec. 3m, 9m

Wagner, *Lohengrin*
Mari Anne Häggander/(11/17) Meredith Mizell (Elsa), Eva Randová (Ortrud)/ Paul Frey/(11/21) William Johns in the wings/(11/26) Ben Heppner (Lohengrin), Sergei Leiferkus** (Telramund), Siegfried Vogel (Heinrich)
Charles Mackerras/(12/8) Ian Robertson
Nov. 11, 17, 21, 26m, 29, Dec. 2, 8

Vivaldi, *Orlando Furioso*
Marilyn Horne (Orlando), Susan Patterson (Angelica), Kathleen Kuhlmann (Alcina), Sandra Walker (Bradamante); Jeffrey Gall (Ruggiero), William Matteuzzi (Medoro), Kevin Langan (Astolfo)
Randall Behr
Nov. 19m, 24, 30, Dec. 3, 6, 9

Strauss,
Die Frau ohne Schatten
Mary Jane Johnson (Empress), Gwyneth Jones (Barak's Wife), Anja Silja (Nurse); William Johns (Emperor), Alfred Muff** (Barak)
Christoph von Dohnányi
Nov. 25, 28, Dec. 1, 4, 7, 10m

SUMMER 1990

Wagner,
Der Ring des Nibelungen
Das Rheingold
Helga Dernesch (Fricka), Birgitta Svendén (Erda); James Morris/(6/20) Robert Hale (Wotan), Jacque Trussel (Loge), Tom Fox/(6/12, 24) Franz Mazura (Alberich) (6/6, 12) Peter Schneider**/ Donald Runnicles
June 6, 12, 20, 24m

Die Walküre
Gwyneth Jones/(6/14) Janis Martin/(6/27) Hildegard Behrens (Brünnhilde),

Rebecca Blankenship** (Sieglinde), Helga Dernesch (Fricka); Gary Lakes (Siegmund), James Morris/(6/21) Robert Hale (Wotan), John Macurdy (Hunding) (6/8, 14) Peter Schneider/ Donald Runnicles
June 8, 14, 21, 27

Siegfried
Gwyneth Jones/(6/16) Janis Martin/(6/29) Hildegard Behrens (Brünnhilde), Birgitta Svendén (Erda); (6/10) Williams Johns/René Kollo (Siegfried), (6/10, 23)Tom Fox /Franz Mazura (Alberich), Helmut Pampuch (Mime), James Morris/(6/23) Robert Hale (Wanderer) (6/10, 16) Peter Schneider/ Donald Runnicles
June 10m, 16, 23, 29

Götterdämmerung
Gwyneth Jones/(6/19) Janis Martin/(7/1) Hildegard Behrens (Brünnhilde), Kathryn Day (Gutrune); (6/13) Williams Johns/ René Kollo (Siegfried), Michael Devlin (Gunther), Eric Halfvarson (Hagen) (6/13, 19) Peter Schneider/ Donald Runnicles
June 13, 19, 26, July 1m

1990

Puccini, *Suor Angelica*
Leona Mitchell (Angelica), Elena Obraztsova (Princess)
Nello Santi
and
Leoncavallo, *Pagliacci*
Marilyn Mims (Nedda); Vladimir Atlantov** (Canio), Matteo Manuguerra/(10/2) Timothy Noble (Tonio), Gino Quilico (Silvio)
Nello Santi
Sept. 16m, 19, 22, 28, Oct. 2

Berg, *Wozzeck*
Judith Forst (Marie); Allan Monk (Wozzeck), Warren Ellsworth (Drum Major), Stuart Kale** (Captain), Siegfried Vogel (Doctor)
Friedemann Layer
Sept. 21, 23m, 26, 29m

Verdi, *Rigoletto*
Ruth Ann Swenson (Gilda), Claire Powell** (Maddalena); Alain Fondary (Rigoletto), Richard Leech (Duke), Kevin Langan (Sparafucile)
John Fiore
Sept. 15, 20, 25, 30m, Oct. 5, 10, 12

Hei-Kyung Hong (Gilda), Catherine Keen (Maddalena); Juan Pons (Rigoletto), Hong-Shen Li (Duke), Mark S. Doss (Sparafucile)
Ian Robertson
Dec. 1m, 7

Mozart, *Die Entführung aus dem Serail*
Susan Patterson (Constanze), Cheryl Parrish (Blondchen); Kurt Streit (Belmonte), Lars Magnusson (Pedrillo), Kurt Moll (Osmin)
Hermann Michael
Sept. 27, Oct. 3, 7m, 9, 13, 16, 19

Massenet, *Don Quichotte*
Katherine Ciesinski (Dulcinée); Samuel Ramey (Don Quichotte), Dennis Petersen (Juan), Michel Trempont (Sancho Pança)
Julius Rudel
Oct. 11, 14m, 18, 20, 23, 26

Strauss, *Capriccio*
Kiri Te Kanawa (Countess), Hanna Schwarz (Clairon), Reri Grist (Italian Soprano); Keith Olsen (Flamand), Håkan Hagegård (Count), William Shimell (Olivier), Victor Braun (La Roche)
Stephen Barlow**
Oct. 21m, 24, 27, Nov. 2, 7, 11m

Verdi,
Un Ballo in Maschera
Deborah Voigt/(10/31) Susan Dunn (Amelia), Tracy Dahl (Oscar), Diane Curry (Ulrica); Ermanno Mauro (Gustavo), Alain Fondary (Renato)
Maurizio Arena
Oct. 28m, 31, Nov. 3, 6, 9, 14, 18m

Strauss, J. Jr.,
Die Fledermaus (in English)
(11/4, 8, 10, 16) Elizabeth Holleque/Nancy Gustafson (Rosalinda), Barbara Kilduff (Adele), (11/4, 8, 10) Hanna Schwarz/Ildiko Komlosi (Orlofsky); (11/4, 8, 25, 27) Håkan Hagegård/Theodore Baerg (Eisenstein), Jorge Lopez-Jañez (Alfred), Timothy Nolen (Falke), Arte Johnson (Frosch)
Julius Rudel/(11/24, 25, 27, 30) Patrick Summers
Nov. 4m, 8, 10, 16, 24m, 25, 27, 30

Patricia Racette (Rosalinda), Janet Williams (Adele), Catherine Keen (Orlofsky); Dennis McNeil (Eisenstein), Craig Estep (Alfred), LeRoy Villanueva (Falke),

Arte Johnson (Frosch)
Patrick Summers
Nov. 10m

Mussorgsky,
Khovanshchina
Dolora Zajick (Marfa); Nicolai Ghiaurov (Khovansky), John Treleaven (Golitsin), Michael Myers (Andrei), Timothy Noble (Shaklovity), Gwynne Howell (Dosifei)
Yuri Simonov
Nov. 17, 20, 24, 29, Dec. 2m, 5, 8

Monteverdi, *Il Ritorno d'Ulisse in Patria*
(Leppard edition)
Frederica von Stade/(11/25) Yanyu Guo (Penelope), Susan Graham (Minerva), Kathryn Cowdrick (Melanto); Thomas Hampson (Ulisse), Vinson Cole (Telemaco), William Lewis (Eumete)
Mario Bernardi
Nov. 23, 25m, 28, Dec. 1, 4, 6, 9m

SUMMER 1991 —
A SEASON OF MOZART

Mozart, *Die Zauberflöte*
Ruth Ann Swenson (Pamina), Sally Wolf (Queen); Jerry Hadley (Tamino), Michael Kraus** (Papageno), Kevin Langan (Sarastro)
Gerard Schwarz
June 1, 4, 7, 13, 16m, 22

Mozart, *Le Nozze di Figaro*
Cheryl Parrish (Susanna), Renée Fleming (Countess), Frederica von Stade (Cherubino); Simone Alaimo (Figaro), Wolfgang Brendel (Count)
Wolfgang Rennert
June 2m, 6, 9m, 15, 19, 21

Mozart, *Così fan tutte*
Susan Patterson (Fiordiligi), Judith Forst (Dorabella), Janet Williams (Despina); Deon van der Walt (Ferrando), James Michael McGuire (Guglielmo), Dale Travis (Don Alfonso)
Patrick Summers
June 14, 18, 20, 23m, 26, 29

Mozart, *Lucio Silla*
(Concert version)
Sally Wolf (Giunia), Alexandra Coku (Celia), Ann Panagulias (Lucio Cinna), Monica Bacelli** (Cecilio); Vinson Cole (Lucio Silla), Hong-Shen Li (Aufidio)
Julius Rudel
June 28, 30

1991

Verdi, *La Traviata*
Carol Vaness/(9/29) Mariana Nicolesco (Violetta), Marcello Giordani (Alfredo), Paolo Coni (Germont)
Maurizio Arena
Sept. 6, 11, 14, 18, 22m, 27, 29

Susan Patterson (Violetta); Jorge Lopez-Yañez/(11/29) Hong-Shen Li (Alfredo), Gaétan Laperrière (Germont)
Ian Robertson
Nov. 25, 29, Dec. 5

Prokofiev, *War and Peace*
(in Russian)
Ann Panagulias (Natasha), Elena Zaremba (Hélène), Irina Bogachova (Marya), Catherine Keen (Sonya); Dimitri Kharitonov (Prince Andrei), Barry McCauley (Pierre), Alexandre Naoumenko** (Platon), Valery Alexeiev** (Napoleon), Vladimir Ognovenko** (Old Prince Bolkonsky, Matveyev), Valery Gergiev**/(10/2) Alexander Anissimov**
Sept. 7, 10, 12, 15m, 20, 26, Oct. 2

Bellini,
I Capuleti e i Montecchi
Cecilia Gasdia (Giulietta), Delores Ziegler (Romeo); (9/19, 21, 25) Vincenzo La Scola**/Hong-Shen Li (Tebaldo), Paul Plishka (Capellio), Philip Skinner (Lorenzo)
Antonio Pappano
Sept. 19, 21, 25, 29m, Oct. 5, 8, 10

Mozart, *Don Giovanni*
Marilyn Mims (Anna), Kallen Esperian (Elvira), Harolyn Blackwell (Zerlina); (9/28) Samuel Ramey/Gino Quilico (Giovanni), Frank Lopardo (Ottavio), Lucio Gallo** (Leporello), Peter Rose** (Commendatore)
Leopold Hager
Sept. 28, Oct. 1, 3, 6m, 11, 13m, 15, 19

Bizet, *Carmen*
(10/12, 25, 29, 11/1) Denyce Graves/Kathleen Kuhlmann (Carmen), (10/12,16, 20, 23, 26) Patricia Racette/ Cynthia Haymon (Micaëla); Barry McCauley/(10/25, 29) Antonio Ordoñez (Don José), (10/12, 16, 25, 11/7, 10) Dimitri Kharitonov/ Robert Hale (Escamillo)
Vjekoslav Šutej
Oct. 12, 16, 20m, 23, 25, 26, 29, Nov. 1, 7, 10m

Wagner,
Tristan und Isolde
Gabriele Schnaut** (Isolde), Hanna Schwarz (Brangäne); William Johns (Tristan), Hartmut Welker/(11/9) Victor Braun (Kurwenal), Alfred Muff (King Marke)
Peter Schneider
Oct. 21, 24, 27m, 30, Nov. 2, 5, 9

Henze,
*Das Verratene Meer***
Ashley Putnam (Fusako); Tom Fox (Ryuji), Craig Estep (Noboru), Brian Asawa (Number Two), LeRoy Villanueva (Number One)
Markus Stenz**
Nov. 8, 13, 17m, 20, 23

Strauss, *Elektra*
Gwyneth Jones (Elektra), Nadine Secunde (Chrysothemis), Helga Dernesch (Klytemnestra); James King (Aegisth), Monte Pederson/(12/1, 4, 7) Tom Fox (Orest)
Christian Thielemann**
Nov. 16, 22, 26, Dec. 1m, 4, 7

Verdi, *Attila*
Elizabeth Connell (Odabella); Samuel Ramey (Attila), Antonio Ordoñez (Foresto), (11/21, 24) Vladimir Chernov/Luis Girón May (Ezio), Craig Estep (Uldino)
Gabriele Ferro
Nov. 21, 24m, 27, 30, Dec. 3, 6, 8m

SUMMER 1992 — A CELE-BRATION OF ROSSINI

Rossini, *Guillaume Tell*
Carol Vaness (Mathilde), Janet Williams (Jemmy); Timothy Noble (Guillaume), Chris Merritt (Arnold), Jeffrey Wells (Fürst), Peter Rose (Gessler)
Donald Runnicles
May 30, June 3, 6, 11, 14m

Rossini,
Il Barbiere di Siviglia
Frederica von Stade (Rosina); Jeffrey Black (Figaro), Jorge Lopez-Yañez (Almaviva), Peter Rose (Basilio), Alfonso Antoniozzi** (Bartolo)
Ion Marin
June 2, 5, 7m, 13, 16, 19

Rossini,
L'Italiana in Algeri
Marilyn Horne (Isabella), Janet Williams (Elvira); Frank Lopardo (Lindoro),

Alfonso Antoniozzi (Taddeo), Simone Alaimo (Mustafà)
Donato Renzetti
June 9, 12, 17, 21m, 24, 27

Rossini, *Ermione***
(Staged Concert Version)
Anna Caterina Antonacci (Ermione), Kathleen Kuhlmann (Andromaca); Hong-Shen Li (Pirro), Jorge Lopez-Yañez (Oreste), Craig Estep (Pilade), Jeffrey Wells (Fenicio)
Patrick Summers
June 26, 28m

1992

Puccini, *Tosca*
Maria Guleghina (Tosca), Sergei Larin** (Cavaradossi), Juan Pons (Scarpia)
Daniel Oren
Sept. 11, 15, 18, 23, 26, Oct. 1, 4m

Leona Mitchell (Tosca); Michael Sylvester (Cavaradossi), Timothy Noble (Scarpia)
Patrick Summers
Dec. 1, 5m, 9, 12m

Mussorgsky,
Boris Godunov (Original version, Shostakovich orchestration, in Russian)
Susan Quittmeyer (Marina); James Morris (Boris), Mark Baker (Dimitri), Gwynne Howell (Pimen), Wieslaw Ochman (Shuisky), Sergei Leiferkus/(9/27, 29, 10/3) Alan Held (Rangoni)
Donald Runnicles
Sept. 12, 16, 19, 24, 27m, 29, Oct. 3

Donizetti, *L'Elisir d'Amore*
Ruth Ann Swenson (Adina); Jerry Hadley (Nemorino), Gino Quilico (Belcore), Simone Alaimo (Dulcamara)
Bruno Campanella
Sept. 20m, 22, 25, 30, Oct. 2, 6, 10, 13

Beethoven, *Fidelio*
Hildegard Behrens (Leonore), Ann Panagulias (Marzelline); Gary Lakes (Florestan), Ekkehard Wlaschiha (Pizarro), Hans Tschammer (Rocco)
Donald Runnicles
Oct. 11m, 14, 17, 20, 23, 29, Nov. 1m

Verdi,
La Forza del Destino
Leona Mitchell (Leonora), Judith Forst (Preziosilla), Lando Bartolini (Don Alvaro), Vladimir Chernov (Don Carlo),

Roberto Scandiuzzi**/ (11/6, 10) Kevin Langan (Padre Guardiano Roberto Abbado**

Oct. 18m, 21, 24, 27, 30, Nov. 6, 10

Verdi, *Don Carlo*
Carol Vaness (Elisabetta), Nina Terentieva (Eboli); Richard Margison (Carlo), Thomas Allen (Rodrigo), Robert Lloyd (Philip II), Gwynne Howell (Grand Inquisitor) Donald Runnicles/(11/18, 21) Ian Robertson

Oct. 31, Nov. 4, 8m, 11, 14, 18, 21

Adams, *The Death of Klinghoffer*
Sheila Nadler (Marilyn Klinghoffer), Stephanie Friedman (Omar), Janice Felty (Swiss Grandmother, Austrian Woman, British Girl); Sanford Sylvan (Leon Klinghoffer), James Maddalena (Captain), Eugene Perry (Mamoud), Thomas Hammons ("Rambo") John Adams

Nov. 7, 13, 15m, 19, 22m, 24

Giordano, *Andrea Chénier*
Aprile Millo (Maddalena), Bruno Beccaria (Chénier), Paolo Gavanelli/(12/13) Robert McFarland (Gérard) Nello Santi

Nov. 20, 25, 28, Dec. 3, 6m, 8, 13m

Britten, *A Midsummer Night's Dream*
Sylvia McNair (Tytania), Susan Patterson (Helena), Catherine Keen (Hermia); Brian Asawa (Oberon), Kurt Streit (Lysander), David Malis (Demetrius), Donald Adams (Bottom) John Mauceri

Nov. 29m, Dec. 2, 4, 6, 10, 12

Milhaud, *Christophe Colomb*
(Stylized concert version) Maria Fortuna (Isabella); Derek Jacobi** (Narrator), Jean-Philippe Lafont (Columbus I), Victor Ledbetter (Columbus II) Kent Nagano

Dec. 11, 13

SUMMER 1993 — A CELEBRATION OF STRAUSS

Strauss, *Salome*
Maria Ewing (Salome), Leonie Rysanek/(6/26) Susan Bickley (Herodias);

Robert Tear (Herod), Tom Fox (Jokanaan) Donald Runnicles

June 4, 10, 13m, 16, 19, 26

Strauss, *Der Rosenkavalier*
Frederica von Stade (Octavian), Felicity Lott (Marschallin), Christine Schäfer** (Sophie); Eric Halfvarson (Ochs), Hong-Shen Li (Italian Singer), David Holloway (Faninal) Charles Mackerras

June 5, 8, 11, 18, 23, 27m

Strauss, *Capriccio*
Kiri Te Kanawa (Countess), Tatiana Troyanos (Clairon); David Kuebler (Flamand), Håkan Hagegård (Count), Simon Keenlyside** (Olivier), Victor Braun (La Roche) Donald Runnicles/ (7/1) Andrew Davis

June 12, 17, 20m, 25, 28, July 1

Strauss, *Daphne*
(Dramatized concert performance) Janice Watson** (Daphne), Gweneth Bean (Gaea); Hong-Shen Li (Leukippos), Jon Fredric West (Apollo), Franz Hawlata (Peneios) Andrew Davis

June 30, July 2

1993

Verdi, *I Vespri Siciliani*
Carol Vaness (Elena); Chris Merritt (Arrigo), Timothy Noble/(9/26) Hector Vasquez (Monforte), James Morris (Procida) Charles Mackerras

Sept. 10, 14, 17, 23, 26m, 29, Oct. 2

Donizetti, *La Fille du Régiment*
Kathleen Battle (Marie), Felicity Palmer (Marquise), Mollie Sugden** (Duchess); Frank Lopardo (Tonio), Michel Trempont (Sulpice) Bruno Campanella

Sept. 11, 15, 18, 21, 24, 26, 30, Oct. 3m

Puccini, *La Bohème*
Verónica Villarroel (Mimì), Ann Panagulias (Musetta); Roberto Aronica**/ (10/6, 9, 13, 16) Fernando De La Mora (Rodolfo), William Shimell/ (10/9, 13, 16) Victor Ledbetter (Marcello), Philip Skinner (Colline) Charles Mackerras/ (10/9, 13) Patrick Summers

Sept. 19m, 22, 25, 28, Oct. 6, 9, 13, 16

Patricia Racette (Mimì), Maria Fortuna (Musetta); Richard Leech (Rodolfo), Victor Ledbetter (Marcello), Robert Milne (Colline) Patrick Summers

Nov. 29, Dec. 2, 5m, 9, 11

Puccini, *Turandot*
Eva Marton/(10/20, 11/2, 5) Ealynn Voss (Turandot), Lucia Mazzaria (Liù); Michael Sylvester/ (10/20, 29, 11/5) Vladimir Popov (Calaf), Kevin Langan (Timur) Donald Runnicles/(11/2, 5) Ian Robertson

Oct. 7, 10m, 12, 15, 18, 20, 23, 26, 29, Nov. 2, 5

Janáček, *Věc Makropulos*
Stephanie Sundine (Emilia Marty); Graham Clark (Albert Gregor), Tom Fox (Prus) Charles Mackerras

Oct. 14, 17m, 22, 27, 30

Wagner, *Die Meistersinger*
Karita Mattila (Eva), Catherine Keen (Magdalene); Ben Heppner (Walther), Bernd Weikl (Hans Sachs), Robert Orth (Beckmesser), Jan-Hendrik Rootering (Pogner), Lars Magnusson (David) Donald Runnicles

Oct. 28, 31m, Nov. 3, 6, 9, 12, 17

Mozart, *La Clemenza di Tito*
Ljuba Kazarnovskaya/ (11/22, 24, 28) Marquita Lister (Vitellia), Frederica von Stade (Sesto); (11/7, 19)Ben Heppner/ Stephen Guggenheim (Titus) Donald Runnicles

Nov. 7m, 11, 13, 19, 22, 24, 28m

Bellini, *I Puritani*
June Anderson (Elvira), Mika Shigematsu (Enrichetta); Gregory Kunde (Arturo), Roberto Frontali (Riccardo), Alastair Miles** (Giorgio) Maurizio Arena

Nov. 16, 21m, 27, 30, Dec. 3, 7, 10

Tchaikovsky, *Pikovaya Dama*
Maria Guleghina (Lisa), Yanyu Guo (Paulina), Leonie Rysanek (Countess); Vladimir Atlantov (Gherman), Vladimir Redkin/(12/4, 8, 12) Gino Quilico (Yeletsky), Valery Alexeiev (Tomsky) Edo de Waart

Nov. 23, 26, Dec. 1, 4, 8, 12m

1994

Verdi, *Macbeth*
Gwyneth Jones (Lady Macbeth); James Morris (Macbeth), Hong-Shen Li (Macduff), Robert Lloyd (Banquo) Donald Runnicles

Sept. 9, 13, 16, 20, 24, 29, Oct. 2m

Susa/Littell, *The Dangerous Liaisons***
Frederica von Stade (Merteuil), Renée Fleming (Tourvel), Mary Mills (Cécile); Thomas Hampson (Valmont), David Hobson** (Danceny) Donald Runnicles

Sept. 10, 15, 18m, 21, 23, 27

Verdi, *Il Trovatore*
(9/17, 22, 25) Claudia Waite/Aprile Millo (Leonora), Dolora Zajick (Azucena); Fabio Armiliato (Manrico), Paolo Gavanelli (Luna) Daniel Oren

Sept. 17, 22, 25m, 28, Oct. 1, 6, 11

Zvetelina Vassileva** (Leonora), Stefania Toczyska (Azucena); Dennis O'Neill (Manrico), Vladimir Chernov/(12/7, 10) Eduardo del Campo (Luna) Ian Robertson

Dec. 1, 4m, 7, 10

Rossini, *Otello*
Cecilia Gasdia (Desdemona), Mika Shigematsu (Emilia); Chris Merritt (Otello), Craig Estep (Iago), Bruce Ford (Rodrigo) Patrick Summers

Oct. 4, 9m, 13, 18, 22, 25, 28

Wagner, *Tannhäuser*
Deborah Voigt (Elisabeth), Catherine Keen (Venus); Wolfgang Schmidt (Tannhäuser), Jorma Hynninen (Wolfram), Victor von Halem (Hermann) Donald Runnicles

Oct. 12, 15, 20, 23m, 26, 29, Nov. 2

Prokofiev, *The Fiery Angel*
(in Russian) Galina Gorchakova (Renata), Larissa Diadkova (Fortuneteller, Mother Superior); Sergei Leiferkus (Ruprecht), Bulat Minzhilkiev (Inquisitor) Valery Gergiev/(10/21) Alexander Polianichko**

Oct. 19, 21, 27, 30m, Nov. 1, 5, 9

Massenet, *Hérodiade*
Dolora Zajick (Hérodiade), Renée Fleming (Salomé); Plácido Domingo/(11/23, 25) John Keyes (Jean), Juan Pons (Hérode), Kenneth Cox (Phanuel) Valery Gergiev/(11/23, 25) Paul Ethuin**

Nov. 8, 12, 15, 18, 20m, 23, 25

Boito, *Mefistofele*
Aprile Millo/(12/3, 6, 9) Patricia Racette (Margherita), Carol Neblett (Elena); Samuel Ramey (Mefistofele), Richard Margison (Faust) Julius Rudel

Nov. 13m, 16, 21, 27m, 30, Dec. 3, 6, 9

Donizetti, *Lucia di Lammermoor*
Ruth Ann Swenson (Lucia); Marcello Giordani (Edgardo), Roberto Servile** (Enrico) Nello Santi

Nov. 19, 22, 26, 29, Dec. 2, 4, 8, 11m

SUMMER 1995

Gluck, *Orphée et Eurydice*
(Concert performance; Berlioz edition) Dawn Upshaw (Eurydice), Jennifer Larmore (Orphée), Alison Hagley (Amour) Donald Runnicles

May 18

Prokofiev, *L'Amour des Trois Oranges*
(Opéra de Lyon) Veronica Cangemi (Ninette), Monique Barscha (Fata Morgana); Jean-Luc Viala (Prince), Jean-Marie Frémeau (Truffaldin), Georges Gautier (Truffaldin), Jules Bastin (Cook) Kent Nagano

June 17, 18m, 21, 22

1995

Donizetti, *Anna Bolena*
Carol Vaness (Anna), Susanne Mentzer (Giovanna Seymour), Patricia Bardon** (Smeton); Giuseppe Sabbatini (Percy), Roberto Scandiuzzi (Henry VIII) Roberto Abbado

Sept. 8, 12, 15, 21, 24m, 27, 30

Glinka, *Ruslan and Lyudmila* (in Russian)
Anna Netrebko** (Lyudmila), Valentina Tsidipova/(9/26, 29) Zvetelina Vassileva (Gorislava), Elena Zaremba (Ratmir), Catherine Cook (Naina);

Jeffrey Wells/(9/17, 22, 26) Vladimir Ognovenko (Ruslan), Vladimir Atlantov (Finn), Yuri Marusin (Bayan), Vladimir Ognovenko/(9/17, 22, 26, 29) Gennadi Bezubenkov (Farlaf) Valery Gergiev/ (9/26, 29) Alexander Titov**

Sept. 9, 14, 17m, 19, 22, 26, 29

Verdi, *La Traviata*
Verónica Villarroel (Violetta); Roberto Aronica (Alfredo), Gregory Yurisich (Germont) Steven Mercurio

Sept. 16, 20, 23, 28, Oct. 1m, 4, 7, 10, 12

Puccini, *Madama Butterfly*
Catherine Malfitano (Cio-Cio-San), Catherine Keen (Suzuki); Richard Leech/(10/20, 22) Alfredo Portilla (Pinkerton), Victor Ledbetter (Sharpless) Donald Runnicles

Oct. 3, 6, 8m, 11, 14, 17, 20, 22m

Yoko Watanabe/(12/9m) Christiane Riel (Cio-Cio-San), Elizabeth Bishop (Suzuki); Richard Margison/(12/9m) Alfredo Portilla (Pinkerton), Theodore Baerg (Sharpless) Charles Mackerras/(12/9m) Donald Runnicles

Dec. 2m, 4, 9m, 9

Rossini, *La Cenerentola*
Olga Borodina (Angelina), Kurt Streit (Don Ramiro), Simone Alaimo (Don Magnifico), Lucio Gallo (Dandini) Carlo Rizzi

Oct. 13, 15m, 18, 21, 25, 28, Nov. 2

Gounod, *Faust*
Nancy Gustafson (Marguerite), Susan Quittmeyer/(10/29, 31) Zheng Cao (Siebel); Richard Leech (Faust), Rodney Gilfry (Valentin), Samuel Ramey (Méphistophélès) Patrick Summers

Oct. 26, 29m, 31, Nov. 3, 5m, 8, 11, 16

Wagner, *Die Walküre*
Jane Eaglen/(11/21) Susan Marie Pierson/ (11/25, 29) Marilyn Zschau (Brünnhilde), Anne Evans (Sieglinde), (11/4, 7, 12) Marjana Lipovšek/ Catherine Keen (Fricka); Poul Elming (Siegmund), (11/4, 7, 12) James Morris/ Willard White (Wotan), Victor von Halem (Hunding) Donald Runnicles

Nov. 4, 7, 12m, 15, 21, 25, 29

Mozart, *Don Giovanni*
Deborah Riedel (Anna), Daniela Dessì (Elvira), Rebecca Evans (Zerlina); (11/14, 18, 20) Samuel Ramey/William Shimell (Giovanni), John Mark Ainsley**/ (12/1, 3, 7) Stanford Olsen (Ottavio), Alfonso Antoniozzi (Leporello), Victor von Halem (Commendatore) Donald Runnicles

Nov. 14, 18, 20, 24, 28, Dec. 1, 3m, 7

Dvořák, *Rusalka*
Renée Fleming (Rusalka), Stephanie Sundine/ (12/6) Claudia Waite (Foreign Princess), Felicity Palmer (Ježibaba); Sergei Larin (Prince), Philip Skinner (Water Spirit) Charles Mackerras

Nov. 26m, 30, Dec. 2, 6, 8, 10m

SUMMER 1996

Puccini, *La Bohème*
(Orpheum Theatre) Patricia Racette (Mimì), (6/7) Nicolle Foland/ Ann Panagulias/ (Musetta); Marcello Giordani/ (6/19m, 21, 23m) Alfredo Portilla (Rodolfo), Earle Patriarco (Marcello), Philip Skinner (Colline) Steven Mercurio/(6/21) Ian Robertson/(6/23m) Marco Armiliato

June 7, 9m, 12, 15, 19m, 21, 23m

Mary Mills (Mimì), Nicolle Foland (Musetta); Roberto Aronica (Rodolfo), Victor Ledbetter (Marcello), Chester Patton (Colline) Steven Mercurio/(6/22, 28, 30m) Marco Armiliato

June 8, 12m, 14, 16m, 20, 22, 28, 30m

Alison Buchanan (Mimì), Peggy Kriha Dye (Musetta); Tito Beltrán/(6/19) Roberto Aronica (Rodolfo), Mark Oswald (Marcello), Daniel Sumegi (Colline) Marco Armiliato/ (6/15m, 19) Ian Robertson

June 13, 15m, 19, 22m

Leontina Vaduva/ (6/26, 29m) Gwynne Geyer, Ann Panagulias/ (6/26, 29m) Peggy Kriha Dye (Musetta); Tito Beltrán/(6/26, 29m) Alfredo Portilla (Rodolfo), Earle Patriarco/(6/26, 29m) Hector Vásquez (Marcello), (6/26) Chester Patton/

John Relyea/(6/29m)
Philip Skinner (Colline)
Marco Armiliato
June 25, 26, 27, 29m, 2

1996-97

Borodin, *Knyaz Igor*
(Prince Igor)
(Bill Graham
Civic Auditorium)
Lauren Flanigan
(Yaroslavna), Elena
Zaremba (Konchakovna);
Sergei Leiferkus (Igor),
Jeffrey Wells (Galitsky),
Mark Baker (Vladimir),
Paata Burchuladze
(Konchak)
Alexander Anissimov
September 6, 10, 13,
15m, 18, 21, 25

Thomas, *Hamlet*
(Orpheum Theatre)
Ruth Ann Swenson (Ophélie),
Judith Forst (Gertrude);
Thomas Hampson (Hamlet),
Robert Lloyd (Claudius),

Kevin Langan (Ghost)
Yves Abel
Sept. 12, 14, 17, 19, 22m,
24, 27, 29m

Wagner, *Lohengrin*
(Bill Graham
Civic Auditorium)
Karita Mattila (Elsa),
Elizabeth Connell (Ortrud);
Ben Heppner/(9/6, 9, 12)
Thomas Sunnegårdh**
(Lohengrin), Tom
Fox (Telramund)
Donald Runnicles
Sept. 28, Oct. 1, 4, 6m,
9, 12

Rossini,
Il Barbiere di Siviglia
(Orpheum Theatre)
Jennifer Larmore (Rosina);
Dmitri Hvorostovsky
(Figaro), (10/10, 13)
Bruce Ford/Roberto
Saccà (Almaviva), John
Del Carlo (Bartolo)

Alastair Miles (Basilio)
Bruno Campanella
Oct. 10, 13, 18,
20m, 23, 26, 28

Mika Shigematsu (Rosina);
Earle Patriarco (Figaro),
(10/11) Roberto Saccà**/
Jorge Lopez-Yañez
(Almaviva), Steven
Condy (Bartolo),
Chester Patton (Basilio)
Patrick Summers
Oct. 11, 19, 24, 26m

Bizet, *Carmen*
(Bill Graham
Civic Auditorium)
Olga Borodina (Carmen),
Mary Mills (Micaëla);
José Cura (Don José),
Richard Paul
Fink (Escamillo)
Donald Runnicles
Oct. 22, 25, 27m, 30,
Nov. 2, 5, 8

Nancy Maultsby (Carmen),
Patricia Racette/(2/15)
Alison Buchanan (Micaëla);
Sergei Larin (Don José),
Gino Quilico (Escamillo)
Emmanuel Joel**
Feb. 12, 15, 19, 22

Wallace/Korie,
Harvey Milk
(Orpheum Theatre)
Juliana Gondek (Dianne
Feinstein), Elizabeth
Bishop (Mother), Jill
Grove (Anne Kronenberg);
Robert Orth (Harvey Milk),
Raymond Very (Dan White),
Bradley Williams (Scott
Smith), Gidon Saks
(Mayor Moscone),
James Maddalena
(Messenger)
Donald Runnicles
Nov. 9, 13, 16, 19,
21, 24m, 27, 30

Offenbach,
Les Contes d'Hoffmann
(Bill Graham
Civic Auditorium)
Tracy Dahl (Olympia),
Patricia Racette (Antonia),
Catherine Keen (Giulietta),
Ruxandra Donose**
(Nicklausse); Jerry
Hadley (Hoffmann),
Samuel Ramey (Villains)
Steven Mercurio
Nov. 17m, 20, 23, 26, 29,
Dec. 1m, 3

Strauss, J., *Die Fledermaus*
(Bill Graham
Civic Auditorium)
Eilana Lappalainen
(Rosalinda), Tracy
Dahl (Adele); Brian
Asawa (Orlofsky),
Theodore Baerg (Eisenstein),
Alfredo Portilla (Alfred),
Michael Chioldi (Falke)
Alexander Sander
Dec. 26, 28m, 29

Nicolle Foland (Rosalinda),
Peggy Kriha Dye (Adele);
Brian Asawa (Orlofsky),
David Okerlund (Eisenstein),
Carlo Scibelli (Alfred),
Earle Patriarco (Falke)
Alexander Sander
Dec. 27, 28

Nicolle Foland (Rosalinda),
Tracy Dahl (Adele);
Brian Asawa (Orlofsky),
Theodore Baerg (Eisenstein),
Alfredo Portilla (Alfred),
Earle Patriarco (Falke)
Alexander Sander
Dec. 31 (Act II only)

Strauss, R., *Salome*
(Bill Graham
Civic Auditorium)
Karen Huffstodt (Salome),
Judith Forst (Herodias);
William Cochran (Herod),
Bernd Weikl (Jokanaan)
Ralf Weikert
Jan. 18, 21, 23, 26m, 29;
Feb. 1

Verdi, *Aida*
(Bill Graham
Civic Auditorium)
Michèle Crider/(2/13, 16, 21)
Marquita Lister (Aida),
Nina Terentieva/(2/13, 16,
21) Eugenie Grunewald
(Amneris); Fabio Armiliato/
(2/11, 14, 21) Walter
Fraccaro (Radames),
Timothy Noble/
(2/13, 20) Christopher
Robertson (Amonasro)
Donald Runnicles
Feb. 8, 11, 13, 14,
16m, 18, 20, 21, 23m

World Premieres

Dello Joio, *Blood Moon,* 1961

Imbrie, *Angle of Repose,* 1976

Susa/Littell,
The Dangerous Liaisons, 1994

U.S. Premieres

Britten, *A Midsummer Night's
Dream,* 1961

Cherubini, *The Portuguese Inn,* 1954

Henze, *Das Verratene Meer,* 1991

Janáček, *The Makropulos Case,* 1966

Orff, *The Wise Maiden,* 1958

Poulenc, *The Dialogues of the
Carmelites,* 1957

Ravel, *L'Enfant et les Sortilèges,* 1930

Reimann, *Lear,* 1981

Rossini, *Maometto II,* 1988

Schuller, *The Visitation,* 1967

Shostakovich, *Katerina Ismailova,*
1964

Strauss, *Die Frau ohne Schatten,*
1959

Tippett, *The Midsummer Marriage,*
1983

Tippett, *King Priam (Opera Center),*
1994

von Einem, *The Visit of the Old
Lady,* 1972

Walton, *Troilus and Cressida,* 1955

Weill, *Royal Palace,* 1968

U.S. Stage Premieres

Cherubini, *Medea,* 1958

Donizetti, *Maria Stuarda,* 1971

Honegger, *Joan of Arc at the Stake,*
1954

Milhaud, *Christopher Columbus,*
1968

Orff, *Carmina Burana,* 1958

Rossini, *Ermione,* 1992

West Coast Premieres

Adams, *The Death of Klinghoffer,*
1992

Wallace/Korie, *Harvey Milk,* 1996

THE SAN FRANCISCO
recipients
OPERA MEDAL

In 1970, San Francisco Opera inaugurated the SAN FRANCISCO OPERA MEDAL to honor artists and members of the company for their long-term contributions to the company. Recipients of the medal, often presented at a post-performance ceremony onstage, have been some of the biggest names in the opera world. The award has also gone to less visible talents treasured by the company—Colin Harvey, a member of the chorus; Otto Guth, a vocal coach; Philip Eisenberg, assistant for artists; and violinist Zaven Melikian, concertmaster. The complete list follows.

1970	Dorothy Kirsten, soprano	1980	Geraint Evans, baritone	1990	Janis Martin, soprano Marilyn Horne, mezzo-soprano
1972	Jess Thomas, tenor	1981	Matthew Farruggio, stage director Birgit Nilsson, soprano	1991	Licia Albanese, soprano
1973	Paul Hager, stage director	1982	Regina Resnik, mezzo-soprano	1993	Walter Mahoney, costume shop
1974	Colin Harvey, chorus	1984	Joan Sutherland, soprano	1994	Zaven Melikian, concertmaster Michael Kane, master carpenter Plácido Domingo, tenor
1975	Otto Guth, musical adviser Alexander Fried, music critic	1985	Thomas Stewart, baritone	1995	Charles Mackerras, conductor
1976	Leonie Rysanek, soprano	1987	Régine Crespin, soprano		
1977	Leontyne Price, soprano	1988	Philip Eisenberg, assistant for artists		
1978	Kurt Herbert Adler, general director	1989	Pilar Lorengar, soprano Bidú Sayão, soprano		

Three of San Francisco Opera's favorite singers, **Stella Roman**,
Licia Albanese, and **Bidú Sayão**, attended the Kurt Herbert
Adler Anniversary Gala on November 19, 1978.

Lotfi Mansouri
General Director

Donald C. Runnicles
Music Director

Michael J. Savage
Managing Director

Sir Charles Mackerras
Principal Guest Conductor

San Francisco Opera
War Memorial Opera House
301 Van Ness Avenue
San Francisco, CA
94102-4509

Web address:
www.sfopera.com